DAVID WHITWELL

MUSIC DURING THE ENGLISH RESTORATION

PHILOSOPHY AND PERFORMANCE PRACTICE

WHITWELL BOOKS

Music during the English Restoration: Philosophy and Performance Practice
Dr. David Whitwell

Copyright © 2015 David Whitwell
All rights reserved.
Published in the United States of America.
These essays were first published between 2000 and 2010.

Cover image: *St Paul's Cathedral, London* by Another Believer, 2014, CC BY-SA 4.0

ISBN-13 9781936512867

Whitwell Publishing
Austin, TX 78701
WWW.WHITWELLPUBLISHING.COM

Contents

I	Society and Music	9
1	Music in the Restoration Court	11
2	Music in the Restoration Church	19
3	Music in the Restoration Theater	47
4	Music in Restoration Poetry	59
5	Music in Restoration Prose	79
II	Philosophers on Music	99
6	Restoration Philosophers on Music	101
7	Isaac Newton on Music	125
8	Dryden on Music	131
9	English Views on Foreign Opera	139
10	Dryden on Opera	157
11	Restoration Journals on Opera	165

III The Public and Music 179

12 Civic Music on the English Baroque 181

13 Music and English Manners 195

14 Pepys on Music 207

15 Restoration Journals on Music 219

Bibliography 231

About the Author 245

About the Editor 249

I want to express my appreciation for my colleague, Craig Dabelstein of Brisbane, Australia, for his contribution to this volume. His own musicianship, broad education and skill in editing is responsible for thus preserving my essays. Any reader who places value in having these essays in his library is in his debt.

Part I

Society and Music

1
Music in the Restoration Court

> This day came in his Majestie Charles the 2d to London after a sad & long Exile, and Calamitous Suffering both of the King & Church: being 17 yeares ... The wayes straw'd with flowers, the bells ringing, the streetes hung with Tapisssry, fountains running with wine ... windows & balconies all set with Ladys, Trumpets, Musick ... [1]

[1] *The Diary of John Evelyn* for May 29, 1660.

WELL, "SUFFERING" was a relative concept for Charles II. Some of his contemporaries called him the "happy king," and well he might have been, having spent fourteen years enjoying Paris with no cares of government. An Italian diplomat said of him,

> His fiercest enemies are diligence and business. He worships comforts, pleasures, and practical jokes, hates implacably all sort of work, and loves with the greatest enthusiasm every kind of play and diversion.[2]

[2] Lorenzo Magalotti, *Relazione d'Inghilterra* (1668).

As a collector of mistresses he was without equal for his generation, thus setting the example for both his court and Restoration theater. One of the most memorable lines of the seventeenth century was spoken by one of his ladies whom the crowd mistook for a newly arrived French (and thus Catholic) mistress. From her coach window she exclaimed, "Be silent, good people, I am the *Protestant* whore!"[3] This young lady was Nell Gwynn (1650–1687), who was born in a coal yard garret in Drury Lane and developed her singing and acting ability in the lowest taverns. She was fortunate

[3] Sir Arthur Bryant, *King Charles II* (London, 1955), 238.

to live at the time when female parts on the stage were first allowed to be played by women and her success on the stage brought her to the attention of the king. She collected considerable funds from the king's purse, but it must be noted that she gave much of this money to private charities, including Chelsea Hospital. A letter by Mme de Sévigné in Paris records the character of this girl, and also mentions a child who is usually overlooked in the literature on Charles II.

> The actress is as haughty as the Duchess of Portsmouth [another mistress of the king]; she insults her, makes faces at her, attacks her, frequently steals the King from her, and boasts of his preference for her. She is young, indiscreet, confident, meretricious, and pleasant; she sings, dances, and acts her part well. She has a son by the king, and wishes to have him acknowledged.[4]

There was of course a great celebration surrounding the coronation of Charles II. One eyewitness mentions the participation of wind bands representing the various trade guilds[5] and pay records document the presence of the king's wind band.[6] One eyewitness, John Ogilby, gives some interesting detail of a group of thirty trumpets and eighteen drums positioned in "Leaden-Hall Street near Lime Street End." It is rather rare to have the actual titles of performances on such ceremonial occasions.

Drums:	Marches of several countries
Trumpets:	Several "Levets"
Drums:	Change to a "Battel"
Trumpets:	Sound a "charge"
Trumpets:	Sound pleasant "Levets"
Drums:	Beat a lofty English march

Ogilby heard, at the "second arch," a number of wind bands, one of twelve players, two of eight players and the rest of six players.

At another arch, the "Naval" arch, on two galleries he heard twelve players of "Winde-Musik," while outside the arch there were two more groups of six winds dressed as sailors. He describes such performance across the town.[7]

[4] Quoted in *Letters of Madame de Sévigné*, ed. Richard Aldington (London: Routledge, 1937), I, 170.

[5] *The Diary of John Evelyn*, for April 22, 1661.

[6] London, Lord Chamberlain Accounts, vol. 741, p. 118.

[7] John Ogilby, *The Relation of His Majestic's Entertainment passing through the City of London to His Coronation* (London, 1661), 2–44.

It appears that some of the compositions in Matthew Locke's "ffor his Majesty's Sagbutts & Cornetts" were used for the coronation.[8] Locke's role in the court music can be seen in a document reading, "Mathew Lock in the place of Alphonso Ferabosco [II], composer for the wind music."[9]

Roger North recalled the musical preferences of Charles II:

> He had lived some considerable time abroad, where the French music was in request, which consisted of an Entry and then Brawles, as they were called, that is motive aires, and dances. And it was, and is yet a mode among the *Monseurs*, always to act the music, which habit the King had got, and never in his life could endure any music that he could not act by keeping the time; which made the common *andante* or else the step-tripla the only musical styles at Court in his time. And after the manner of France, he set up a band of 24 violins to play at his dinners, which disbanded all the old English music at once. He was a lover of slight songs, and endured the accompaniment very well, provided he could keep the time.[10]

As North indicated, Charles II developed an even larger musical establishment, with twenty-four violins (modeled after the "24 Violons du Roi" of Paris),[11] a wind band which grew to sixteen players by 1663, and in addition to an assortment of lutes, voices, trumpets and drummers. The overall responsibility for performance fell to Nicholas Lanier and one document refers to his authority over rehearsals.

> Nicholas Lanier ... hath power to order and convocate [his Majesty's musick] at fitt time of practize and service ... If any of them refuse to wayte at such convenient tymes of practize and service ... I shall punish them either in their persons or their wages.[12]

The king's "24 violins" took over some of the burden of functional music during the second half of the seventeenth century, supplying the dinner music for the king,[13] as well as dance music—"after supper some fiddles and so to dance."[14] The king's wind band appears in the records of all official occasions. They were present in 1662 for the arrival of the Russian ambassador:

---

[8] Grove, *Dictionary of Music* (1980), XI, 109.

[9] London, Lord Chamberlain Accounts, vol. 479, 99–100.

[10] Quoted in John Wilson, *Roger North on Music* (London: Novello, 1959), 299ff.

[11] Peter Holman, in "London: Commonwealth and Restoration," in *The Early Baroque Era*, (Englewood Cliffs: Prentice Hall, 1994), 312, points out that the violin, at the beginning of the seventeenth century, was used only by players of dance music. Then he suggests it began to be used in the string fantasias of Coprario, Lupo, et. al. All English scholars make this assumption, even though most of the actual manuscripts bear no designation of instruments. The appearance of the "French violin clef" is no proof, for this same clef was also used for the oboe in the *Le Grands Hautbois* in Paris. Holman states that the violin "became acceptable in serious musical circles ... in the late 1650s." Curiously, as proof he offers a quotation by an eyewitness who actually says the contrary.

> [Gentlemen in private meetings] play'd three, four, and five parts all with *viols*, as treble-viol, tenor, counter-tenor and bass, with either an organ or virginals or harpsicon joy'nd with them: and they esteemed a *violin* to be an instrument only belonging to a common fidler, and could not indure that it should come among them for feare of making their meetings seem to be vain and fidling.

Roger North [see John Wilson, *Roger North on Music*, 222] made the interesting observation that it was the superiority of the new violin which helped change the multi-part style into the melody-bass character of the new *galant* style. In a viol consort, he says, everyone felt comfortable playing any part, but after the appearance of the violin "few or none cared to play under it, as supposing all the spirit of the consort lay in that."

[12] Lord Chamberlain Accounts, vol. 741, p. 316.

[13] Pepys *Diary*, August 28, 1667, for example.

[14] Ibid., February 23, 1669.

> ... his retinue being numerous, all clad in vests of several Colours, & with buskins after the Eastern manner ... Wind musick playing all the while in the Galleries above.[15]

And again for the celebration of St. George's Day at Whitehall in 1667:

> ... and lastly proceeded to the Banqueting house to a greate feast: The King sate on an elevated Throne at the upper end, at a Table alone ... at the lowere end the Musick: on the balusters above the Wind musique, Trumpets & kettle drums.[16]

On occasion, no doubt for political reasons, Charles II loaned out his players to other lords, as we see in a court record.

> Warrant to provide and deliver to the earl of Oxford or his assignes, eight cornets with stands and other necessaries thereunto belonging, seventeen bannerols for trumpeters with the Jolley Boyes and cordage to them, with tassels, one payre of handerolls for the kettle-drummers ...[17]

Surprisingly, according to the Samuel Pepys diary, an individual citizen could even engage the royal trumpets.

> Up: and called up by the King's trumpets, which cost me 10s.[18]

One reads, during this reign, of a trumpet player being killed while on diplomatic duty, in this case, "John Christmas, who was attending Lawrence Hyde on his embassy to Poland." This document has as its main concern the consequent loss of one of the king's silver trumpets.[19]

A document of June 18, 1669, announced the "retrenchment of his Majesty's musick."[20] From this time on the numbers of players are dramatically reduced. The wind band, for example, falls to ten and by 1679 to five. An engraving of the coronation of James II shows a fife player and four drummers, eight royal trumpeters (among them a pathetic figure bent over under the weight of two timpani on his back) and the wind band, which is now only three players![21] The

---

[15] *The Diary of John Evelyn*, for December 29, 1662.

[16] Ibid., for April 23, 1667.

[17] Lord Chamberlain Papers, Bundle 8.

[18] Entry for December 28, 1668.

[19] Richard McGrady, "The Court Trumpeters of Charles I and Charles II," *The Music Review* (1974), 227.
[20] Holman, "London," 314, incorrectly says "the Wind Music effectively ceased to exist" at this time.

[21] Contained in Francis Standford, *The History of the Coronation of ... James II* (London, 1687). Curiously the wind band is identified as "Two Sackbuts and a double Courtal," whereas in fact there is pictured two slide trumpets and a cornett.

Diary of John Evelyn records his dining with the king, as well as the absence of more sophisticated music to accompany the meal, as part of an entertainment given for the Venetian ambassadors.

> The dinner was most magnificent and plentiful, at four tables, with music, kettle-drums, and trumpets, which sounded upon a whistle at every [toast].[22]

[22] *The Diary of John Evelyn*, for December 18, 1685.

Roger North, in his autobiography, comments on the influence of various national styles heard in the court music at this time.

> The court about this time entertained only the theatrical music and French melody in song, but that somewhat softened and variegated; so also was the instrumental more vague and with a mixture of caprice ... But we found most satisfaction in the Italian, for their measures were just and quick, set off with wonderful solemn *Grave's*, and full of variety. The old English Fancys were in imitation of an elder Italian sort of sonata ... At length the time came off the French way and fell in with the Italian, and now that holds the ear. But still the English singularity will come in and have a share.[23]

[23] Quoted in John Wilson, *Roger North on Music*, 25.

During the reign of William and Mary (1689–1694) an order was given to the Dean of the Chapel Royal, on February 23, 1689, that there was to be no further instrumental music in the Chapel, except for the organ.[24] On the other hand, a new ensemble appears at this time, an Hautboisten band modeled after the famous one in Paris. There is a record of them accompanying the king on a visit to Holland in 1690[25] and another record describing four rehearsals and a subsequent performance at a ball for the king's birthday in 1695.[26] It was this ensemble which performed the funeral music for Queen Mary by Henry Purcell. We share, even today, the reaction of one who heard the original performance of this music.

[24] Donald Burrows, "London: Commercial Wealth and Cultural Expansion," in *The Late Baroque Era* (Englewood Cliffs: Prentice Hall, 1994), 355.

[25] Lord chamberlain Accounts, vol. 724.

[26] Ibid., vol. 776, 31b.

> I appeal to all that were present, as well such as understand Music, as those that did not, whither they ever heard any thing so rapturously fine and solemn & so Heavenly in the Operation, which drew tears from all; & yet a plain, Naturall

Composition; which shows the power of Music, when 'tis rightly fitted & Adapted to devotional purposes.

Anyone who has not heard the unaccompanied choral works by Purcell which were part of this ceremony has missed some of the most extraordinary music of the Baroque. There were companion works for this ceremony, both entitled "Queen's Farewell," also for oboe band, by Thomas Tollet and James Paisible.

This ensemble appears to remain the basic royal wind band until 1750 and its repertoire included a dozen or so works by Handel.[27]

With the accession of Anne in 1702 the musical establishment in the court began to expand again and Burrows points to the regular employment of more than 60 musicians at this time.[28] The patronage of opera under George I during the next decade continued this growth in activity and during the 1730s it expanded further as various members of the royal family pursued their own support of music.

One scholar suggests that marches in the oratorios and operas of Handel, such as *Rinaldo*, *Scipione*, *Deidamia* and the *Occasional Oratorio*, not to mention the two versions of "See the Conquering Hero Comes," from *Joshua* and *Judas Maccabaeus*, can be performed without the doubling string parts, leaving perhaps original marches for oboes and bassoons. We might add that the oratorio, *Deborah* (1733), contains the mention of a "Military Symphony" as a prelude to Act Three, although the music has not survived.

In the poetry of the Restoration we have some interesting glimpses of the daily music at the court. We may be sure there was much music directed toward the praise of various English nobles. Pope, in his "The Dunciad," addresses this practice as part of his satire of writers who seek to flatter the great.

> With horns and trumpets now to madness swell,
> Now sink in sorrows with a tolling bell;
> Such happy arts attention can command,
> When fancy flags, and sense is at a stand.
> Improve we these. Three Cat-calls be the bribe

[27] Handel's "Fireworks Music," originally, *Grand Overture of Warlike Instruments*, was composed for nine-part Hautboisten with the addition of the trumpets and drums referred to in the title. Because its first performance was given with some sixty players doubling the parts, it is always thought of today as a composition for a large ensemble. Handel was also familiar with a wind band piece played in Naples during Christmas by the civic wind band [*pifferari*]. This became the "Pastoral Symphony" of the *Messiah* and Handel has conscientiously acknowledged this by writing the abbreviation *pifa* at the beginning of this music in his autograph score.

[28] Burrows, "London," 364.

Of him, whose chattering shames the monkey-tribe;
And his Drum, whose hoarse heroic bass
Drowns the loud clarion of the braying Ass ...
So swells each wind-pipe; Ass intones to Ass;
Harmonic twang! of leather, horn, and brass;
Such as from laboring lungs the Enthusiast blows,
High Sound, attempered to the vocal noise;
Or such as bellow from the deep Divine ...
All hail him victor in both gifts of song,
Who sings so loudly, and who sings so long.[29]

Swift writes of a duke who has come under depressed circumstances.

His wings are clipped: he tries no more in vain
With bands of fiddlers to extend his train.[30]

Hunting remained a popular form of court entertainment and there are numerous references to the hunting horns, as for example in Alexander Pope, in his "Windsor Forest":

Now range the hills, the gameful woods beset,
Wind the shrill horn, or spread the waving net.[31]

William Somerville wrote a long poem called "The Chase," which covers an entire day of hunting.[32] He begins by inviting the reader to abandon the theaters and its music for the more manly pursuit of hunting.

While crowded theaters, too fondly proud
Of their exotic minstrels, and shrill pipes,
The price of manhood, hail thee with a song,
And airs soft-warbling; my hoarse-sounding horn
Invites thee to the Chase, the sport of kings;
Image of war, without its guilt.[33]

The hunting day begins with a musical wakeup call, which also serves to excite the hunting dogs, who in turn excite the horses.

Thy early meal, or thy officious maids,
The toilet placed, shall urge thee to perform
The important work. Me other joys invite,
The horn sonorous calls, the pack awaked

[29] "The Dunciad," Book II, lines 227ff, in *The Works of Alexander Pope* (New York: Gordian Press, 1967), IV, 147ff. Alexander Pope (1688–1744) was born to the family of a prosperous merchant, but as he was also born Catholic he was denied an education at any of the great universities. Thus, the greatest English poet of the eighteenth century was the product of his own education through reading. An illness as a child left him a four foot high hump-back.

[30] "The Dean and Duke" (1734).

[31] "Windsor Forest," lines 95ff, in *The Works of Alexander Pope*, I, 346.

[32] William Somerville (1682–1742) was born a wealthy nobleman in Warwickshire.

[33] "The Chase," I, lines 1-ff.

Their matins chant, nor brook my long delay.
My courser hears their voice; see there with ears
And tail erect, neighing he paws the ground;
Fierce rapture kindles in his reddening eyes,
And boils in every vein.[34]

[34] Ibid., II, 86ff.

The hunting horns play as the company rides through the fields,

What gay heart-cheering sounds
Urge through the breathing brass their mazy way![35]

[35] Ibid., IV, 410ff.

and as a Requiem of sorts for the death of the animals:

Bid the loud horns, in gaily warbling strains,
Proclaim the felon's fate; he dies, he dies.[36]

[36] Ibid., IV, 461ff.

2
Music in the Restoration Church

Music is the only science allowed in the doors of the church.[1]
John Playford

WHEN CHARLES II RETURNED from his exile in France to begin the Restoration, he brought back much culture, including the concept of the large string ensemble, known in Paris as the "Twenty-four Violins of the King." Subsequently we find in the diary of John Evelyn, for December 21, 1662, a record of the first introduction of strings in the royal chapel.

> One of his Majesty's chaplains preached; after which, instead of the ancient, grave, and solemn wind music accompanying the organ, was introduced a concert of twenty-four violins between every pause, after the French fantastical light way, better suiting a tavern, or a playhouse, than a church. This was the first time of change, and now we no more heard the cornett which gave life to the organ; that instrument quite left off in which the English were so skillful.

Another eyewitness who recorded the arrival of strings in the English church was Samuel Pepys. In an entry in his famous diary for September 14 he appears to document the first use of strings.

> I heard Captain Cookes new Musique; this the first day of having Vialls and other Instruments to play a Symphony between every verse of the Anthem; but the Musique more full then it was the last Sunday, and very fine it is.[2]

[1] John Playford, *An Introduction to the Skill of Music* [1674] (Ridgewood: Gregg Press, 1966), 1. Playford (1623–1686) was a publisher and amateur composer and theorist.

[2] Pepys *Diary*, Sept 14, 1662. Some historians date the appearance of the first strings two months later, with a December, 1662, entry in the diary of John Evelyn.

For the uninformed reader we might explain that for centuries wind players had been the professional musicians and string players the amateurs, often called "beer fiddlers." Beyond this tradition, at least one writer explained that besides only the winds are always in tune and for this reason should be maintained in the church.

> [String instruments] ar often out of tun; (Which soomtime happeneth in the mids of the Musik, when it is neither good to continue, nor to correct the fault) therefore, to avoid all offence (where the least shoolde not bee givn) in our Chyrch-solemnities onely the Winde-instruments (whose Notes ar constant) bee in use.[3]

[3] Charles Butler, *Principles of Musick* (1636).

Although the arrival of the string ensemble concept initiated a new chapter of both church and court music in England, so wonderfully represented in the music of Purcell, there was an ill-wind beginning to blow which would have dramatically harmful political consequences in England and on all later music of the English-speaking world. A radical, fundamentalist religious movement had begun during the sixteenth century and within it there began to appear voices who wanted to sever the connection of music and the church. We read this, for example, in Spinoza, who knows only a God who recognizes no emotion.

> God is without passions, neither is he affected by any emotion of pleasure or pain.[4]

[4] Spinoza, *The Ethics*, "Of the Power of the Understanding, or of Human Freedom," Proposition XVII.

Why, he says, "there are men lunatic enough to believe that even God himself takes pleasure in [hearing] harmony."[5]

[5] Ibid., "Concerning God," Appendix.

More harmful were the Puritans, who looked back to the early world of the New Testament as a model for their faith. As there are no descriptions of instrumental music used in the service in the New Testament, instruments must go—and so, in England, they destroyed all church organs. The actual order (Lords and Commons Ordinance of 1644) called for,

> the speedy demolishing of all organs, images and all matters of superstitious monuments in all Cathedrals ... throughout the kingdom of England and the Cominion of Wales, the

better to accomplish the blessed reformation so happily begun and to remove offences and things illegal in the worship of God.

In the spirit of this ordinance, we have an account from Exeter, for example, that records that soldiers,

> brake down the organs, and taking two or three hundred pipes with them in a most scorneful and contemptuous manner, went up and down the streets piping with them; and meeting with some of the Choristers of the Church, whose surplices they had stolne before, and imployed them to base servile offices, scoffingly told them, "Boyes, we have spoyled your trade, you most goe and sing hot pudding pyes."[6]

To a terrible extent, the seventeenth century Puritans in England achieved one of their goals, eliminating instrumental music from the church service. Due to them organs were suppressed and destroyed and organs did not reappear generally in England until 1860! During this interval many smaller churches organized church bands, consisting of a half-dozen or so wind instruments with an occasional cello to serve as a surrogate organ.[7]

A few men who considered themselves strong Puritans nevertheless argued for the value in the use of music in religion. One was the famous John Milton (1608–1674). In his treatise on "Church-Government," Milton, after pointing to the numerous instances of songs and lyric poetry in the Old Testament, defines the purpose of church music. Music, he says, should be a,

> power beside the office of a pulpit, to inbreed and cherish in a great people the seeds of virtue, and public civility, to allay the perturbations of the mind, and set the affections in right tune.[8]

One of his poems, "Il Penseroso," is a testimonial to his being moved by the emotional power of music.

> But let my due feet never fail,
> To walk the studious Cloisters pale,
> And love the high embowed Roof,

[6] Peter Holman, in "London: Commonwealth and Restoration," in *The Early Baroque Era* (Englewood Cliffs: Prentice Hall, 1994), 307.

[7] K. H. MacDermott, *The Old Church Gallery Minstrels* (London, 1948) and his manuscript correspondence, "The Old Church Gallery Minstrels," in GB-Lbm [MS. Add. 47775].

[8] "Church-Government," in *The Works of John Milton,* ed. Frank Patterson (New York: Columbia University Press, 1931–1938), III, 238.

> With antique Pillars massy proof,
> And storied Windows richly dight,
> Casting a dim religious light.
> There let the pealing Organ blow,
> To the full voiced Choir below,
> In Service high, and Anthems clear,
> As may with sweetness, through mine ear,
> Dissolve me into extasies,
> And bring all Heaven before mine eyes.[9]

[9] "Il Penseroso," in Ibid., I, 45.

Another religious theme, under which Milton discusses music at length, is the creation of the world. All musicians must take pleasure in the discovery in Milton's "Paradise Lost" that on the seventh day God rested, as we are told in the Old Testament, but, says Milton, he did not rest in silence—he listened to a concert!

> But not in silence holy kept; the Harp
> Had work and rested not, the solemn Pipe,
> And Dulcimer, all Organs of sweet stop,
> All sounds on Fret by String or Golden Wire
> Tempered soft Tunings, intermixt with Voice
> Choral or Unison ...
> Creation and the six Days acts they sung ...[10]

[10] Ibid., VII, 594ff.

In addition to the Puritans desire to eliminate music from the church service because it was not mentioned in the New Testament, there is some evidence to suggest that perhaps the quality of the professional singing had fallen to a level which may have contributed to their hostility to church music. Consider, for example, John Earle's characterization of "The Common Singing-men in Cathedral Churches." They are, he says,

> a bad society, and yet a company of good fellows, that roar deep in the choir, deeper in the tavern. They are the eight parts of speech, which go to the Syntaxis of Service, and are distinguished by their noises much like bells, for they make not a consort but a peal. Their pastime or recreation is prayers, their exercise drinking, yet herein so religiously addicted that they serve God oftenest when they are drunk ... Though they never expound the scripture they handle it much, and pollute the Gospel with two things, their conversation and

their thumbs. Upon work-days they behave themselves at prayers as at their pots, for they swallow them down in an instant. Their gowns are laced commonly with streamings of ale, the superfluities of a cup or throat above measure.[11]

In the view of Thomas Mace the reason for this state of affairs was the poor pay given cathedral singers, which Mace found "very low, inconsiderable, insufficient, unbecoming and uncomfortable." As a consequence, the singers often were forced to take other jobs. Why should we be surprised, Mace asks, that when they sing in church they "make sour faces, and cry, or roar out aloud." He concludes,

> Now I say, these things considered how certainly true they are, first in reference to the [singers] pitiful-poor-wages, and likewise to the general dead-heartedness, or zeal-benumbed-frozen-affections in these our time, toward the encouragement of such things; how can it be imagined that such [singers] should be fit and able performers in that duty, which necessarily depends upon education, breeding and skill in that quality of music, which is both a costly, careful and a laborious-attainment, not at all acquirable (in its excellency) by an inferior-low-capacitated men.[12]

Mace was also disturbed by the intonation of the singers and declared it better not to sing at all than to sing out of tune. This, because of the close relationship he perceived between music and the divine.

> For as I often used to say, that as concording unity in music is a lively and very significant simile of God, and Heavenly joys, and felicities, so on the contrary, jarring discords are as apt a simile of the Devil, or Hellish tortures.[13]

Another difficulty for the choir was that since the time that Henry VIII closed all the Catholic schools in England, a primary source of the training of boy singers, England, in effect, began to run out of boy singers for the churches. This is one reason why Roger North proposes that now perhaps is the time to allow women to sing.

> One might without a desperate solescisme maintain that if females were taken into the choirs instead of boys, it would

[11] John Earle, *Microcosmography* [1628] (St. Clair Shores: Scholarly Press, 1971), 94. John Earle (1600–1665) was a chaplain to Charles II, during the King's exile, and a Dean of Westminster during the Restoration.

[12] Thomas Mace, *Musick's Monument* [1676] (Paris: Editions du Centre National de la Recherche Scientifique, 1966), 23 ff. Mace (1613–1709) was a "clerk" at Trinity College, Cambridge.

[13] Ibid., 3.

be a vast improvement of choral music, because women come to a judgment as well as voice, which the boys's do not arrive at before their voices perish ... But both text[14] and morality are against it; and the Roman usage of castration is utterly unlawful, and a scandalous practice where it is used.[15]

There is one eyewitness account we know which suggests the congregation itself shared the poor discipline associated above with the singers. It is found in, of all places, Defoe's *Robinson Crusoe*, when he recalls attending a special religious service celebrating the victory of the English over the French at Ramillies.

> But I observed these grave people, in the intervals of their worshiping God, when it was not their turn to sing, or read, or pray, bestowed some of the rest of their time in taking snuff, adjusting their perukes, looking about at the fair ladies, whispering, and that not very softly neither, to one another, about this fine lady, that pretty woman, this fine duchess, and that great fortune, and not without some indecencies, as well as words as of gestures.[16]

As we have pointed out in other essays, and contrary to the almost total lack of discussion found on this subject in music history texts, improvisation had been practiced in churches for centuries. There is evidence to suggest that this practice was also found in England during the Baroque. A complaint in the famous *Spectator* for October 25, 1711, describes a visiting woman from the city who improvises during village church music.

> But what gives us the most offense is her theatrical manner of singing the psalms. She introduces above fifty Italian melodies into the Hunderdth Psalm, and whilst we begin "All People" in the old solemn tune of our fore-fathers, she in quite a different key runs divisions on the vowels, and adorns them with the graces of Nicolini ... we are certain to hear her quavering them half a minute after us to some sprightly airs of the opera.

A contemporary poem by George Herrick is especially interesting for its reference to improvisation by a singer and an instrumentalist together.

[14] I Corinthians 14:34:
> As in all the churches of the saints, the women should keep silence in the churches.

[15] Quoted in John Wilson, *Roger North on Music* (London: Novello, 1959).

[16] Daniel Defoe, *Robinson Crusoe*, (Garden City: Doubleday, n.d.), III, 151ff.

> What sweeter musick can we bring,
> Than a Carol, for to sing
> The Birth of this our heavenly King?
> Awake the voice! Awake the string!

Curiously enough, while the Puritan preachers were working to eliminate all instrumental music from the service, there were a group of poets who were Puritans but who nevertheless spoke in support of instrumental music in their poems. One which calls upon a number of musical instruments for this purpose is by George Wither.

> Come, oh come in pious Laies [songs],
> Should we God-Almighty's praise.
> Hither bring in one consent,
> Heart, and voice, and instrument.
> Musick-add of every kind;
> Sound the Trumpet, the Cornet winde.
> Strike the Viol, touch the Lute.
> Let nor Tongue, nor String be mute.[17]

Richard Creshaw's Hymn, "The Name of Jesus," also calls upon a number of instruments to praise Jesus.

> Wake Lute and Harp
> And every sweet-lipped thing
> That talks with tuneful string;
> Start into life, and leap with me
> Into a hasty Fitt-tuned Harmony
>
> ......
>
> Complaining Pipes, and prattling Strings,
> Bring all the store
> Of Sweets you have; And murmur that you have no more.
> Come, near to part,
> Nature and Art!
>
> ......
>
> Bring all your Lutes and Harps of Heaven and Earth;
> What ever cooperates to the common mirth
> Vessels of vocal Joys,
> Or you, more noble architects of Intellectual Noise,
> Cymbals of Heaven, or Human spheres,
> Solicitors of Souls or Ears ... [18]

[17] *Works of George Wither* (New York: Franklin, 1967), Spenser Society, Nr. 26–27, "Halelviah," Hymn I. George Wither (1588–1667), one of the so-called Cavalier Poets was an officer in the Puritan army and most of his poetry is political in nature.

[18] "The Name of Jesus," in *The Complete Poetry of Richard Crashaw*, ed. George Williams (New York: New York University Press, 1972), 32ff.

In another poem, Crashaw makes a rare reference to string instruments in Heaven.

> When some new bright Guest
> Takes up among the stars a room,
> And Heaven will make a feast,
> Angels with crystal viols come ... [19]

[19] "The Weeper," in Ibid., 129.

The strict Puritan, George Wither, in his book of emblems, under the title, "Though Music be of some abhorred, She, is the Handmaid of the Lord," seems to reserve music's purpose primarily for the church.

> To Music, and the Muses, many bear
> Much hatred; and, to whatsoever ends
> Their soul-delighting-raptures tuned are,
> Such peevish dispositions, it offends.
> Some others, in a moral way, affect
> Their pleasing strains (or, for a sensual use)
> But, in God's Worship, they the same suspect;
> (Or, tax it rather) as a great abuse.
> The first of these, are full of Melancholy;
> And, Pity need, or Comfort, more than blame;
> And, soon, may fall into some dangerous folly,
> Unless they labor, to prevent the same.
> The last, are giddy things, that have befooled
> Their judgments, with beguiling *fantasies*,
> Which (if they be not, by discretion, schooled)
> Will plunge them into greater vanities.
>
> For, Music, is the Handmaid of the Lord,
> And, for his Worship, was at first ordained:
> Yea, therewithall she fitly doth accord;
> And, where devotion thrives, is retained.
> She, by a natural power, helps to raise,
> The mind of God, when joyful Notes are sounded:
> And, passions fierce distemperatures, allays;
> When, by grave tones, the melody is bounded.
> It, also may in mystic-sense, imply
> What music, in ourselves, ought still to be;
> And, that our jarring-lives to certify,
> We should in voice, in hand, and heart, agree:
> And, sing out, faith's new songs, with full consent,
> Unto the Laws, ten-stringed instrument.[20]

[20] Wither, *A Collection of Emblemes*, 65. In a "Hymn for a Musician," [Spenser Society, vols. 26–27], Wither appears to use the "ten string law" as a metaphor for the Ten Commandments.

This same poet, in a Hymn composed in 1650, comments on the importance of sincerity of spirit in church music.

> There is no musick in our Songs,
> That's worthy to be heard of thee;
> Because, our hearts, eyes, ears, and tongues,
> Profaned, and untuned be.[21]

A similar observation is made by George Herbert, who contends that church music is not effective unless the heart of the listener is in the right place.

> The fineness which a hymn or psalm affords
> Is, when the soul unto the lines accord.[22]

A poem by George Herrick on the subject of Christmas is especially interesting for its reference to improvisation.

> What sweeter musick can we bring,
> Than a Carol, for to sing
> The Birth of this our heavenly King?
> Awake the voice! Awake the string!
> Heart, ear, and eye, and everything
> Awake! the while the active finger
> Runs divisions with the singer.[23]

In another poem which comments on performance practice in church music, Herrick writes,

> Comely acts well; and when he speaks his part,
> He doth it with the sweetest notes of Art:
> But when he sings a *Psalm*, there's none can be
> More cursed for singing out of tune than he.[24]

We must assume that artists of all kinds were very nervous in the climate created by the Puritans, but some were also brave enough to satirize the church. Samuel Butler wrote a long epic poem, "Hudibras," inspired by *Don Quixote*, which was extremely popular and enjoyed many editions. It is a strange work, with little plot, which found its popularity in its coarse and bigoted satire of the Puritans. One of the characters is Crowdero, an itinerant fiddler. We first meet him as a metaphor for the Puritan's distaste for instrumental music. Here we see the fiddler [Music] blamed for its ill-effect on society.

---

[21] *Wither*, Spenser Society, Nr. 22, "Hymne 1."

[22] "A True Hymn," in *The Poems of George Herbert*, ed. Ernest Rhys (London: Walter Scott, 1885), 175. George Herbert (1593–1633) devoted most of his poetry to the Church of England, which he served as a rector near Salisbury. None of his poetry was published during his lifetime. Some publications refer to him as a "late orator of the University of Cambridge."

[23] *The Poetical Works of Robert Herrick* (Oxford: Clarendon Press, 1963), 364. Herrick (1591–1674) is considered one of the most gifted of the so-called Cavalier Poets. He was a graduate of Cambridge and became a prior in Devonshire.

[24] Ibid., 266.

> But to that purpose first surrender
> The Fiddler, as the prime offender,
> The incendiary vile, that is chief
> Author and engineer of mischief;
> That makes division between friends,
> For profane and malignant ends.
> He and that engine of vile noise,
> On which illegally he plays,
> Shall (*dictum factum*) both be brought
> To condign punishment, as they ought.[25]

Later, when Butler is discussing this fiddler, he takes the opportunity to satirize the predilection of the Catholic Church princes for entertainment.

> … they hold their luxuries,
> Their dogs, their horses, whores, and dice,
> Their riots, revels, masks, delights,
> Pimps, buffoons, fiddlers, parasites;
> All which the Saints have title to.[26]

North also made a passing object to the Catholic church, in this case on the nature of chant.

> Now to give a censure of this kind of music, I must own myself far from approving it, because there is no scheme or design in it; for beginning middle and ending are all alike, and it is rather a murmur of accords, than music.[27]

Some poets and playwrights took what seems like a very strange turn, writing of pagan religious ceremonies. One wonders if they felt this was a safe way to write of religion in this Puritan environment, or were they more subtle and were suggesting that the Puritans were taking society back to primitive times. We find several references to pagan ceremonies involving the moon. But one must remember that in the Old Testament, which was assembled from several sources, and perhaps hurriedly, that a strange reference to such a pagan ceremony exists in Psalm 81, something completely out of character with the rest of the Psalms.

> Raise a song, sound the timbrel,
>   The sweet lyre with the harp.

---

[25] Samuel Butler (1612–1680), "Hudibras," Part I, Canto ii, lines 667ff. The reader will notice the pun on "division," a standard element of improvisation at this time.

[26] Ibid., I, ii, lines 1013ff.

[27] Roger North, *The Musicall Gramarian* (Oxford: Oxford University Press, 1925), 9.

> Blow the trumpet at the new moon,
>   At the full moon, on our feast day.

Dryden makes such a reference in his play, *Aureng-Zebe* (V, i):

> Trumpets and Drums shall fright her from the Throne,
> As sounding Cymbals aid the laboring Moon.

Nathaniel Lee, in his play, *Oedipus* (II, i), refers to military music participating in a Greek cult ceremony, although in historical practice this was actually a Roman tradition. Oedipus calls out,

> A vast Eclipse darkens the laboring Planet:
> Sound there, sound all our instruments of war;
> Clarions, and Trumpets, Silver, Brass, and Iron,
> And beat a thousand drums to help her labor.

In George Villiers' *The Rehearsal* (V, i) this same ancient cult ceremony is satirized in a scene where, instead of the war-like instruments, the moon is serenaded by a series of popular songs, including "Robin Hood," "Trenchmore," and "Dance the Hey."

A poem of Swift also refers to the legend of the ancient Roman religious cult which tells of using cymbals and drums in a worship service of the moon.

> Wise people, who believed with reason
> That this eclipse was out of season,
> Affirmed the moon was sick, and fell
> To cure her by a counter spell.
> Ten thousand cymbals now begin,
> To rend the skies with brazen din;
> The cymbals rattling sounds dispel
> The cloud, and drive the hag to hell.
> The moon, delivered from her pain,
> Displays her silver face again.[28]

There are a few other references to very untraditional religious practices in the Restoration drama repertoire. In Behn's play, *Sir Patient Fancy* (III, vii) there is a reference to spirits which haunt a house, allowing the playwright an opportunity for anti-Catholic sentiment.[29]

---

[28] "A Simile on our Want of Silver."

[29] Mrs. Aphra Behn (1640–1689) was the first English woman to earn a living by writing. After the death of her merchant husband, her experiences included service as a spy in the Netherlands and a period of time in prison for debts.

SIR PATIENT. Ah, the house is beset, surrounded and confounded with profane tinkling, with Popish Horn-pipes, and Jesuitical Cymbals, more Antichristian and Abominable than organs, or anthems.

NURSE. Yea verily, and surely it is the spawn of Cathedral Instruments played on by Babylonish Minstrels, only to disturb the Brethren.

In this same playwright's *The Widow Ranter* (IV, i), which is set in Virginia, there is an Indian religious ceremony, for which there are extensive stage directions. It begins with,

> *[The Musick playing louder, the Priests and Priestesses dance about the Idol with ridiculous Postures, and crying . . .]*

Then "soft musick" is called for, followed by,

> *[The Musick changes to confused Tunes, to which the Priests and Priestesses dance . . .]*

Some poets, again perhaps fearful of the Puritans, kept their religious references to Heaven and the angels. We especially enjoy Edward Young's refusal to sing in the Heavenly choir unless it is conduced by the artist, Raphael!

> But sing no more—no more I sing,
> Or reassume the lyre,
> Unless vouchsafed an humble part
> Where Raphael leads the choir.[30]

James Thomson writes of the music of the angels in two of his poems.

> Whose flaming love their tuneful harps employ
> In solemn hymns Jehovah's praise to sing,
> And make all heaven with hallelujahs ring.[31]

> . . . . . .

> Methinks I hear the full celestial choir,
> Through Heaven's high dome their awful anthem raise;
> Now chanting clear, and now they all conspire
> To swell the lofty hymn from praise to praise.[32]

Alexander Pope, in his poem, "The Dying Christian," hears the music of heaven and pens one of his most famous lines.

[30] Edward Young, "Resignation," in *Edward Young: The Complete Works* (Hildesheim: Olms, 1968), II, 123.

[31] 'Upon Happiness," in *The Poetical Works of James Thomson* (London: Bell and Daldy, c. 1860), I, 98. James Thomson (1700–1748) was highly respected by both Voltaire and Lessing, but has never been esteemed by his own countrymen, II, 171.

[32] "An Ode on Aeolus's Harp," in Ibid., II, 228.

> The world recedes; it disappears!
> Heaven opens on my eyes! my ears
> With sounds seraphim ring:
> Lend, lend your winds! I mount! I fly!
> O Grave! where is thy Victory?
> O Death! where is thy Sting?[33]

Gradually, as the English society began to gain a bit more self confidence after the Puritan disruption, poets and playwrights began again to praise the relationship between music and the divine. There is little reference to church music in Dryden, however, in the preface to his play *Tyrannick Love*, while discussing the potential of dramatic poetry in influencing the audience in matters of religion, he digresses to comment on church music.

> By the harmony of words we elevate the mind to a sense of devotion, as our solemn musick, which is inarticulate poetry, does in churches; and by the lively images of piety, adorned by action, through the senses allure the soul: which while it is charmed in a silent joy of what it sees and hears, is struck at the same time with a secret veneration of things Celestial, and is wound up insensibly into the practice of that which it admires.[34]

In *Love in a Nunnery* (IV, iii) a scene set in a chapel begins with a stage direction reading "Instrumental and vocal music." Dryden gives us some idea of the music he had in mind when he has the duke reflect,

> You have treated me with harmony so excellent, that I believed myself among a choir of angels.

A more conventional view is found in a line in Alexander Pope's "Eloisa to Abelard," which finds the "swelling organs lift the rising soul."[35]

Due to the disruption of the church boy's schools, after the Restoration it was found that there was a shortage of boys to sing the upper parts and so the cornett was called upon to fill these voices. This problem is discussed by Matthew Locke in a treatise, "The Present Practice of Music Vindicated," in 1673.

---

[33] "The Dying Christian to his Soul" (1712), in *The Works of Alexander Pope* (New York: Gordian Press, 1967), IV, 409. Alexander Pope (1688–1744) was born to the family of a prosperous merchant, but as he was also born Catholic he was denied an education at any of the great universities. Thus, the greatest English poet of the eighteenth century was the product of his own education through reading. An illness as a child left him a four foot high hump-back.

[34] *The Works of John Dryden*, ed. Edward Hooker (Berkeley: University of California Press, 1956), X, 109.

[35] "Eloisa to Abelard," line 272.

For above a year after the opening of His Majesty's Chappell the orderers of the musick there were necessitated to supply the superior part of their musick with cornets and men's feigned voices, there being not one lad for all that time capable of singing his part readily.

A similar complaint was made by Hawkins:

Upon the revival of the choral service, in the royal chapel especially, they were necessitated for want of treble voices, to make use of cornets, and on particular occasions sacbuts and other instruments.[36]

A petition made to the government by a group of composers in 1657 took a broader view in their concerns of the negative impact of the Puritans.

By reason of the late dissolution of the Choirs in the Cathedrals where the study and practice of the Science of Music was especially cherished, Many of the skillful Professors of the said Science have during the late Wars and troubles died in want, and there being now no preferment or Encouragement in the way of Music, no man will breed his child in it, so that it must needs be, that the Science itself, must die in this Nation, with those few Professors of it now living, or at least it will degenerate much from that perfection lately attained unto.[37]

But the use of cornetts to perform the upper voices were not the only winds in the church after the Restoration, indeed a wide variety was beginning to appear, as we see in another diary which mentions the festival of St. George at Windsor in 1661.

...the hymn was composed and set with verse and chorus by Capt. Cook—by whose direction some instrumental loud musick was at that time introduced, namely, two double sackbuts and two double courtalls—one sackbut and courtal before the four petty canons who began the hymn, and the other two immediately before the prebends of the College.[38]

This same eyewitness gives us another valuable comment on the actual placement of the winds in the church in his record of a service in 1674.

[36] Quoted in Henry De Lafontaine, *The King's Musick* (London, 1909), 482.

[37] Quoted in Peter Holman, in "London: Commonwealth and Restoration," in *The Early Baroque Era* (Englewood Cliffs: Prentice Hall, 1994), 307ff.

[38] Elias Ashmole, quoted in Lafontaine, *The King's Musick*, 448.

> There were placed in the middle of the Choristers two Cornets & behind them a Sackbote, & last of all a Sackbut ... & Doctor Child the Organist alone in his Doctors habit.[39]

According to Roger North, the regional cathedrals of Durham and York continued to depend on wind instruments, even to substitute for missing voices.

> They have ordinary wind instruments in the choirs, as the cornett, sackbut, double curtal and others, which supply the want of voices, very notorious there; and nothing can so well reconcile the upper parts in a choir, since we can have none but boys and those none of the best, as the cornett (being well sounded) doth; one might mistake it for a choice eunuch.[40]

As the seventeenth century progressed one finds a number of philosophers and musicians who registered objections not to music in the service, but to the quality of the performance. Thomas Mace was one who pointed to the importance of emotions in church music, especially for reaching the common man.

> All things in the church, and in its service, would be contrived and ordered, that the common-poor-ignorant-people might be so much capable as it is possible of apprehending, discerning or understanding; so, as they might unite their voices, hearts and affections together with the congregation and the service.[41]

Mace mentions the affections of the congregation in the above, and indeed he places considerable emphasis on the importance of the church composer reflecting emotions, especially with regard to the words of the Psalms, in his music. This entire relationship, of music and words, and of their impact on man, was regarded by Mace as little studied.

> There being a very great affinity, nearness, naturalness or sameness between language and music, although not known to many. And it is a bemoanable pity to consider how few there are who know, but fewer who consider, what wonderful-powerful-efficacious virtues and operations of music has upon the souls and spirits of men divinely-bent.[42]

[39] *The Autobiographical Notes of Elias Ashmole*, ed. C. H. Josten (Oxford, 1966), IV, 1380.

[40] Quoted in John Wilson, *Roger North on Music* (London: Novello, 1959), 40.

[41] Thomas Mace, *Musick's Monument* [1676] (Paris: Editions du Centre National de la Recherche Scientifique, 1966), 232ff. Mace (1613–1709) was a "clerk" at Trinity College, Cambridge.

[42] Ibid., 3.

In this regard, Mace concluded his book with the thought that music might be the form of communication used in heaven.

> And I am subject to believe (if in Eternity we shall make use of any languages, or shall not understand one another, by some more spiritual conveyances, or infusions of perceptions, than by verbal language) that music itself may be that eternal and celestial language.[43]

[43] Ibid., 272.

When Mace turns his attention to country churches, he finds the Psalms tortured and tormented, the Service dishonored, coarse and made ridiculous by the quality of the music. He was particularly exercised by the quality of the singing and declared it better not to sing at all than sing out of tune. This, because of the close relationship he perceived between music and the divine.

> For as I often used to say, that as conchording unity in music is a lively and very significant simile of God, and Heavenly joys, and felicities, so on the contrary, jarring discords are as apt a simile of the Devil, or Hellish tortures.[44]

[44] Ibid., 3.

Considering that if even one with an absolute voice is "uncertain of singing in tune," he wonders what can one expect from "the unskilfull-inharmonious-coarse-grained-harsh-voice?" Certainly God takes no pleasure from such "halt, lame and blind sacrifices." Mace's solution for helping the country congregation is the organ and he writes at length explaining the kind of instrument needed, how the funds can be raised and how to find an organist.

The cathedral churches Mace also found wanting, with insufficient numbers of singers. The small numbers were further decimated by frequent absences,

> by reason of sickness, indispositions, hoarseness, colds, business, and many other accidents, and necessary occasions, men must be absent, disabled, or impeded from doing their duties; so that at such times, the Service must suffer: and such like accidents happen too often.[45]

[45] Ibid., 23ff.

And, of those present, "few of them are (or can possibly be) masters in the art of song, or singing; much less in the art of music in general."

The reason for this state of affairs was the poor pay given cathedral singers, which Mace found "very low, inconsiderable, insufficient, unbecoming and uncomfortable." As a consequence, the singers often were forced to take other jobs. Why should we be surprised, Mace asks, that when they sing in church they "make sour faces, and cry, or roar out aloud." He concludes,

> Now I say, these things considered how certainly true they are, first in reference to the [singers] pitiful-poor-wages, and likewise to the general dead-heartedness, or zeal-benumbed-frozen-affections in these our time, toward the encouragement of such things; how can it be imagined that such [singers] should be fit and able performers in that duty, which necessarily depends upon education, breeding and skill in that quality of music, which is both a costly, careful and a laborious-attainment, not at all acquirable (in its excellency) by an inferior-low-capacitated men.

Avison, whose entire discussion of musical expression was based on the communication of emotions, even stressed that the church organist must feel the appropriate emotions while he plays if he is to succeed.

> If our organist is a lover of poetry, without which, we may dispute his love for music; or indeed, if he has any well-directed passions at all, he cannot but feel some elevation of mind, when he hears the psalm preceding his voluntary, pronounced in an awful and pathetic strain: It is then he must join *his* part, and with some solemn air, relieve, with religious cheerfulness, the calm and well-disposed heart. Yet, if he feels not this divine energy in his own breast, it will prove but a fruitless attempt to raise it in that of others.[46]

He also finds the congregation does not sing with enough emotion and makes the interesting observation that he wishes they sang as they do when they visit a foreign church, without reading line by line.

In his "Solomon's Temple Spiritualized," John Bunyan reviews at length the descriptions of church singing mentioned in both the Old and New Testaments. The only comments which Bunyan makes regarding church music of his own

[46] Charles Avison, *An Essay on Musical Expression* [London, 1753] (New York: Broude Reprint, 1967), 88. Avison (1709–1770) was an organist and composer.

time are that the music should be contemporary in its themes and that it should be sung in the proper spirit and with understanding.

> And answerable to this, is the church to sing now new songs, with new hearts for new mercies. New songs, I say, are grounded on new matter, new occasions, new mercies, new deliverances, new discoveries of God to the soul, or for new frames of heart; and are such as are most taking, most pleasing, and most refreshing to the soul ...
>
> I pray God it be done by all those that now-a-days get into churches, in spirit and with understanding.[47]

Another important contemporary document we have for insight into the quality of Restoration church music is the Samuel Pepys diary. He was an amateur musician, but one of some experience. In his diary Pepys makes numerous observations on the music of the church which he heard in person. Sometimes he primarily comments on the quality of the choir, as in 1664 when he calls the choir at the famous St. Pauls "the worst that ever I heard."[48] On the other hand, after hearing the service at Windsor, St. George's Chapel in 1666, he writes,

> And here, for our sakes, had this anthem and the great service sung extraordinary, only to entertain us ... A good Choir of voices.[49]

In the early years covered by the diary there are some unusual descriptions. In September 1660 he reports hearing "a dull Anthem,"[50] and the following month, at Whitehall, an anthem "ill sung, which made the king laugh."[51] Three months later he reports "a long Psalm was set that lasted an hour while the Sexton gathered his year's contribution through the whole church."[52]

With regard to the court church music, his comments would seem to indicate that the music of the Queen's Chapel was the more progressive. In 1666 he writes that he does not like the music at the Queen's Chapel,[53] but two weeks later he makes the first of several references to what must have been some form of unusual instrumental accompaniment (the "Musique").

---

[47] "Solomon's Temple Spiritualized," in *The Works of John Bunyan*, ed. George Offor (London: Blackie and Son, 1853), III, 496. John Bunyan (1628–1688) is considered the greatest prose writer among the Puritans of the seventeenth century. Only the Bible was so widely read in English homes for the subsequent three centuries. Bunyan was also the epitome of the "hell and brimstone" preacher.

[48] Pepys Diary, February 28, 1664.

[49] Ibid., February 26, 1666.

[50] Ibid., September 2, 1660.
[51] Ibid., October 14, 1660.

[52] Ibid., January 6, 1661.

[53] Ibid., April 1, 1666.

> [I] heard a good deal of their mass and some of their Musique, which is not so contemptible, I think, as our people would make it, it pleasing me very well.[54]

One wonders if by "contemptible" there was some form of movement by the instrumentalists. Otherwise, what could he possibly mean when he writes,

> but that they do jump most excellently with themselves and their instrument—which is wonderful pleasant.[55]

An entry a few months later also possibly refers to unusual instrumental accompaniment. On this occasion he liked the composition but found the voices harsh and suspected it was their choice of instruments that caused it[56]

It is in the Queen's Chapel as well, where he also heard Italian singers. In 1667 he mentions the Italian music, "whose composition is fine, but yet the voices of the Eunuchs I do not like." He goes on to make one of his favorite contentions, that vocal music can only really be understood by the people who speak the language of the text.[57] The following year, however, he seems quite delighted.

> To the Queen's chapel and there did hear the Italians sing; and indeed, their music did appear most admirable to me, beyond anything of ours—I was never so well satisfied in my life with it.[58]

With regard to the King's Chapel, during the early years Pepys appears most complimentary. He frequently praises the anthems of Henry Cooke[59] and one such reference describes a rehearsal.

> After dinner to White-hall chappell with Mr. Childe; and there did hear Captain Cooke and his boy make a trial of an anthem against tomorrow, which was rare Musique.[60]

An entry of September 1662 may refer to the use of wind instruments, "a most excellent Anthem (with Symphony's between) sung by Captain Cooke."[61]

Later entries in the diary, following the return of Humfrey and the introduction of more complex contrapuntal styles, find Pepys not so pleased.

---

[54] Ibid., April 15, 1666.

[55] Ibid., April 7, 1667.

[56] Ibid., September 8, 1667.

[57] Ibid., April 7, 1667.

[58] Ibid., March 22, 1668.

[59] Captain Henry Cooke (1615–1672) composed in all styles, including opera. He must have been an exceptional teacher, for his students included Blow, Humfrey and Purcell.

[60] Pepys Diary, February 23, 1661.

[61] Ibid., September 7, 1662.

> [To White-hall] and heard a fine Anthem, made by Pelham [Humfrey] who is come over in France, of which there was great expectation; and indeed is a very good piece of Musique, but still I cannot call the Anthem anything but Instrumental music with the Voice, for nothing is made of the words at all.[62]

A similar entry the following year reads,

> To the Chapel and did hear an Anthem of Silas Taylors making—a dull old-fashion thing of six and seven parts that nobody could understand.[63]

Finally, we might cite a reference of September 1667 to performance practice in church music.

> I went to the King's Chapel ... and there I hear Cresset sing a Tenor part along with the Church music; very handsomely, but so loud that people did laugh at him—as a thing done for ostentation.[64]

When the king appeared at important festivities in the church one may assume he arrived with his royal trumpets. The royal pay accounts for 1630 indicate seventeen trumpets performed during a Pentecost ceremony.[65] An eyewitness has left a similar record of a Te Deum sung in church celebrating the Peace of Utrecht in 1743.

> ...as it was composed for a military triumph, the 14 trumpets, two pair of common kettle drums, two pair of double drums from the Tower, and a pair of *double bass drums*, made expressly for this commemoration ... were introduced with great propriety. Indeed the last-mentioned drums, except in their destruction, had all the effect of the most powerful artillery.[66]

The great Italian opera movement, one of the distinguishing hallmarks of the Baroque Period, was very late in being embraced by England. Once it began to appear there were complaints, as indeed there were in other countries, of its bad influence on church music. The chief complaints were against music which sounded popular or theatrical and also against improvisation. Typical of these objections are some articles

[62] Ibid., November 1, 1667.

[63] Ibid., June 28, 1668.

[64] Ibid., September 8, 1667.

[65] Lord Chamberlain Accounts, London (vols. 799, 459).

[66] W. T. Parke, *Musical Memoirs* (New York, 1970), 38.

which appeared in the new popular journals at the end of the Baroque. A correspondent to the *Spectator* issue of March 28, 1712, complains about the introduction of lighter music in the church.

> For a great many of our Church Musicians being related to the theater, they have, in imitation of these epilogues, introduced in their farewell Voluntaries a sort of Musick quite foreign to the design of church services, to the great prejudice of well-disposed people. Those fingering gentlemen should be informed, that they ought to suit their Airs to the place and business; and that the musician is obliged to keep to the text as much as the preacher ... For when the preacher has often, with great piety and art enough handled his subject ... I have found in my self, and in the rest of the pew, good thoughts and dispositions, they have been all in a moment dissipated by a merry Jig from the organ loft ... Pray Sir do what you can to put a stop to these growing evils.

Addison, writing in the *Spectator* for June 14, 1712, wishes as much attention could be given to the improvement of church music as has been devoted to the music of the stage in recent years. He wonders why the excellent texts, in both Hebrew and English, available to composers do not inspire them to greater efforts. As we have seen before, Addison is thinking of the purpose of music being to support language and finds its virtue there, rather than from any inherent qualities.

> Since we have such a treasury of words, so beautiful in themselves, and so proper for the Airs of Musick, I cannot but wonder that persons of distinction should give so little attention and encouragement to that kind of Musick, which would have its foundation in Reason, and which would improve our virtue in proportion as it raised our delight. The passions that are excited by ordinary compositions, generally flow from such silly and absurd occasions, that a man is ashamed to reflect upon them seriously; but the fear, the love, the sorrow, the indignation that are awakened in the mind by hymns and anthems, make the heart better, and proceed from such causes as are altogether reasonable and praise-worthy. Pleasure and duty go hand in hand, and the greater our satisfaction is, the greater is our religion.

Addison then briefly reviews the use of music in the Old Testament and in the religious rites of the ancient Greeks, after which he wishes,

> Had we frequent entertainments of this nature among us, they would not a little purify and exalt our passions, give our thoughts a proper turn, and cherish those divine impulses in the soul, which every one feels that has not stifled them by sensual and immoderate pleasures.
>
> Musick, when thus applied, raises noble hints in the mind of the hearer, and fills it with great conceptions. It strengthens devotion, and advances praise into rapture.

Steele published a fictional letter to the editor of the *Spectator* of October 7, 1712, which describes a gentleman attending a church service in London in which he reports on "a young lady in the very bloom of youth and beauty, dressed in the most elegant manner imaginable." Except for the fact that she chose to stand during the entire service, everyone noticed that she was the very picture of modesty, goodness, sweetness and "ardent devotion."

> Well, now the organ was to play a voluntary, and she was so skillful in Musick, and so touched with it, that she kept time, not only with some motion of her head, but also with a different air in her countenance. When the Musick was strong and bold, she looked exalted, but serious; when lively and airy, she was smiling and gracious; when the notes were more soft and languishing, she was kind and full of pity. When she had now made it visible to the whole congregation, by her motion and ear, that she could dance, and she wanted now only to inform us that she could sing too, when the Psalm was given out, her voice was distinguished above all the rest, or rather people did not exert their own in order to hear her. Never was any heard so sweet and so strong. The organist observed it, and he thought fit to play to her only, and she swelled every note; when she found she had thrown us all out, and had the last verse to herself in such a manner, as the whole congregation was intent upon her, in the same manner as you see in cathedrals they are on the person who sings alone the anthem.

Finally, we will append here some examples of the poems in honor of St. Cecilia's Day, which celebrated not a religious theme exactly, but the worship of music. Perhaps, in its own way, it was this literature which was the ultimate answer to the Puritans. Joseph Addison has written two such poems.[67] In his "A Song for St. Cecilia's Day," he begins in praise of the patron saint.

[67] Joseph Addison (1672–1719) was a fellow at Magdalen College, Oxford, and was very active in politics, eventually becoming Secretary of State.

> Let all Cecilia's praise proclaim,
> Employ the echo in her name,
> Hark how the flutes and trumpets raise,
> At bright Cecilia's name, their lays;
> The organ labors in her praise.
> Cecilia's name does all our numbers grace,
> From every voice the tuneful accents fly,
> In soaring trebles now it rises high,
> And now it sinks, and dwells upon the base.
> Cecilia's name through all the notes we sing,
> The work of every skillful tongue,
> The sound of every trembling string,
> The sound and triumph of our song.

Now he turns to the purposes of music, treating in turn emotions, character development and religion.

> For ever consecrate the day,
> To music and Cecilia;
> Music, the greatest good that mortals know,
> And all of heaven we have below.
> Music can noble hints impart,
> Engender fury, kindle love;
> With unsuspected eloquence can move,
> And manage all the man with secret art . . .

> Music religious heats inspires,
> It wakes the soul, and lifts it high,
> And winds it with sublime desires,
> And fits it to bespeak the Deity.
> The Almighty listens to a tuneful tongue,
> And seems well-pleased and courted with a song.
> Soft moving sounds and heavenly airs
> Give force to every word, and recommend our prayers.

He concludes with a poetic reference to the Day of Judgment.

> When time itself shall be no more,

> And all things in confusion hurled,
> Music shall then exert its power,
> And sound survive the ruins of the world.

The second poem on this subject by Addison is called "Ode for St. Cecilia's Day," written in 1699 and set to music by Daniel Purcell. In this work he concentrates on aesthetic characterizations of the violin, flute, organ and trumpet.

> First let the sprightly violin
> The joyful melody begin,
> And none of all her strings be mute;
> While the sharp sound and shriller lay
> In sweet harmonious notes decay,
> Softened and mellowed by the flute.
>
> Next, let the solemn organ join
> Religious airs, and strains divine,
> Such as may lift us to the skies,
> And set all Heaven before our eyes.
>
> Let then the trumpet's piercing sound
> Our ravished ears with pleasure wound.
> The soul overpowering with delight,
> As, with a quick uncommon ray,
> A streak of lightening clears the day,
> And flashes on the sight.
> Let Echo too perform her part,
> Prolonging every note with art,
> And in a low expiring strain
> Play all the concert over again ...
>
> And now the choir complete rejoices,
> With trembling strings and melting voices.
> The tuneful ferment rises high,
> And works with mingled melody.
> Quick divisions run their rounds,
> A thousand trills and quivering sounds
> In airy circles over us fly,
> Till, wafted by a gentle breeze,
> They faint and languish by degrees,
> And at a distance die.

As in the above case, most of these St. Cecilia Odes were set to music. William Congreve wrote a poem, "A Hymn to Harmony," in honor of St. Cecilia's Day of 1701, which was set to music of "John Eccles, Master of Her Majesties Musick." John Oldham's "Ode for an Anniversary of Musick on St. Cecilia's Day," was set to music by "Dr. Blow."

> Begin the song, your instruments advance
> Tune the voice, and tune the flute,
> Touch the silent, sleeping lute,
> And make the strings to their own measures dance.
> Being gentlest thoughts, that into language glide,
> Bring softest words, that into numbers slide.
> Let every hand, and every tongue,
> To make the noble consort, throng.
> Let all in one harmonious note agree
> To frame the mighty song,
> For this is musick's sacred Jubilee.
>
> Hark, how the wakened strings resound,
> And break the yielding air,
> The ravished sense, how pleasingly they wound,
> And call the listening soul into the ear;
> Each pulse beats time, and every heart,
> With tongue, and fingers, bears a part.
> By harmony's entrancing power,
> When we are thus wound up to ecstasy;
> Methinks we mount, methinks we tower,
> And seem to antedate our future bliss on high.
>
> How dull were life, how hardly worth our care,
> But for the charms that musick lends!
> How faint its pleasures would appear,
> But for the pleasure which our art attends!
> Without the sweets of melody,
> To tune our vital breath,
> Who would not give it up to death,
> And in the silent grave contented lie?
>
> Musick's the cordial of a troubled breast,
> The softest remedy that grief can find;
> The gentle spell, that charms our care to rest,
> And calms the ruffled passions of the mind.
> Musick does all our joys refine,
> It gives the relish to our wine,
> 'Tis that gives rapture to our love,
> And wings devotion to a pitch divine;
> 'Tis our chief bliss on earth, and half our heaven above.
>
> Come then, with tuneful throat and string,

The praises of our art let's sing;
Let's sing to blest Cecilia's fame,
That graced this art, and gave this day its name;
With musick, wind and mirth conspire
To bear a consort, and make up the choir.[68]

Alexander Pope also contributed an Ode to St. Cecilia's Day, one which begins with a call to the Muses:

Descend, ye Nine! descend and sing;
The breathing instruments inspire,
Wake into voice each silent string,
And sweep the sounding lyre!
In a sadly-pleasing strain
Let the warbling lute complain:
Let the loud trumpet sound,
Till the roofs all around
The shrill echoes rebound:
While in more lengthened notes and slow,
The deep, majestic, solemn organs blow.
Hark! the numbers soft and clear,
Gently steal upon the ear;
Now louder, and yet louder rise,
And fill with spreading sounds the skies;
Exulting in triumph now swell the bold notes,
In broken air, trembling, the wild music floats;
Till, by degrees, remote and small,
The strains decay,
And melt away,
In a dying, dying fall.[69]

Next Pope offers a catalog of the purposes and virtues of music.

By Music, minds an equal temper know,
Nor swell too high, nor sink too low.
If in the breast tumultuous joys arise,
Music her soft, assuasive voice applies;
Or when the soul is pressed with cares,
Exalts her in enlivening airs.
Warriors she fires with animated sounds;
Pours balm into the bleeding lover's wounds:
Melancholy lifts her head,
Morpheus rouses from his bed,
Sloth unfolds her arms and wakes,

[68] In *The Works of John Oldham* (London: Bettenham, 1722), II, 254. John Oldham (1653–1683) was a satirist best remembered for his "Satyrs Upon the Jesuits," of 1681.

[69] "Ode on St. Cecilia's Day," in *The Works of Alexander Pope*, IV, 397ff.

Listening Envy drops her snakes;
Intestine war no more our Passions wage,
And giddy Factions hear away their rage.

......

Music the fiercest grief can charm,
And fate's severest rage disarm:
Music can soften pain to ease,
And make despair and madness please ...

Jonathan Swift offers a strange addition to the repertoire of Odes to St. Cecilia.

Grave Dean of St. Patrick's, how comes it to pass,
That you, who know music no more than an ass,
That you who so lately were writing of drapiers,
Should lend your cathedral to players and scrapers [violinists]?
To act such an opera once in a year,
So offensive to every true Protestant ear,
With trumpets, and fiddles, and organs, and singing,
Will sure the Pretender and Popery bring in,
No Protestant Prelate, his lordship or grace,
Durst there show his right, or most reverend face:
How would it pollute their crosiers and rochets,
To listen to minims, and quavers, and crotchets![70]

[70] "Dr. Swift to Himself on St. Cecilia's Day."

3
Music in the Restoration Theater

> ... profane babblings and fabulous stories ...
> fit only for Heathens.
> *William Penn, on seventeenth century English plays*

THE SEVENTEENTH CENTURY PLAYWRIGHT, Sir Charles Sedley, in the prologue to his *Bellamira*, gives a playwright's answer to the above preacher's complaint.

> Is it not strange to see in such an age
> The Pulpit get the better of the Stage?
> Not through rebellion as in former days,
> But zeal for sermons and neglect for plays.

John Hawkins, looking back from 1776, saw Restoration drama as a medium focused on low entertainment, which he attributed in part to its association with popular music.

> The Restoration was followed by a total change in the national manners; that disgust which the rigor of the preceding times had excited, drove the people into the opposite extreme of licentiousness; so that in their recreations and divertissements they were hardly to be kept within the bounds of moderation ...
> The [Reformation theaters] were truly and emphatically styled theaters, as being constructed with great art, adorned with painting and sculpture, and in all respects adapted to the purposes of scenic representation. In the entertainments there exhibited music was required as a necessary relief, as well

to the actors as the audience, between the acts: compositions for this purpose were called Act-tunes, and were performed in concert; instruments were also required for the dances and the accompaniment of songs. Hence it was that, upon the revival of stage-entertainments, music became attached to the theaters, which from this time, no less than formerly the church had been, became the nurseries of musicians; insomuch, that to say of a performer on any instrument that he was a playhouse musician, or of a song, that it was a playhouse song, or a playhouse tune, was to speak of each respectively in terms of the highest commendation.[1]

All this notwithstanding, the reader must remember that since the time of Elizabethan theater it had been a goal of the plays to be life-like, to reflect London life as it was. It is for this reason that it is important that one not forget to look at these plays for clues to seventeenth century musical life in England.

Before looking at the plays we should like to mention an essay by a leading playwright, William Congreve, "Amendments of Mr. Collier's," in which he writes of the association of "inspiration" with the "Divine" and makes a remarkable contemporary definition.

> The word *inspiration* when it has *divine* prefixed to it, bears a particular and known signification. But otherwise, to *inspire* is no more than to *Breathe into*; and a man without profaneness may truly say, that a trumpet, a fife, or a flute deliver a musical sound, by the help of Inspiration.[2]

Many observers during the seventeenth century blamed the popularity of opera for the decline of drama in both Italy and England. It is no surprise, therefore to find some of these playwrights making rather negative comments about opera. In Richard Steele's *The Conscious Lovers* (II, iii), Indiana suggests the "entertainment" of opera does not compare with drama.

> Though in the main, all the pleasure the best opera gives us, is but mere Sensation. Methinks it's pity the mind can't have a little more share in the Entertainment. The Musick's certainly fine; but, in my thoughts, there's none of your composers come up to old Shakespeare and Otway.

[1] John Hawkins, *A General History of the Science and Practice of Music* (1776) (New York: Dover Reprint, 1963), II, 684ff.

[2] *The Complete Works of William Congreve* (New York: Russell & Russell, 1964), III, 184. William Congreve (1670–1729) is considered the best of the Restoration writers of comedy and was particularly admired by Voltaire. He studied at Trinity College, Dublin, and worked in various government offices in London.

In Vanbrugh's *A Journey to London* (II, i), Arabella suggests that dice make better music than a "sleepy Opera!" Opera is mentioned again in his *The Provoked Husband* (V, iii), where Lord Townly infers that the high price of tickets in the theater keeps the poor people out. Then, the subject of opera is introduced.

> MASQUERADER. Right, my Lord. I suppose you are under the same astonishment, that an Opera should draw so much good company.
> LADY GRACE. Not at all, Madam; it is an easier matter sure to gratify the ear, than the understanding.[3]

We might also mention that Congreve, in the introduction to his *Opera of Semele*, explains that since his work is intended to be set to music, he has not felt obligated to observe the "equality of measure" in his lines which were intended to be used in Recitative. He adds,

> For as that style in Musick is not confined to the strict observation of time and measure, which is required in the composition of Airs and Sonatas, so neither is it necessary that the same exactness in numbers, rhymes, or measure, should be observed in words designed to be set in that manner, which must ever be observed in the formation of Odes and Sonnets. For what they call Recitative in Musick, is only a more tuneable speaking, it is a kind of Prose in Musick; its Beauty consists in coming near Nature, and in improving the natural accents of words by more Pathetick or Emphatical Tones.

It should be added that Congreve has written the words for a brief masque, *The Judgment of Paris*, with music by "Mr. John Eccles, Mr. Finger, Mr. Purcel, and Mr. Weldon." It appears, on the basis of its publication, that this entire work was sung, with the exception of a number of "symphonies."

On the Purpose of Music

THE MOST COMMON PURPOSE of music found in early literature is to soothe the listener or player. A typical example is found in Otway's *Alcibiades* (V, lines 108ff),[4] where the king

[3] *The Complete Works of John Vanbrugh* (London: Nonesuch Press, 1927), III, 264, 266 contains the music for two songs of Act IV, one with an optional version for flute.

[4] Thomas Otway (1652–1685) was highly esteemed by his contemporaries as a playwright.

(just before he is murdered!) calls for his page:

> Boy take thy Lute, and with a pleasing Air
> Appease my sorrows, and delude my care.

A similar instance is found in Nathaniel Lee's *Gloriana*, a play covering the life of Augustus Caesar, which begins with a banquet scene. After a stage direction,

> *[Ovid enters followed by Musick, and sings
>   while the Emperor sits melancholy.]*

A song begins:

> Let Business no longer usurp your High mind,
> But to dalliance give way, and to pleasure be kind.

When a song is called for in Nathaniel Lee's *Rival Queens* (IV, ii), we are reminded of a frequent criticism in ancient Greece that music made one effeminate.

> ALEXANDER. Ha! let me hear a song.
> CLYTUS. Musick [is] for Boys—Clytus would hear the groans
>   Of dying persons, and the Horses neighings;
>   Or if I must be tortured with shrill voices,
>   Give me the cries of Matrons in sacked towns.

Beginning with the Renaissance one finds mention of the value of music for use in courtship. But this purpose is satirized in George Etherege's Comedy of Manners, *The Man of Mode* (V, ii). Busy, a waiting woman, volunteers to sing a song, "As Amoret with Phillis sat." Harriet observes "She has a voice that will grate your ears worse than a cat-call." After she sings, two listeners observe,

> MR. DORIMANT. Musick so softens and disarms the mind.
> HARRIET. That not one arrow does resistance find.[5]

A humorous comment on this purpose is found in Congreve's *The Old Batchelour* (III, ii), where, after the lyrics of a love song are given, Silvia tells her suitor, the old bachelor, "If you could sing and dance so, I should love to look upon you too." The bachelor, Heartwell, answers,

[5] Sir George Etherege (1633–1691) is known for his emphasis on manners. Regarding this song, the original publication carried a note reading "Song by Sir C.S."

Why it was I sung and danced; I gave Musick to the voice, and life to their measures—Look you here, Silvia, [*Pulling out a Purse and chinking it*] here are Songs and Dances, Poetry and Musick—hark! how sweetly one Guinea rhymes to another— And how they dance to the Musick of their own Chink. This buys all together ...

The most important purpose of music, of course, is to communicate emotions. In an atmosphere where drama was focused on entertainment, this purpose is rarely mentioned. We do find in Congreve a brief hint into the contemporary perception of the power of music to incite the emotions, when he cites a Mr. Collier, who used the expression "Gun-Powder-Treason Plot upon Musick and Plays." Congreve adds that he concluded, "Musick is as dangerous as Gun-Powder."[6]

[6] "Amendments of Mr. Collier," in *The Complete Works of William Congreve*, III, 206.

We do find an interesting observation on the presence or absence of emotion in the actual performance of music in Richard Steele's *The Tender Husband* (III, i), where the point seems to be that the English perform without emotion. Here, after listening to a lady sing, her music teacher, a "Spinet-Master," responds,

You sing it very well; but, I confess, I wish you'd give more into the French Manner. Observe me, Hum it *A-la-Francoise*.

    With Studied Airs, etc.

The whole person, every limb, every nerve sings—The *English* way is only being for that time a mere musical instrument, just sending forth a sound without knowing they do so—Now, I'll give you a little of it, like an *English* woman— You are to suppose I've denied you 20 times, looked silly, and all that—Then with hands and face insensible—I have a mighty cold.

    With Studied Airs, etc.[7]

A similar comment on French singing suggests that the French songs are all skill and passion, but without thought. In George Etherege's *The Man of Mode* (IV, ii), Sir Fopling is urged to sing and he admits he studied in Paris with

[7] Richard Steele (1672–1729) attended Oxford, but left before graduating. He entered the army under an assumed name, for which he was disinherited. He became a very influential writer, especially in his collaboration with Joseph Addison.

"Lambert, the greatest master in the world, but I have his own fault, a weak voice." He finally sings the song, which he believes was composed by "Baptist," an illusion to Lully. The heart of this passage is found in the reaction by the listeners.

> MR. DORIMANT. I shall not flatter you, Sir Fopling, there is not much thought in it. But it is passionate and well turned.
> MR. MEDLEY. After the French way.

Regarding instrumental practice, we might add that in William Wycherley's *The Gentleman Dancing-Master* (III, i)[8] violinists are associated with dancing-masters and barbers. Don Diego adds the reflection, "indeed all that deal with Fiddles are given to impertinency."

During the seventeenth century in France the small bagpipe, called a musette, became a favorite instrument among aristocratic players who enjoyed pretending they were poor peasants. The royal oboists, who also played this instrument sometimes took off the canter, playing it as a small oboe—which, of course, it is. We know some professional oboists in Europe who therefore consider the musette as part of the oboe family. With this perspective, our attention was attracted to a point in John Vanbrugh's *The Relapse* (V, v), where the stage direction reads, "To the *Hautboys*," but the next dialogue, by Sir Tunbelly Clumsy, begins, "*Bag-pipes*, make ready there."[9]

On Music in the Plays

DURING THE JACOBEAN PERIOD there was almost no music used in Tragedy, but in the works of Nathaniel Lee we find music again employed. His stage directions call for an interesting variety of music to open scenes, including "soft Musick"[10]; a "lofty March," played by trumpets[11]; two child singers[12] and a "plaintive Tune, representing the present condition of Thebes."[13] But what is meant at the beginning of *Mithridates* by the stage direction, "A noise of Musick and *tuning* Voices is heard?" Sometimes a play begins with a stage direction reading simply, "fiddles playing."[14]

[8] William Wycherley (1641–1715) studied at Oxford, joined the court in exile in France and on his return to London was imprisoned for his debts.

[9] In Congreve's *Squire Trelooby* (I, xi) there is a comic scene with two musicians playing on "Glyster-pipes."

[10] *Sophonisba* (I, ii) and *Caesar Borgia* (IV, i), followed by a wedding song.
[11] *Sophonisba* (III, iii).
[12] *Theodosius* (IV, ii).
[13] *Oedipus* (I, i).

[14] *The Princess of Cleve* (I, i). The opening dialogue includes "prithe leave off playing fine in Consort, and stick to Time and Tune."

James Thomson wrote a masque, *Alfred*, for which the music was composed by Thomas Arne.[15] Thomson's stage direction for the beginning of Act I, scene iii, is unusually complex for the period.

> [Solemn music is heard at a distance.
> It comes nearer in a full symphony: after which
> a single trumpet sounds a high and awakening air.
> Then the following stanzas are sung by two aerial spirits unseen.]

Act II, scene iv, begins with a stage direction calling for a "Symphony of martial music."

In Congreve's *Semele*, a libretto intended to be used for an opera, Act III, scene one, begins with a stage direction which indicates prelude music in the character of a more modern overture. Congreve uses "movement" here in the Baroque style, meaning a change in emotion.

> [The God of Sleep lying on his Bed.
> A soft Symphony is heard.
> Then the Musick changes to a different Movement.]

A program direction at the beginning of III, vii, calls for "a mournful Symphony."

In Aphra Behn's *The Forced Marriage*, Act II begins with a stage direction which indicates that music "softly plays," until a curtain is lowered, and then "the Musick plays aloud till the Act begins."[16]

In some cases the music was used to establish a specific mood for the action which follows. In George Villiers *The Rehearsal* (V, i), for example, a stage direction reads "Soft Music," which is followed by this dialogue.

KING USHER. What sound is this invades our ears?
KING PHYSICIAN. Sure 'tis the Musick of the moving
  Spheres.[17]

A particularly curious example of establishing mood is found in John Vanbrugh's *Aesop* (V, i),[18] where we find the unusual stage direction,

> [The Trumpets sound a Melancholy Air until Aesop appears; and
> then the violins and hautbois strike up a Lanchashire Hornpipe.]

[15] James Thomson (1700–1748) was highly respected by both Voltaire and Lessing, but has never been esteemed by his own countrymen.

[16] Mrs. Aphra Behn (1640–1689) was the first English woman to earn a living by writing. After the death of her merchant husband, her experiences included service as a spy in the Netherlands and a period of time in prison for debts.

[17] George Villiers, Duke of Buckingham (1628–1687), intended this work as a satire on the current heroic drama style.

[18] Sir John Vanbrugh (1664–1726) was not only a playwright but a celebrated architect, whose work included Blenheim Palace and the Haymarket Opera—which he also managed.

Vanburgh's *The Pilgrim* (V, iii) contains "strange Musick" off stage, which one character supposes has its origin with fairies.

In Aphra Behn's *The Forced Marriage* (V, ii) we find a very rare instance where a stage direction indicates the music is to "continue all this scene." More common is the use of music only while some necessary stage movement is accomplished, as in "A Symphony playing all the while," as a god descends from the ceiling in Behn's *The Emperor of the Moon* (III, iii).

Music, usually trumpets, is often used to introduce a high ranking character onto the stage. A typical example is found in Nathaniel Lee's *Rival Queens* (II, i), where the arrival of Alexander the Great is announced by the "Noise of Trumpets sounding far off."[19] Surely, therefore, satire (or insult?) was intended in *Theodosius* (I, i) where the leading noble is announced by "Recorders flourish." On the other hand, a grandiose example is found in Congreve's *The Mourning Bride* (I, i), where a stage direction, before the entrance of the king, calls for a "Symphony of Warlike Musick."

The reader will recall the ancient Roman cult festival of the Moon, in which trumpets and percussion played a central role. This provides the occasion of a humorous moment in Behn's *The Emperor of the Moon* (III, ii), when Harlequin perceives the arrival of the emperor:

But hark, the sound of Timbrels, Kettle-Drums and Trumpets—
The Emperor, Sir, is on his way, prepare for his reception.

But the stage direction suggests a broader percussion section,

> *[A strange Noise is heard of Brass Kettles,*
> *and Pans, and Bells, and many tinkling things.]*

In contrast, in Act III, scene iii, of this play, the emperor's arrival in a procession is accompanied by "the Flutes playing a Symphony."

[19] Other instances in *Oedipus* (I, i) and in *Constantine the Great*. Trumpets announce arrival of Sulpitius, in Otway's *History and Fall of Caius Marius* (II, line 414).

Art Music

THE RESTORATION PLAYS are filled with the lyrics for songs, sometimes with an indication of the composer who "set" the words.[20] Curiously, these songs often have no relationship with the plot, rather they seem to be simply interpolated as if it were felt there was some need for musical entertainment. This can clearly only be taken as a feeble attempt to compete with the popular interest in Italian opera.

Some songs carry the interesting stage direction indicating a specific song is to be *notated*. A stage direction in Nathaniel Lee's *Oedipus* (III, i), for example, reads, "Musick first. Then Sing." To this stage direction is appended a further note, "This to be set through."[21] Such a specific indication invites one to wonder if the rest of the songs were sung with the music improvised. In fact, there is a specific request for an improvised song in Sir Charles Sedley's *The Mulberry Garden* (III, ii), where we find the following dialogue:

> VICTORIA. Are not these Verses somewhat too weak to stand alone?
>
> JACK WILDISH. Faith, Madam, I am of your mind, put a Tune to them, it is an easy Stanza.
>
> *[Victoria sings.]*

Perhaps this is also what is meant by a song in Richard Steele's *The Tender Husband*, which was published with a note reading, "Designed for the Fourth Act, but not Set."[22]

Some references to songs in these plays indicate a known song, as in Congreve's *Love for Love* (V, i), when Valentine requests, "I would have Musick— Sing me the Song that I like." After the song, he reflects, "No more, for I am melancholy." We suspect that such references are to the popular repertoire of broadside ballads, as seems likely in Farquhar's *The Beaux Stratagem* (III, iii), which contains the lyrics of a love song, which the stage direction indicates is to be sung to the tune of "Sir Simon the King." This is a rare instance where, before the action resumes, the singer is paid.

[20] In Congreve's *Love for Love* we are given the lyrics for two songs, together with the information that the music was written by John Eccles and another by Mr. Finger. Congreve's *The Way of the World* (III, i) tells us the composer was Eccles and names the singer as "Mrs. Hodgson." Farquhar's *Love and a Bottle* (III, i) includes a song for which the stage direction tells us the composer was "Mr. Richardson" and his *The Inconstant* includes a song composed by Daniel Purcell. Daniel Purcell is named as composer again in Richard Steele's *The Funeral* (V, iv). Aphra Behn's *The Lucky Chance* (III, i) includes a song with the indication, "made by Mr. Cheek."

[21] His tragedy, *Theodosius* was published with art songs composed by Henry Purcell which were sung after each act. The music is reproduced in *The Works of Nathaniel Lee* (Metuchen: Scarecrow Reprints, 1968), II, 305ff. This volume also includes a song sung in Act V of *The Duke of Guise*, the play co-authored with Dryden [Ibid., 473].

[22] The lyrics are given in *The Plays of Richard Steele* (Oxford: Clarendon Press, 1971), 213.

There are numerous instances in these plays in which there is a specific request for a *new* song. In Congreve's *The Old Batchelour* (II, ii), for example, Araminita requests, "O I am glad we shall have a Song to divert the discourse—Pray oblige us with the latest new Song." In his *The Double-Dealer* (II, i), before a song is sung, Mellefont not only requests a new song, but asks to hear it in a rehearsal.

> What's here, the Musick? Oh, my Lord has promised the Company a New Song ... [*Musicians crossing the Stage*] Pray let us have the favor of you to practice the Song before the Company hear it.

In William Wycherley's *Love in a Wood* (I, ii) a lady, Flippant, announces she will sing a new song, and the lyrics are given. After this song she observes that it is "the fashion for women of quality to sing any Song whatever, because the words are not distinguished." In his *The Gentleman Dancing-Master* (II, i) a lady has sung "a new Song" the previous evening and another character reflects "Madam, I dreamed all night of the Song you sung last."

In Vanbrugh's *The Provoked Wife* (II, ii) Lady Fancyfull asks her private singing teacher, "Is the town so dull, Mr. Treble, that it affords us never another New Song?" He gives her a new song which he acquired the day before and makes the comment, "Make what Musique you can of this Song, here." A reference to a song "a newly married Lady made within this week" concludes Vanbrugh's *The Provoked Wife*.

Finally, in Otway's *The Orphan* (III, lines 452ff), a page offers to sing the "last new song" he has learned, one about "my Lord and Lady, who were caught together, you know where." Lord Castalio is shocked.

> CASTALIO. You must be whipped Youngster, if you get such songs as these ...
> PAGE. Why, what must I sing, pray, my dear Lord?
> CASTALIO. Psalms, Child, Psalms.
> PAGE. Oh dear me! Boys that go to school learn Psalms, but Pages that are better bred sing Lampoons.

In the plays of Aphra Behn there are some curious and rare examples of music which has a negative impact on the listener. Her *Abdelazer* begins with "still Musick" followed by a love song. The Moor Abdelazer reacts "On me this Musick lost?—this sound on me, that hates all Softness?" The Queen of Spain wants to make love, the music continues playing softly, but again Abdelazer complains, "Cease that ungrateful Noise."[23] In *The Young King* (II, i), Orsames's philosophy teacher, Geron, plays an instrumental piece on the lute, but Orsames responds,

[23] A similar instance of music which is not appreciated is found at the beginning of Behn's *The Emperor of the Moon*.

> I do not like this Musick;
> It pleases me at first,
> But every touch thou giv'st that is soft and low
> Makes such impressions here,
> As puzzles me beyond Philosophy
> To find the meaning of;
> Begets strange notions of I know not what,
> And leaves a new and unknown thought behind it,
> That does disturb my quietness within.

There is one instance where we find a description of the private singing of a lady. In Vanbrugh's Comedy, *The Provoked Wife* (II, ii), we find this dialogue between a lady and her private singing teacher.

MR. TREBLE. I know no body sings so near a Cherubin as your Ladyship.
LADY FANCYFULL. What I do I owe chiefly to your skill and care, Mr. Treble. People do flatter me indeed, that I have a voice, and a *je-ne-scai quoy* in the conduct of it, that will make Musick of anything. And truly I begin to believe so, since what happened the other night: would you think if, Mr. Treble; walking pretty late in the park, a whim took me to sing *Chevy-Chase*, and would you believe it? Next morning I had three copies of Verses ...
MR. TREBLE. Are there any further commands for your Ladyship's humble servant?
LADY FANCYFULL. Nothing more at this time, Mr. Treble. But I shall expect you here every morning for this month.

Finally, there are a few references to serenades in these plays and they are generally uncomplimentary with respect to the music. In Aphra Behn's *Sir Patient Fancy* (I, i) there is a discussion of a potential serenade.

SIR CREDULOUS EASY. What think you then of the Bagpipe, Tongs, and Gridiron, Cat-calls, and loud-sounding Cymbals?

LODWICK KNOWELL. Naught, naught, and of known use; you might as well treat her with viols and flute-doux, which are enough to disoblige her forever.

Next, there is a discussion of perhaps hiring the king's Musick. When Lodwick reminds Sir Credulous that he must obtain a song, the latter responds,

A Song! hang it, it is but rummaging the Play-books, stealing thence is lawful Prize.

This serenade, when it occurs, is only mentioned in a stage direction reading, "A confused Noise of the Serenade."

Later in this same play (III, ix) there is another serenade, preceded by a procession in the street for which the stage direction calls for an elephant (!) and "others playing on strange confused instruments." When the first song is ineffective, Sir Credulous calls out "you Ballad-singers, have you no good songs of another fashion?" A musician wryly recommends a ballad called "Ill-wedded Joys, how quickly do you fade."[24]

[24] In *The Amorous Prince* (II, iii) a serenade is sung by the drunk Lorenzo, who tells his musicians, "Let them be soft low notes, do you hear?"

4
Music in Restoration Poetry

For thousands of years most poetry was sung. Now, while most poetry was no longer sung, it is interesting to find poets still speaking as if it were. Not only do the English Restoration poets speak of the "harmony" of their verses and begin by writing rhetorically "I sing of . . . ," but they also actually *call* their poetry *music*. Mark Akenside, for example, writes,

> . . . Attend, ye gentle powers
> Of musical delight! and, while I sing . . . [1]

While the Restoration poets continued to contribute to the overwhelming interest among Baroque artists in understanding and improving the goal of the communication of feeling as the most important role of the arts, after nearly two centuries of the opposite influence by the Church, now we also begin to see a broader interest. Following the progress in science made during the Enlightenment, we now see some evident interest in the actual physical associations with poetry. In other essays we have cited numerous examples of philosophers who, on purely an intuitive or deductive basis, seemed to perceive the basic bicameral nature of our brain and its function. A poem by Thomas Sheridan (1687–1738), a priest and schoolmaster friend of Swift, is a remarkable example. He is absolutely, and astonishingly, correct in his

[1] "The Pleasures of Imagination," I, lines 6ff, in *The Poetical Works of Mark Ekenside* (London: Bell and Daldy, 1845). Mark Akenside (1721–1770) was born of humble origins and eventually became a physician and activist in Scottish affairs.

assigning of right or left eye and ear functions vis-a-vis their actual relationship with the brain hemispheres.

> With my left eye, I see you sit snug in your stall,
> With my right I'm attending the lawyers that scrawl.
> With my left I behold your bellower a cur chase;
> With my right I'm reading my deeds for a purchase.
> My left ear's attending the hymns of the choir,
> My right ear is stunned with the noise of the crier.[2]

James Thomson also makes a reference to these separate faculties, but finding understanding in the head and music in the heart:

> To show us artless reason's moral reign,
> What boastful science arrogates in vain;
> The obedient passions knowing each their part;
> Calm light the head, and harmony the heart![3]

Alexander Pope, in a poem which he called "An Essay on Criticism," reflects on the similarities between music and poetry and suggests the highest art is that which goes to the heart.

> Music resembles poetry; in each
> Are nameless graces which no methods teach,
> And which a master hand alone can reach.
>
> ......
>
> Great wits sometimes may gloriously offend,
> And rise to faults true critics dare not mend;
> From vulgar bonds with brave disorder part,
> And snatch a grace beyond the reach of art,
> Which, without passing through the judgment, gains
> The heart, and all its end at once attains.[4]

In a poem of Mark Akenside we can see how firmly accepted was the dogma which still pervades our Western world today: that the subjects of the left hemisphere of the brain are valued considerably above those of the right hemisphere.

---

[2] Quoted in *The Poetical Works of Jonathan Swift* (London: Bell and Daldy, n.d.), III, 245.

[3] "Epitaph on Miss Stanley," in *The Poetical Works of James Thomson* (London: Bell and Daldy, c. 1860), II, 225. James Thomson (1700–1748) was highly respected by both Voltaire and Lessing, but has never been esteemed by his own countrymen.

[4] "An Essay on Criticism," lines 143ff, in *The Works of Alexander Pope* (New York: Gordian Press, 1967), II, 42ff. Alexander Pope (1688–1744) was born to the family of a prosperous merchant, but as he was also born Catholic he was denied an education at any of the great universities. Thus, the greatest English poet of the eighteenth century was the product of his own education through reading. An illness as a child left him a four foot high hump-back.

> For man loves knowledge, and the beams of Truth
> More welcome touch his understanding's eye,
> Than all the blandishments of sound his ear ...⁵

And in Gay's "Daphnis and Chloe," the lady is interested in speech above music.

> 'Tis true, thy tuneful reed I blamed,
> That swelled thy lip and rosy cheek;
> Think not thy skill in song defamed,
> That lip should other pleasures seek:
> Much, much thy musick I approve;
> Yet break thy pipe, for more I love,
> Much more to hear thee speak.⁶

On the other hand we see some poets returning to the subjects raised by the ancients such as the influence of the arts on morals and on society at large. The poet Mark Akenside makes the interesting suggestion that it was because early poetry was sung, that it was able to enter the world of philosophy.

> Armed with the lyre, already have we dared
> To pierce divine Philosophy's retreats,
> And teach the Muse her lore; already strove
> Their long divided honors to unite,
> While, tempering this deep argument, we sang
> Of Truth and Beauty.⁷

James Thomson, in his poem "Liberty," discusses the progress of music after the Dark Ages as it revived and the culture moved north and suggests that it is the heart, not Reason, which affects morals.

> ...Music again
> Her universal language of the heart
> Renewed; and, rising from the plaintive vale,
> To the full concert spread, and solemn choir.
> Even bigots smiled; to their protection took
> Arts not their own, and from them borrowed pomp:
> For in a tyrant's garden these awhile
> May bloom, though freedom be their parent soil.
> And now confessed, with gently growing gleam
> The morning shone, and westward streamed its light.

---

⁵ "The Pleasures of Imagination," II, lines 100ff, in *The Poetical Works of Mark Ekenside*.

⁶ In *The Works of John Gay* (London: Edward Jeffery, 1745), III, 145. John Gay (1685–1732) was born of humble stock and worked for a while as a silk merchant. He became one of the most beloved of English literary figures.

⁷ "The Pleasures of Imagination," II, lines 62ff, in *The Poetical Works of Mark Ekenside*.

> The Muse awoke. Not sooner on the wing
> Is the gay bird of dawn. Artless her voice,
> Untaught and wild, yet warbled through the woods
> Romantic lays. But as her northern course
> She, with her tutor Science, in my train,
> Ardent pursued, her strains more noble grew:
> While Reason drew the plan, the Heart informed
> The moral page, and Fancy lent it grace.[8]

[8] "Liberty," IV, in *The Poetical Works of James Thomson*, II, 73ff.

Alexander Pope includes in his poetry several references to the poor musical taste of nobles. In the Epilstle III of his "Moral Essays":

> Who starves by Nobles, or with Nobles eats?
> The wretch that trusts them, and the rogue that cheats.
> Is there a Lord, who knows a cheerful noon
> Without a fiddler, flatterer, or buffoon?
> Whose table, wit or modest merit share,
> Unelbowed by a gamester, pimp, or player?[9]

[9] "Moral Essays," Epistle III, lines 237ff, in *The Works of Alexander Pope*, III, 149.

A similar criticism of the taste of the noble is found in Epistle IV:

> Light quirks of music, broken and uneven,
> Make the soul dance upon a jig to Heaven.[10]

[10] Ibid., Epistle IV, lines 143ff.

Quite a different view of the enlightened noble's taste is found in Patrick Delany:

> A soul ennobled and refined
> Reproaches every baser mind:
> As strains exalted and melodious
> Make every meaner music odious.[11]

[11] Patrick Delany (c. 1685–1768), Chancellor of St. Patrick's, "The Pheasant and the Lark" (1730), quoted in *The Poetical Works of Jonathan Swift*, II, 182.

John Gay wonders why England does not support music as other countries do:

> Why must we climb the Alpine mountain's sides
> To find the seat where Harmony resides?
> Why touch we not so soft the silver lute,
> The cheerful haut-boy, and the mellow flute?
> 'Tis not the Italian clime improves the sound,
> But there the Patrons of her sons are found.[12]

[12] "Epistle IV," in *The Works of John Gay*, III, 34.

Music was a frequent vehicle for figures of speech during the English Baroque. One example we like is by Jonathan Swift and it is addressed to the Prince of Wales, who would become King George II.

> Now take your harp into your hand,
> The joyful strings, at your command,
>   In doleful sounds no more shall mourn.
> We, with sincerity of heart,
> To all your tunes shall bear a part,
>   Unless we see the tables turn.[13]

We also find it interesting that one still finds reference to the fabled Music of the Spheres in Restoration poetry. James Thomson, as had occasional writers over a long period before him, suggests that composers may find their inspiration in this celestial music.

> O yon high harmonious spheres,
> Your powerful Mover sing;
> To Him your circling course that steers,
> Your tuneful praises bring.
>
> Ungrateful mortals, catch the sound,
> And in your numerous lays,
> To all the listening world around,
> The God of nature praise.[14]

Pope also mentions the music of the spheres in his poem, "An Essay on Man," arguing that God was wise in not making man's senses more sensitive than they are, as he would likely be miserable. Of music, he says,

> If nature thundered in his opening ears,
> And stunned him with the music of the spheres,
> How would he wish that heaven had left him still
> The whispering zephyr, and the purling rill?[15]

On the Purpose of Music

AS MENTIONED ABOVE, the great interest among musicians in particular during the Baroque Period was in understanding

[13] "Parody on the Speech of Dr. Benjamin Pratt." Jonathan Swift (1667–1745) is the best known prose writer at the end of the English Baroque and shared a grandfather with Dryden. He rarely deals with artistic matters, preferring to satirize manners. Reared in Ireland, he became active in English politics until he returned to Dublin as Dean of St. Patrick's.

[14] "Hymn to God's Power," in *The Poetical Works of James Thomson*, II, 141.

[15] "An Essay on Man," lines 201ff, in *The Works of Alexander Pope*, II, 363.

the role of music in the expression of emotions. We find a number of poems, for example which focus on the very power of the emotions and the ability of music to help relieve these. Abraham Cowley finds that even the birds have to sing to soothe themselves.

> And when no Art affords me help or ease,
> I seek with verse my griefs to appease.
> Just as a bird that flies about
> And beats itself against the cage,
> Finding at last no passage out,
> It sits and sings, and so overcomes its rage.[16]

Another reference to the communication of rather strong emotions is found in Richard Lovelace's poem called "Dialogue for Lute and Voice."

> What sacred charm may this then be in harmonie,
> That thus can make the angels wild, the devils mild,
> And teach low Hell to Heaven to swell,
> And the high Heaven to stoop to Hell.[17]

A poem by Robert Herrrick entitled "To Musick" also points to the expression of strong emotions by music.

> Begin to charm, and as thou strike mine ears
> With thy enchantment, melt me into tears.
> Then let thy active hand scu'd over thy Lyre:
> And make my spirits frantic with the fire.
> That done, sink down into a silvery strain;
> And make me smooth as balm, and oil again.[18]

Quite different, is another poem by Herrick.

> The mellow touch of musick most doth wound
> The soul, when it doth rather sigh, then sound.[19]

Several poems in this literature concentrate on the expression of grief through music, as for example one by Edmund Waller.

> GALATEA. You that can tune your sounding strings so well
>   Of ladies beauties, and of love to tell;
>   Once change your note, and let your lute report

[16] "Friendship in Absence," in *The Complete Works of Abraham Cowley*, ed. Alexander Grosart (New York: AMS Press, 1967), II, 139. Abraham Cowley (1618–1667) attracted great attention as a young poet, but little later in his life.

[17] "A Dialogue. Lute and Voice," in *The Poems of Richard Lovelace*, ed. C. H. Wilkinson (Oxford: Clarendon Press, 1930), 161. Richard Lovelace (1618–1657), one of the Cavalier Poets, was devoted to the king and imprisoned by the Puritans.

[18] *The Poetical Works of Robert Herrick*, 67.

[19] Ibid., 12.

> The justest grief that ever touched the court.
> THIRSIS. Fair Nymph, I have in your delights no share,
>   Nor ought to be concerned in your care,
>   Yet would I sing if I your sorrows knew,
>   And to my aid invoke no Muse but you.
> GALATEA. Hear then, and let your song augment our grief
>   Which is so great, as not to wish relief.[20]

[20] 'Thirsis, Galateat," in *Edmund Waller, Poems* (Menston: Scolar Press, 1971), 49ff. Edmund Waller (1606–1687) came from a royalist family, but took the side of the Puritans. He became very popular during the Restoration.

Similarly, Ben Jonson, in lyrics for a song by Henry Youll published in 1608, reads,

> Slow, slow, fresh fount, keep time with my salt tears,
> Yet slower, yet, o faintly gentle springs:
> Listen to the heavy part the musique bears,
> "Woe weeps out her division, when she sings . . ."[21]

[21] *The Complete Poetry of Ben Jonson*, 328.

John Donne finds such strong emotions can be described by poetry, but need music to be fully expressed and to provide a sense of catharsis.

> But when I have done so,
> Some man, his art and voice to show,
> Doth set [to music] and sing my pain,
> And, by delighting many, frees again
> Grief, which verse did restrain.
> To Love, and Grief tribute of verse belongs,
> But not of such as pleases when 'tis read,
> Both are increased by such song . . .[22]

[22] "The triple Foole," *The Complete Poetry of John Donne* (New York: New York University Press, 1968), 99.

In the poetry of George Wither, we find two interesting references to the ancient Greek concept that music could change manners. In one poem, which he disseminated by passing it out a loophole in the Tower of London where he was imprisoned, he decided it "would better stir up the hearts of some, by being sung, than read." In this complaint on the manners of London, the stern Puritan poet implores London to turn to music to help improve the behavior of the citizens.

> Thou, London, whofoe're doth weep,
> Do, on thy viol, play and sing;
> Thy children, daily revel keep . . .[23]

[23] *Wither*, Spenser Society, Nr. 18, "A Warning-Piece to London," 34.

Before his "Hymn for a Musician," Wither writes a comment suggesting that some musicians have manners which might be improved by changing their repertoire.

> Many musicians are more out of order than their instruments: such as are so, may by singing this Ode, become reprovers of their own untunable affections. They who are better tempered, are hereby [reminded] what music is most acceptable to God, and most profitable to themselves.[24]

There are considerably more poems which refer to music and well-being. While the ancient Greeks used harmony as a metaphor to represent the well-ordered person, Henry Vaughan begins at an earlier point in suggesting that God designed man of music. Curiously, the latest research in physics in England and Switzerland has confirmed that man indeed consists of specific vibrating tones.

> Thus doth God *Key* disordered man
> (Which none else can,)
> Tuning his breast to rise, or fall;
> And by a sacred, needful art
> Like strings, stretch every part
> Making the whole most Musical.[25]

George Wither also was thinking of some remote time, writing of "He that first taught his Musicke such a strain":

> He in his troubles eased the body's pains,
> By measures raised to the souls ravishing … [26]

And in another poem,

> Teach me the skill,
> Of him, whose Harp assuaged
> Those passions ill,
> Which oft afflicted Saul.
> Teach me the strain
> Which calms mind's enraged;
> And, which from vain
> Affections, doth recall.[27]

A similar plea is found in Robert Herrick's poem called "To Musick, to becalm a sweet-sick-youth."

[24] Ibid., Nr. 26-27, "Halelviah," Hymn XXXVIII.

[25] "Affliction," in *The Works of Henry Vaughan*, ed. L. C. Martin (Oxford: At the Clarendon Press, 1957), 460.

[26] *Wither*, Spenser Society, Nr. 10, "The Shepheards Hunting," 506.

[27] Ibid., Nr. 26-27, "Halelviah," Hymn XXXVIII.

> Charms, that call down the moon from out her sphere,
> On this sick youth work your enchantments here:
> Bind up his senses with your numbers, so,
> As to entrance his pain, or cure his woe.
> Fall gently, gently, and a while him keep
> Lost in the civil Wilderness of sleep:
> That done, then let him, dispossessed of pain,
> Like to a slumbering Bride, awake again.[28]

Richard Crashaw, in a tribute to the Dutch philosopher, Leonard Lessius (1554–1623), and his book on "Life and Health," states that a healthy man has no need of medicine [physick], especially if he has money and music.

> That which makes us have no need
> Of physick, that's Physick indeed.
> Hark hither, Reader! wilt thou see
> Nature her own physician be?
> Wilt' see a man, all his own wealth,
> His own musick, his own health;
> A man whose sober soul can tell
> How to wear her garments well.[29]

The most extended discussion of music therapy is found in the work of Abraham Cowley. In his poem on the troubles of David, "Davideis," he mentions the passage in the Old Testament in which David and his harp cure the rage of Saul. He then pauses in his story of David to wonder how it is that music has this great power and concludes that the answer must lie in some close relationship to Nature and the subsequent unity of physics and the body.

> And true it was, soft Musick did appease
> The obscure fantastic Rage of Saul's disease.
> Tell me, oh Muse (for thou, or none canst tell
> The mystic powers that in blessed verse [*Numbers*] dwell,
> Thou their great Nature knows, not is it fit
> This noblest gem of thine own crown to omit)
> Tell me from whence these heavenly charms arise;
> Teach the dull world to admire what they despise.
> As first a various unformed hint we find
> Rise in some god-like poet's fertile mind,
> Until all the parts and words their places take,

[28] *The Poetical Works of Robert Herrick*, 99.

[29] "To the Reader," in *The Complete Poetry of Richard Crashaw*, 511.

And with just marches Verse and Musick make;
Such was God's poem, this world's new essay;
So wild and rude in its first draught it lay;
The ungoverned parts no correspondence knew,
An artless war from thwarting motions grew;
Until they to number and fixed rules were brought
By the eternal mind's poetic thought.
Water and air be for the tenor chose.
Earth made the bass, the treble flame arose;
To the active moon a quick brisk stroke he gave,
To Saturn's string a touch more soft and grave.
The motions straight, and round, and swift, and slow,
And short, and long, were mixed and woven so,
Did in such artful figures smoothly fall,
As made this decent measured Dance of All.
And this is Musick; sounds that charm our ears,
Are but one dressing that rich science wears.
Though no man heard it, though no man rehearse,
Yet will there still be musick in my verse.
In this great world so much of it we see;
The lesser, man, is all over harmony.
Storehouse of all proportions! single Choir!
Which first God's breath did tunefully inspire![30]

From hence blessed musick's heavenly charms arise,
From sympathy which them and to man allies.
Thus they our souls, thus they our bodies win.
Not by their force, but party that's within.
Thus the strange cure on our split blood applied,
Sympathy to the distant wound does guide.
Thus when two brethren strings are set alike,
To move them both, but one of them we strike.
Thus David's lyre did Saul's wild rage control,
And tuned the harsh disorders of his soul.[31]

In his own notes for this passage, Cowley clearly desired to go into more detail on this question. He began by reviewing several of the more familiar anecdotes in ancient literature in which music affected behavior.

> Neither should we wonder, that passions should be raised or suppressed ... But that it should cure settled diseases in the body, we should hardly believe, if we had not both human and divine testimony for it.[32]

[30] "Inspire," at this time in England was a synonym for "to blow," as to inspire a flute.

[31] "Davideis," in *The Complete Works of Abraham Cowley*, I, 49.

[32] Ibid., 67.

Cowley then adds, in addition to the testimony in the Old Testament, the well-known and documented instances in which music had cured the poison left by the bite of the Tarantula spider. But how does one explain it? He provides a virtual bibliography of early explanations before turning to speculation which had occurred in more modern times.

> For the explication of the reason of these cures, the Magicians fly to their *Colcodea*; the Platonicks to their *Anima Mundi*; the Rabbis to Fables and Prodigies not worth the repeating. Baptista Porta in his *Natural Magick*, seems to attribute it to the *Magical Power of the Instrument*, rather than of the Musick; for he says, that Madness is to be cured by the Harmony of a Pipe made of Hellobore, because the juice of that plant is held good for that purpose; and the Sciatique by a musical instrument made of Poplar, because of the virtue of the Oil of that tree to mitigate those kind of pains. But these, and many sympathetical experiments are so false, that I wonder at the negligence or impudence of their Relators. Picus. Mirand. says, That Musick moves the spirits to act upon the soul, as medicines do to operate upon the body, and that it cures the body by the soul, as medicine does the soul by the body.

At this point, Cowley offers his own explanation for the power of music to heal the body, which appears to have been based on the writings of the German philosopher, Athanasius Kircher (1601–1680).

> I conceive the true natural Reason to be, that in the same manner as musical sounds move the outward air, so that does the inward, and that the spirits, and they the Humors (which are the seat of diseases) by Condensation, Rarefaction, Dissipation, or Expulsion of Vapors, and by virtue of that sympathy of proportion, which I express afterwards in verse. For the producing of the effect desires, Athan. Kercherus requires four conditions: 1. Harmony. 2. Number and Proportion. 3. Efficacious and pathetical words joined with the harmony (which—by the way—were fully and distinctly understood in the musick of the ancients) And 4. an adapting of all these to the constitution, disposition, and inclinations of the patient. Of which, and all things on this subject, he is well worth the diligent reading, [in his] *Liber de Arte magna Consoni et Dissoni*.

In a Hymn which George Wither called, "A Hymn after a Feast," we find a reference to the ancient custom of a brief concert after a banquet, after the tables have been cleared.

> When is it fitter to begin
> The Song intended, now,
> Then when our Table spread hath bin
> And Cups, did overflow?[33]

[33] Wither, Spenser Society, Nr. 26-27, "Halelviah," Hymn XXXIII.

There are in this literature some interesting humorous descriptions of performers of art music. Andrew Marvel presents a poem in satire of an English priest and amateur musician.

> Now as two instruments to the same key
> Being tuned by art, if the one touched be,
> The other opposite as soon replies,
> Moved by the air and hidden sympathies;
> So while he with his gouty fingers crawls
> Over the lute, his murmuring belly calls,
> Whose hungry guts, to the same straightness twined,
> In echo to the trembling strings repined.[34]

[34] "Fleckno, an English Priest at Home," in *The Complete Works of Andrew Marvell*, I, 229ff.

Richard Lovelace composed a humorous poem in response to a woman who wished to sing a duet with him.

> This is the prettiest motion:
> Madam, the Alarms of a Drum
> That calls your Lord, set to your cries,
> To mine are sacred *Symphonies*.
>
> What, though 'tis said I have a voice;
> I know 'tis but that hollow noise
> Which (as it through my pipe doth speed)
> Bitterns do Carol through a Reed;
>
> In the same key with Monkeys Jiggs,
> Or Dirges of Proscribed Pigs,
> Or the soft Serenades above
> In calm of night, when cats make love ...
>
> Yet can I Musick too; but such,
> As is beyond all voice or touch;
> My mind can in fair order chime,
> Whilst my true heart still beats the time:
> My soul so full of Harmonie,

That it with all parts can agree:
If you winde up to the highest fret
It shall descend an [octave] from it,
And when you shall vouchsafe to fall
Sixteen above you it shall call,
And yet so dis-affenting one,
They both shall meet an unison.

Come then bright Cherubin begin!
My loudest Musick is within:
Take all notes with your skillful eyes,
Hark if mine do not sympathize!
Sound all my thoughts, and see expressed
The *Tablature* of my large breast,
Then you'll admit that I too can
Musick above dead sounds of man;
Such as alone doth bless the spheres,
Not to be reached with human ears.[35]

And then, a curious reference to a most unique occasion for performance is mentioned in the preface to Wither's Hymn LIX:

> It is usual for prisoners brought to suffer for death, to sing at the place of their execution, that they may testify their hope of a joyful Resurrection.[36]

We have, in these essays, argued that the presence of a contemplative listener is a requirement for true art music. The poet, Robert Herrick, describes such a listener in two poems based on ancient subjects. In his "A Canticle to Apollo," we read,

Play Phoebus on thy Lute;
And we will all sit mute:
By listening to thy Lyre,
That sets all ears on fire.[37]

And, in a song to Sapho,

When thou do'st play, and sweetly sing,
Whether it be the voice or string,
Or both of them, that do agree
Thus to entrance and ravish me:
This, this I know, I'm oft struck mute;
And die away upon thy Lute.[38]

[35] "To a Lady that desired me I would beare my part with her in a Song," in *The Poems of Richard Lovelace*, ed. C. H. Wilkinson (Oxford: Clarendon Press, 1930), 90ff.

[36] Wither, Spenser Society, Nr. 26-27, "Halelviah," Hymn LIX.

[37] *The Poetical Works of Robert Herrick*, 151.

[38] Ibid., 142.

In yet another poem, Herrick mentions the listeners in Hell!

> So smooth, so sweet, so silvery is thy voice,
> As, could they hear, the Damned would make no noise,
> But listen to thee, (walking in thy chamber)
> Melting melodious words, to Lutes of Amber.[39]

[39] Ibid., 22.

George Wither observes that one can see the impact of the music on a listener simply by observing his face.

> And, by the same it may appear
> What music most affects your ear.
> Deny it not; for (by your leave)
> We by your looks, your heart perceive.[40]

[40] Wither, *A Collection of Emblemes*, 117.

Edmond Waller has a character announce that he will impact the listener in the tradition of Orpheus.

> There while I sing, if gentle love be by
> That tunes my lute, and winds the strings so high;
> With the sweet sound of *Sacharissa's* name,
> I'll make the listening savages grow tame.[41]

[41] "The Battel of the Summer Islands," in *Edmund Waller, Poems*, 54.

His own reaction to hearing his lady sing is equally dramatic.

> Such moving sounds, from such a careless touch,
> So unconcerned herself, and we so much.
> What Art is this, that with so little pains,
> Transports us thus, and over the spirit reigns?
> The trembling strings above her fingers proud,
> And tell their joy for every kiss aloud.
> Small force there needs to make these tremble so,
> Touched by that hand; who would not tremble through?
> Here Love takes stand, and while she charms the ear
> Empties his quiver on the listening Deer.
> Musick so softens and disarms the mind,
> That not an arrow does resistance find.[42]

[42] "On my Lady Isabella playing on the Lute," in Ibid., 78.

We find a similar reaction by Andrew Marvell, who is completely conquered by a lovely singer.

> To make a final conquest of all me,
> Love did compose so sweet an enemy,

In whom both beauties to my death agree,
Joining themselves in fatal harmony;
That, while she with her eyes my heart does bind,
She with her voice might captivate my mind.

I could have fled from one but singly fair;
My disentangled soul itself might save,
Breaking the curled trammels of her hair;
But how should I avoid to be her slave,
Whose subtile art invisibly can wreath
My fetters of the very air I breathe?[43]

Finally, let us not forget that some of the poems of this literature are written in honor of composers famous to their day. Robert Herrick has written poems in honor of Henry Lawes,[44] and William Lawes.[45] Phineas Fletcher has left a poem which is a tribute to Thomas Tomkins.

For thee the Muses leave their silver well,
And marvel where thou all their art hast found.

Richard Crashaw has written a poem, "Upon the death of a friend," in honor of a musician whose identity is unknown.

He, that once bore the best part, is gone.
Whose whole life Musick was; wherein
Each virtue for a part came in.
And though that Musick of his life be still
The Musick of his name yet soundeth shrill.[46]

For many Restoration poets the purposes of music mentioned in their poetry is more in the older tradition of the joys and pleasures of music. In a poem called "Song," Sir Charles Sedley finds comfort in the pleasure of music.

Let us indulge the joys we know
Of Musick, Wine and Love;
Were sure of what we find below,
Uncertain what's above.[47]

James Thomson, in his "The Castle of Indolence," wonders of God,

Yet the fine arts were what he finished least.
For why? They are the quintessence of all ...[48]

[43] "The Fair Singer," in *The Complete Works of Andrew Marvell* (New York: AMS Press, 1966), I, 110.

[44] *The Poetical Works of Robert Herrick*, 276.
[45] Ibid., 288.

[46] "Upon the Death of a Friend," in *The Complete Poetry of Richard Crashaw*, 477ff.

[47] *The Poetical and Dramatic Works of Sir Charles Sedley* (New York: AMS Press, 1969), II, 196.

[48] In *The Poetical Works of James Thomson*, II, 293ff.

Later in this poem he observes of musicians themselves,

And where they nothing have to do but please:
Ah! gracious God! thou knowest they ask no other fees.

The purpose of music most frequently mentioned in early literature is to soothe the listener or player. James Thomson's "The Castle of Indolence," mentions this purpose among other virtues of music.

A certain music, never known before,
Here lulled the pensive, melancholy mind;
Full easily obtained. Behoves no more,
But sidelong, to the gently waving wind,
To lay the well-tuned instrument reclined;
From which, with airy flying fingers light,
Beyond each mortal touch the most refined,
The gods of winds drew sounds of deep delight:
Whence, with just cause, the harps of Aeolus it heights.

Ah me! what hand can touch the string so fine?
Who up the lofty diapason roll
Such sweet, such sad, such solemn airs divine,
Then let them down again into the soul:
Now rising love they fanned; now pleasing dole
They breathed, in tender musings, through the heart;
And now a graver sacred strain they stole,
As when seraphic hands a hymn impart:
Wild warbling nature all; above the reach of art![49]

Sometimes we find this purpose contained in references to the Greek gods, as in Matthew Prior:

If Wine and Musick have the power,
To ease the sickness of the soul;
Let Phoebus every string explore;
And Bacchus fill the sprightly bowl.[50]

Similarly, in Joseph Addison:

When Orpheus tuned his lyre with pleasing woe,
Rivers forgot to run, and winds to blow,
While listening forest covered as he played,
The soft musician in a moving shade.[51]

[49] In *The Poetical Works of James Thomson*, II, 274. The "harp of Aeolus" was in instrument devised to be placed in the window and played by the wind.

[50] "A Song," *The Literary Works of Matthew Prior* (Oxford: Clarendon, 1959), I, 196. Matthew Prior (1664–1721) was a friend of Gay and Swift and liked to call himself "only a poet by accident."

[51] "Epilogue to the British Enchanters," lines 1ff.

On the other hand, some poems refer to this purpose as directed to specific contemporaries. Gay, in a poem to the dutchess of Marlborough, on the death of her famous husband, observes,

> Numbers [verse], like musick, can even grief control,
> And lull to peace the tumults of the soul.[52]

Epistle X of Pope's "Moral Essays" concludes,

> Vexed to be still in town, I knit my brow,
> Look sour, and hum a tune, as you may now.[53]

In Congreve's hymn to St. Cecilia, the poet comments on the immediacy of music's impact in achieving his purpose.

> While Reason stilled by Hopes or Fears betrayed,
> Too late advances, or too soon retreats.
> Musick alone with sudden charms can bind
> The wandering sense, and calm the troubled mind.

The most fundamental purpose of music is to express feelings, a purpose which is curiously infrequently mentioned among these poems. One would expect to find more examples such as Shenstone's poem, "Love and Music," which begins,

> Shall Love alone for ever claim
> An universal right to fame,
> An undisputed sway?
> Or has not Music equal charms,
> To fill the breast with strange alarms,
> And make the world obey?[54]

James Thomson, in his "The Seasons," suggests that the purpose of music to express love is so universal that it serves the same purpose even among the animal kingdom.

> 'Tis love creates their melody, and all
> This waste of music is the voice of love;
> That even to birds, and beasts, the tender arts
> Of pleasing teaches.[55]

In another poem, "An Ode on Aeolus's Harp," his focus is the woe of love.

[52] "Epistle V," in *The Works of John Gay*, III, 39.

[53] "Moral Essays," Epistle X, lines 49ff, in *The Works of Alexander Pope*, III, 227.

[54] William Shenstone, "Love and Music," in *The Poetical Works of William Shenstone* (Edinburgh: James Nichol, 1854), 144. William Shenstone (1714–1763) was one of the minor figures in English literature of the early eighteenth century, but was possessed of a perceptive intelligence.

[55] "Spring," in "The Seasons," *The Poetical Works of James Thomson*, I, 22.

> Those tender notes, how kindly they upbraid,
> With what soft woe they thrill the lover's heart![56]

Finally, there is an occasional reference which touches on music therapy. A poem by William Wycherley contains an interestingly specific observation in this regard.

> Your verse, like your prescriptions, is so mean,
> That, like bad Musick, it provokes the Spleen.[57]

In another poem, we are closer to the Greek concept of the affect of music on character, as Edward Young refers to music as the parent of good actions.

> How Music charms! How Meter warms!
> Parent of actions good and brave!
> How Vice it tames, and worth inflames,
> And hold proud empire over the grave![58]

Among the references to art music in Restoration poetry there are two which include mention of Handel. Shenstone's "Ode" which was intended to be performed by a chorus of citizens, with an instrumental part for viol d'amour, includes the lines,

> Hear but this strain—'twas made by Handel,
> A wight of skill and judgment deep![59]

Alexander Pope was critical of the ever larger forces of musicians used in performance and, it seems to us, suspicious of the impact the music had on the audience.

> Joy to great Chaos! let division reign:
> Chromatic tortures soon shall drive them hence,
> Break all their nerves, and fritter all their sense:
> One Trill shall harmonize joy, grief, and rage,
> Wake the dull Church, and lull the ranting Stage;
> To the same notes thy sons shall hum, or snore,
> And all thy yawning daughters cry, *encore*.
> Another Phoebus, thy own Phoebus, reigns,
> Joys in my jigs, and dances in my chains.
> But soon, ah soon, Rebellion will commence,
> If Music meanly borrows aid from Sense.
> Strong in new Arms, lo! Giant Handel stands,

---

[56] In Ibid., II, 227.

[57] "To a Doctor of Physick, on his Writing a Satyr against Wit," in *The Complete Works of William Wycherley* (New York: Russell & Russell, 1964), IV, 177. William Wycherley (1641–1715) studied at Oxford, joined the court in exile in France and on his return to London was imprisoned for his debts.

[58] Edward Young, "Ode to the King," in *Edward Young: The Complete Works* (Hildesheim: Olms, 1968), I, 412. Edward Young (1683–1765), best known for his poetry, was born in his father's rectory and later became Dean of Salisbury.

[59] William Shenstone, "Ode," in *The Poetical Works of William Shenstone*, 142.

> Like bold Briareus, with a hundred hands;
> To stir, to rouse, to shake the soul he comes,
> And Jove's own Thunders follow Mar's Drums.
> Arrest him, Empress; or you sleep no more—[60]

In other countries one finds among the repertoire of art songs a number of love songs. The representatives of such repertoire in England include a wide variety. Samuel Butler's focus is on music's aid to those troubled in love.

> All writers, though of different fancies,
> Do make all people in romances,
> That are distressed and discontent,
> Make songs and sing to an instrument.[61]

An unusual love poem by Richard Steele is addressed to his lover's spinet.

> Thou soft Machine that do'st her Hand obey,
> Tell her my Grief in thy harmonious lay.[62]

Pope safely depersonalizes the subject by placing it in the context of a pastoral setting.

> Where Thames reflects the visionary scene:
> Thither, the silver-sounding lyres
> Shall call the smiling loves, and young desires;
> There, every Grace and Muse shall throng,
> Exalt the dance, or animate the song;
> There youths and nymphs, in consort gay,
> Shall hail the rising, close the parting day.[63]

---

[60] "The Dunciad," Book IV, lines 54ff, in *The Works of Alexander Pope*, IV, 193ff.

[61] Unnamed poem in *The Poetical Works of Samuel Butler* (New York: Appleton, 1854), II, 256.

[62] Richard Steele, "The Lying Lover." This work was published in 1704 with music by William Crofts. It was advertised as "with figured bass. Symphony at the end for the flute." The actual music for another of Steele's poems, "The Conscious Lovers," with music by Johann Ernst Galliard, is reproduced in *The Occasional Verse of Richard Steele* (Oxford: Clarendon, 1952), 27. It is interesting that this particular song was intended for the premiere of a play, but no singer could be found. [Ibid., 86]

[63] "Imitations of Horace," Book IV, Ode I, lines 24ff, in *The Works of Alexander Pope*, III, 416.

5
Music in Restoration Prose

The first half of the seventeenth century in England, with its civil wars and the aggressive influence of the Puritans, offered a poor climate for fine prose. This is not to say great numbers of works were not published, but prose by fine writers was not abundant. Although the writers we quote here make philosophical comments, they are not by real philosophers. They are rather reflections on contemporary Jacobean life, made by doctors, preachers, playwrights and writers of prose.

Jacobean Prose

Sir Thomas Browne, in his "Religio Medici," reminds us of some of the ancient philosophers when he offers the personal perspective that all music has something of the divine in it.

> For there is a music wherever there is a harmony, order, or proportion; and thus far we may maintain "the music of spheres" for those well-ordered motions, and regular paces, though they give no sound unto the ear, yet to the understanding they strike a note most full of harmony. Whatsoever is harmonically composed delights in harmony, which makes me much distrust the symmetry of those heads which declaim against all church music. For myself, not only from my obedience but my particular genius I do embrace it: for even that vulgar and tavern music, which makes one man

merry, another mad, strikes in me a deep fit of devotion, and a profound contemplation of the first composer. There is something in it of divinity more than the ear discovers: it is an hieroglyphical and shadowed lesson of the whole world, and creatures of God,—such a melody to the ear, as the whole world, well understood, would afford the understanding. In brief, it is a sensible fit of that harmony which intellectually sounds in the ears of God. I will not say, with Plato, the soul is an harmony, but harmonic, and has its nearest sympathy with music ... [1]

[1] *Sir Thomas Browne's Works*, ed. Simon Wilkin (London: Pickering, 1836), II, 106ff. A few pages later [Ibid., 32]. Sir Thomas Browne (1605–1682), one of the best prose writers of the period, was educated at Oxford and became a provincial doctor in Norwich.

Izaak Walton reminds his readers that one's experience as a listener has a very direct relationship with the kind of music one enjoys.

What musick doth a pack of dogs then make to any man, whose heart and ears are so happy as to be set to the tune of such instruments?[2]

[2] Izaak Walton, *The Compleat Angler* (London: Oxford University Press, 1935), 31. Izaak Walton (1593–1683) is best known for his biographies of contemporary English writers.

In this strict Puritan environment stories such as Noah and the Flood, and the subsequent necessity of rebuilding the human species, were taken quite seriously. Someone must have wondered, what happened to the accumulated knowledge of music before the flood? Walton offers an explanation for how the early knowledge of music survived the Flood. "Others say," he reports, that Seth, one of the sons of Adam engraved the knowledge of mathematics and music, and the rest of previous knowledge, on pillars.[3]

[3] Ibid., 38.

Modern philologists believe that vocal music, as a form of communicating feeling, must have preceded even the most primitive of languages. It is from this perspective that our eye was drawn to Thomas Dekker's essay on lowlife in London, in which he discusses a slang speech of the underworld, of which little is known today, called *canting*. In this passage we get little more than a kind of etymology of the word.

This word *canting* seems to be derived from the Latin verbe (*canto*) which signifies in English, to sing, or to make a sound with words, that is to say to speake. And very aptly may *canting* take his *derivatio a cantando*, from singing, because amongst these beggarly consorts that can play upon no better instruments, the language of *canting* is a kinde of musicke, and he that in such assemblies can *cant* best, is counted the best Musician.[4]

The familiarity of the general English society with music was such that one finds in ordinary discussion an extraordinary range of musical metaphors. Consider, for example, the broad variety of such metaphors by a single writer, Thomas Dekker:

To represent the well-together person:

> ...what monsters they please to set [on] all the world and all the people in it out of tune, and the worse Musicke they make, the more sport it is for him.[5]

As a metaphor for the four winds:

> East, West, North, and South, the foure Trumpetters of the Worlde, that never blow themselves out of breath ...[6]

To describe a papal representative who tries to be all things to all people:

> He's like an Instrument of sundry strings,
> Not one in tune, yet any note he sings.[7]

To describe "cooperation" between two people:

> As strings of an instrument, though we render several sounds, yet let both our sounds cadence [*close up*] in sweet concordant Musicke.[8]

To represent the Spanish and French conspiring against the English:

> To be short, such strange mad musick doe they play upon their Sacke-buttes ...[9]

On the reader's sympathy with his writing:

> If the Notes please thee, my paines are well bestowed. If to thine ear they found untuneable, much are they not to be blamed, in regard they are the melodies [Aires] of a Sleeping Man.[10]

---

[4] Thomas Dekker, "Lanthorne and Candle-Light" [1609], Grosart, *The Non-Dramatic Works of Thomas Dekker* (New York, Russell & Russell, 1963), III, 194. Thomas Dekker (b. 1570) was a very fluent writer, producing plays of his own and in collaboration with others, in addition to "entertainments" and pamphlets on a variety of subjects. It has been said that no writer gave a more vivid picture of London at this time. He, however, failed to earn a living and was often in prison—once for three years. Nothing is known of him after the 1630s.

[5] Thomas Dekker, "The Divels Last Will and Testament" [1609], Ibid., III, 357.

[6] Thomas Dekker, "The Seven Deadly Sinnes of London" [1606], Ibid., II, 97

[7] Thomas Dekker, "A Papist in Armes' [1606], Ibid., II,174.

[8] Thomas Dekker, "The Dead Tearme" [1608], Ibid., IV, 71.

[9] Thomas Dekker, "The Seven Deadly Sinnes of London" [1606], Ibid., II, 44.

[10] Thomas Dekker, "Dekker his Dream," [1620, III, 12.

Other writers were equally creative in their use of music in figures of speech. Thomas Fuller, in warning the reader to beware of "boisterous and over-violent exercise," writes,

> Ringing oftentimes has made good musick on the bells, and puts mens bodies out of tune.[11]

Thomas Overbury uses music as a metaphor to characterize the duties of the lawyer, a profession associated with amateur music making in seventeenth century England.

> He knows so much in Musique, that he affects only the most and cunningest discords; rarely a perfect concord, especially sung, except in *fine*.[12]

Finally, we don't know what else it could be but a nice pun, when John Earle describes a Puritan mother who would not allow her daughters to study the virginals, "because of their affinity with organs."[13]

On the Purpose of Music

THOMAS BROWNE OFFERS, as an example of the frequently mentioned capacity of music to soothe, a strange and modern interpretation of the myth of Orpheus.

> There were a crew of mad women retired unto a mountain, from whence, being pacified by his music, they descended with boughs in their hands; which, unto the fabulosity of those times, proved a sufficient ground to celebrate unto all posterity the magic of Orpheus's harp.[14]

Thomas Dekker also mentions this purpose of music in one passage where he writes of "Musicke charming thine ear,"[15] but in another place he refers to the absence of music to soothe those in prison.

> What musicke hath he to cheer up his Spirits in this sadness? none but this, he hears wretches (equally miserable) breaking their heart-strings every night with groans, every day with sighs, every hour with cares ...[16]

---

[11] Thomas Fuller, *The Holy State and the Profance State* [1642], ed. Maximilian Walten (New York: AMS Press, 1966), II, 184. Thomas Fuller (1608–1661) was a chaplain to Charles II.

[12] *The "Conceited Newes" of Sir Thomas Overbury and His Friends*, ed. James Savage (Gainesville: Scholars' Facsimiles, 1968), 119. Sir Thomas Overbury (1581–1613) was also a poet.

[13] "A She Precise Hypocrite," in John Earle, *Microcosmography* [1628] (St. Clair Shores: Scholarly Press, 1971), 73. John Earle (1600–1665) was a chaplain to Charles II, during the King's exile, and a Dean of Westminster during the Restoration.

[14] *Sir Thomas Browne's Works*, II, 220.

[15] Thomas Dekker, "The Seven Deadly Sinnes of London" [1606], II, 128.

[16] Thomas Dekker, "Jests to Make you Merrie" (1607), Ibid., II, 341.

Thomas Browne is perplexed by the strange nature of dreams and points to music as a soothing means of preparing for trouble-free sleep.

> Half our days we pass in the shadow of the earth; and the brother of death exacts a third part of our lives. A good part of our sleep is peered out with visions and fantastical objects, wherein we are confessedly deceived. The day supplies us with truths; the night with fictions and falsehoods, which uncomfortably divide the natural account of our beings. And, therefore, having passed the day in sober labors and rational enquiries of truth, we are fain to betake ourselves into such a state of being, wherein the soberest heads have acted all the monstrosities of melancholy, and which unto open eyes are no better than folly and madness.
>
> Happy are they that go to bed with grand music, like Pythagoras, or have ways to compose the fantastical spirit, whose unruly wanderings take off inward sleep.[17]

[17] *Sir Thomas Browne's Works*, IV, 355.

Another traditional purpose of music is to attract the ladies, as we see in Thomas Overbury, in a character sketch of a Lover, where he suggests the lover's education must include music. It is important to note, as well, his point here, that through music you reveal yourself, because music is a form of truth.

> His fingers are his Orators, and he expresses much of himself upon some instrument.[18]

[18] *The "Conceited Newes" of Sir Thomas Overbury and His Friends*, 78.

We find one interesting reference to music therapy, where Sir Thomas Browne, a physician as well as a writer of prose, could find no reason to question the folk legends of the use of music to cure bite of the Tarantula.

> Some doubt many have of the *tarantula*, or poisonous spider of Calabria, and that magical cure of the bit thereof by music. But since we observe that many attest it from experience; since the learned Kircherus has positively averred it, and set down the songs and tunes solemnly used for it; since some also affirm the *tarantula* itself will dance upon certain strokes, whereby they set their instruments against its poison, we shall not at all question it.[19]

[19] "Enquiries into Vulgar and Common Errors," in *Sir Thomas Browne's Works*, II, 536.

Restoration Non-Fiction

SOME OF THE MOST IMPORTANT discussions of music representative in Restoration non-fiction prose will be found in works on philosophy and the journals. Here we include a few comments on music from treatises and essays.

Jonathan Swift, in a fragment of a treatise on the spirit, makes some interesting comments. First he tries to explain why it is that a poet, like a composer, in creating a work that sings will find little use for the rules of grammar. The final comment on this subject is a classic observation!

The second subject he addresses is again *canting*. His attempt to describe the musical effect of canting only makes us wish for a seventeenth century recording!

> It is to be understood, that in the language of the spirit, *cant* and *droning* supply the place of *sense* and *reason*, in the language of men Because, in spiritual harangues, the disposition of the words according to the art of grammar, has not the least use, but the skill and influence wholly lie in the choice and cadence of the syllables. Even as a discreet composer, who in setting a song, changes the words and order so often, that he is forced to make it nonsense, before he can make it music . . .
>
> Now, the art of *Canting* consists in skillfully adapting the voice, to whatever words the spirit delivers, that each may strike the ears of the audience, with its most significant cadence. The force, or energy of this eloquence, is not to be found, as among ancient orators, in the disposition of words to a sentence . . . but agreeable to the modern refinements in music, is taken up wholly in dwelling, and dilating upon syllables and letters. Thus it is frequent for a single vowel to draw sighs from a multitude; and for a whole assembly of saints to sob to the music of one solitary liquid.[20]

In a more humorous vein, Sir Charles Sedley, in "An Essay on Entertainments," discusses how to plan a supper. Don't invite just old men, he advises, they talk only of the past; and don't invite just young men, for they talk only of their "debauches."

---

[20] "A Discourse Concerning the Mechanical Operation of the Spirit," in *The Prose Works of Jonathan Swift* (Oxford: Blackwell, 1957), I, 182ff. Jonathan Swift (1667–1745) is the best known prose writer at the end of the English Baroque and shared a grandfather with Dryden. He rarely deals with artistic matters, preferring to satirize manners. Reared in Ireland, he became active in English politics until he returned to Dublin as Dean of St. Patrick's.

> The conversation should not dwell upon state affairs, private business, or matters of interest, which men are apt to dispute with more heat, concern and animosity, than is consistent with the good humor and mirth principally intended at such meetings; in which we should rather talk of pleasant, cheerful and delightful subjects, such as Beauty, Painting, Musick, Poetry, and the Writers of the past and present Age; whereby we may at once improve and refresh our Wits.[21]

In the opening remarks of a proposal to create a music academy in London, Defoe speaks of the meaning of music to him, in particular its ability to soothe and its positive influence on manners. It seems odd to us that in seventeenth century England there were people still talking about music as a branch of mathematics.

> I have been a lover of [music] from my infancy, and in my younger days was accounted no despicable performer on the viol and lute, then much in vogue. I esteem it the most innocent amusement in life; it generally relaxes, after too great a hurry of spirits, and composes the mind into a sedateness prone to everything that is generous and good; and when the more necessary parts of education are finished, it is a most genteel and commendable accomplishment; it saves a great deal of drinking and debauchery in our sex, and helps the ladies off with many an idle hour, which sometimes might probably be worse employed otherwise.
>
> Our quality, gentry, and better sort of traders must have diversions; and if those that are commendable be denied, they will take to worse; now what can be more commendable than music, one of the seven liberal sciences, and no mean branch of mathematics?[22]

Matthew Prior, in writing of the purpose of music, reaches back to the ancient Greek belief regarding the influence of music on behavior.

> If six bells, as John Keil tells me, can make more than a thousand millions of changes, what must be the result of the jangling of ten or twelve passions sustained by an infinite variety of objects in minds upon which every thing can operate. The dawning of light excites us into cheerfulness, the approach of night depresses us into melancholy; a different weight of air raises or depresses our spirits, a trumpet alarms

[21] *The Poetical and Dramatic Works of Sir Charles Sedley* (New York: AMS Press, 1969), II, 99.

[22] Daniel Defoe, "Augusta Triumphans: or, the Way to make London the Most Flourishing City in the Universe," in *The Works of Daniel Defoe* (New York: Henson, 1905),

us to an ardor and action of war, and a flute softens us again into thoughts of love and delight.[23]

Restoration Fiction

IT IS ONLY AT THE END of the English Baroque that the full-length novel first appears. Earlier efforts tended to be prose-romances, by such writers as Sidney, Greene and Nashe. These later novels, reflecting as they do real life in English society, offer interesting insights regarding musical practice. Indeed, Samuel Richardson, in the preface to his novel, *Clarissa Harlowe*, states that an important purpose in his novel is that it is "addressed to the public as a history of *life* and *manners*."[24] At the end of this novel, Richardson again reminds the reader that the various letters and conversations he has created "are presumed to be *characteristic*."[25]

Henry Fielding, in his novel, *The Adventures of Joseph Andrews*, describes an English society divided into two classes, whom he classifies as "high people (people of fashion) and low people those of no fashion." The entertainments of the "high people" he lists as courts, assemblies, operas and balls, whereas the people of no fashion ... hops, fairs, revels, etc.[26] Later in this same novel, Fielding provides an important insight to the definition of a gentleman in English society at this time. In the sixteenth century the aristocracy considered the playing of a musical instrument part of their definition of a gentleman or lady. But at the end of the century, due in large part to the influence of the Puritans, rather suddenly a new definition appears: it is OK to listen to music, but not to actually play it. This is what Fielding points to in the final sentence below, that it is socially acceptable to be knowledgeable of music without any actual ability as a musician.

> The character I was ambitious of attaining was that of a fine gentleman; the first requisites to which, I apprehended, were to be supplied by a tailor, a perriwig-maker, and some few more tradesmen, who deal in furnishing out the human body ...

[23] "Opinion," in *The Literary Works of Matthew Prior* (Oxford: Clarendon, 1959), I, 592. Matthew Prior (1664–1721) was a friend of Gay and Swift and liked to call himself "only a poet by accident."

[24] Samuel Richardson, *Clarissa Harlowe* (New York: AMS Press Reprint, 1972), V, xliii. Samuel Richardson (1689–1761) was reared in the company of spinsters and his novels are considered to reflect unusual knowledge of female psychology.

[25] Ibid., XII, 360.

[26] Henry Fielding, *The Adventures of Joseph Andrews*, II, xiii. Henry Fielding (1707–1754) became a successful novelist after an unsuccessful period of writing farces and comedies.

> The next qualifications, namely, dancing, fencing, riding the great horse, and music, came into my head: but, as they required expense and time, I comforted myself, with regard to dancing, that I had learned a little in my youth, and could walk a minuet genteelly enough ... as to the horse, I hoped it would not be thought of; and for music, I imagined I could easily acquire the reputation of it; for I had heard some of my school-fellows pretend to knowledge in operas, without being able to sing or play on the fiddle.[27]

Similarly, a gentleman is described in Samuel Richardson's novel, *Sir Charles Grandison*, as being,

> generally engaged four months [of Winter] in the diversions of this great town; and was the common patron of all the performers, whether at plays, operas, or concerts.[28]

Alexander Pope, in his "The Art of Sinking in Poetry," attributed to the fictitious "Martinus Scriblerus," a variety of humorous proposals relative to the building of an ideal theater to hold ten thousand spectators. In a reflection about the behavior of the audience, he suggests that just as there is a conductor[29] who controls the performance by hand "signs," another one is needed to make signs for the audience. The point suggests that the audiences of the rapidly expanding public concerts were somewhat timid in knowing how to act.

> It may be convenient to place the Council of Six in some conspicuous situation in the theater, where, after the manner usually practiced by composers in musick, they may give signs (before settled and agreed upon) of dislike or approbation. In consequence of these signs the whole audience shall be required to clap or hiss, that the town may learn certainly when and how far they ought to be pleased.[30]

On the Purpose of Music

THE MOST COMMONLY GIVEN PURPOSE of music in early literature is to soothe the listener or performer. A typical example is found in Samuel Richardson's novel, *Sir Charles Grandison*, where he relates of a lady, "One lesson upon her

---

[27] Ibid., III, iii.

[28] Samuel Richardson, *Sir Charles Grandison*, (New York: AMS Press Reprint, 1972), V, 128

[29] He says "composer," but this was a time when the composer was also the conductor of compositions written for a single performance.

[30] "The Art of Sinking in Poetry," in *The Works of Alexander Pope* (New York: Gordian Press, 1967), X, 407. Alexander Pope (1688–1744) was born to the family of a prosperous merchant, but as he was also born Catholic he was denied an education at any of the great universities. Thus, the greatest English poet of the eighteenth century was the product of his own education through reading. An illness as a child left him a four foot high hump-back.

harpsichord sets everything right with her."[31] He means that playing a single composition allows her enough emotional release to experience a kind of catharsis. In his novel, *Clarissa Harlowe*, we find another young lady attempting to calm her emotions by expressing them through music.

> I have been forced to try to compose my angry passions at my harpsichord; having first shut close my doors and windows that I might not be heard below.[32]

The young lady goes on to compose an "Ode to Wisdom," which she sets to music. The original publication includes this music.

In his novel, *The Life of Mr. Jonathan Wild*, Henry Fielding presents even the lowest criminal as being in need of the soothing quality of music.

> He spent his time in contemplation, that is to say, in blaspheming, cursing, and sometimes singing and whistling.[33]

It is in satire of music's ability to soothe that Dafoe, in his "Memoirs of a Cavalier," has a Cavalier comment on the "soothing" atmosphere created by pounding timpani while his mother was in labor.

> The very evening before I was born, she dreamed she was brought to bed of a son, and that all the while she was in labor a man stood under her window beating on a kettledrum, which very much discomposed her.[34]

The most important purpose of music is the communication of emotions. We find a particularly vivid illustration in the brief novel, *Adventures of Covent-Garden*, by George Farquhar, as a song is being performed by a very sad lady.

> He found her in an undress sitting on her beds-feet in a very melancholy posture; her nightgown carelessly loose discovered her snowy breasts, which agitated by the violence of her sighs, heaved and fell with a most languishing motion; her eyes were fixed on the ground, and without regarding Peregrine, she raised her voice in a mournful and moving sweetness, singing, "Fool, Fool, that considered not when I was well," concluding which with a deep sigh, she cast a complaining look on Peregrine, intimating that he alone had occasioned her sorrows.

---

[31] Samuel Richardson, *Sir Charles Grandison*, XV, 41.

[32] Samuel Richardson, *Clarissa Harlowe*, VI, 64. The music is found on page 67. In Ibid., XII, 189, the will is given for Clarissa Harlowe and she wills another young lady "my harpsichord, my chamber-organ, and all my music-books."

[33] Henry Fielding, *The Life of Mr. Jonathan Wild*, II, xiii.

[34] Daniel Defoe, "Memoirs of a Cavalier," in *The Works of Daniel Defoe* (New York: Henson, 1905), V, 1. Daniel Dafoe (1660–1731), a staunch Presbyterian, was the son of a London butcher and spent some years in that trade himself. Eventually he produced hundreds of literary works, while on the side serving as a spy.

Farquhar also gives us a portrait of the contemplative listener, Peregrine:

> He heard that tuneful start of grief which made his ravished soul strike unison with the complaining harmony.35

[35] *The Complete Works of George Farquhar* (New York: Gordian Press, 1967), II, 212. George Farquhar (1677–1707) studied at Trinity College in Dublin and was an actor and a soldier.

There are also, in this literature, some examples of performers who are not emotionally in the mood to perform. Samuel Richardson, in his novel *Pamela*, describes a young lady not in the emotional mood to play, even for herself.

> And, indeed, these and my writing will be all my amusement: for I have no work given me to do; and the spinnet, if in tune, will not find my mind, I am sure, in tune to play upon it.36

[36] Samuel Richardson, *Pamela*, I, 117.

And, similarly, we find later,

> When I was at my devotion, Mrs. Jewkes came up, and wanted me sadly to sing her a psalm, as she had often on common days importuned me for a song upon the spinnet: but I declined it, because my spirits were so low I could hardly speak, nor cared to be spoken to.37

[37] Ibid., I, 150.

Henry Fielding, in his novel *Tom Jones*, pauses to comment on the practice by playwrights to use music to emotionally prepare the audience for the scene to be presented and it seems almost as premeditated as cinema music. His comments suggest that there was a much greater use of such music in the plays of this period than is reflected in the printed texts.

> This is an art well known to, and much practiced by our tragic poets; who seldom fail to prepare their audience for the reception of their principal characters.
>
> Thus the hero is always introduced with a flourish of drums and trumpets, in order to rouse a martial spirit in the audience, and accommodate their ears to bombast and fustian ... Again, when lovers are coming forth, soft music often conducts them on the stage, either to soothe the audience with the softness of the tender passion, or to lull and prepare them for that gentle slumber in which they will most probably be composed by the ensuing scene.38

[38] Henry Fielding, *The History of a Foundling*, IV, i.

The advent of humanism during the Renaissance included much discussion regarding the values of ancient music and modern music. This is the background of the satire by Johathan Swift in his contribution to the fictional "Memoirs of Scriblerus," in which he bemoans the loss of ancient principles

> The bare mention of music threw Cornelius into a passion. How can you dignify (quoth he) this modern fiddling with the name of Music? Will any of your best Hautboys encounter a wolf now days with no other arms but their instruments, as did that ancient piper Pythocaris? ... Does not Aelian tell us how the Libyan mares were excited to [mating] by Music? (which ought in truth to be a caution to modest women against frequenting Operas; and consider, brother, you are brought to this dilemma, either to give up the virtue of the ladies, or the power of your Music). Whence proceeds the degeneracy of our morals? Is it not from the loss of ancient music, by which (says Aristotle) they taught all the virtues? Else might we turn Newgate [prison] into a college of Dorian musicians, who should teach moral virtues to those people ...

After citing a number of familiar testimonials found in ancient literature to the power of music, Swift continues his satire by having a character attempt a trial by playing his Lyra from his balcony.

> The uncouth instrument, the strangeness of the man and of the music, drew the ears and eyes of the whole mob that were got about the two female champions, and at last of the combatants themselves. They approached the balcony, in as close attention as Orpheus's first audience of cattle, or that of an Italian Opera, when some favorite melody is just awakened ... The mob laughed, sung, jumped, danced, and used many odd gestures, all which he judged to be caused by the various strains and modulations. "Mark (quoth he) in this the power of the Ionian, in that you see the effect of the Aeolian." But in a little time they began to grow riotous, and throw stones. Cornelius then withdrew, but with the greatest air of triumph in the world.[39]

[39] "Memoirs of Scriblerus," in *Satires and Personal Writings of Jonathan Swift* (London: Oxford University Press, 1956), 126ff.

Art Music

IT IS IN THE NOVELS of the Restoration Period that we get for the first time a picture of the growing new phenomenon of middle class music making. Samuel Richardson, in his novel, *Sir Charles Grandison*, provides an unusually detailed picture of domestic music in a gentleman's home in Restoration England.[40] A room, the "music-parlor," is devoted to music and it is described as "adorned with a variety of fine carvings, on subjects that do honor to poetry and music." The company retreats to this room after a "sumptuous and well-ordered" dinner. Several of the guests participate in the music-making, which begins with the request of Sir Charles:

> "May I ask you, my Harriet?" pointing to the harpsichord. I instantly sat down to it. It is a fine instrument. Lord G—— took up a violin; my uncle, a bass-viol; Mr. Deane, a German flute; and we had a little concert of about half an hour.

Next a gentleman performed a work on an organ, while he sang. The reaction of one listener is remarkable.

> How did our friends look upon one another as the excellent man proceeded!—I was astonished. It was happy I sat between my aunt and Lucy!—They each took one of my hands. Tears of joy ran down my cheeks. Every one's eyes congratulated me. Every tongue, but mine, encored him. I was speechless. Again he obliged us. I thought at the time, I had a foretaste of the joys of heaven!—How sweet is the incense of praise from a husband; that husband a good man; my surrounding friends enjoying it!

In these novels, such domestic music-making usually entails the performance by a young lady. The young lady we find in Henry Fielding's novel, *Tom Jones*, has the additional difficulty of performing before a father who has no taste.

> It was Mr. Western's custom every afternoon, as soon as he was drunk, to hear his daughter play on the harpsichord; for he was a great lover of music, and perhaps, had he lived in town, might have passed for a connoisseur; for he always

[40] Samuel Richardson, *Sir Charles Grandison*, XIX, 45ff.

excepted against the finest compositions of Mr. Handel. He never relished any music but what was light and airy; and indeed his most favorite tunes were "Old Sir Simon the King," "St. George he was for England," "Bobbing Joan," and some others.

His daughter, though she was a perfect mistress of music, and would never willingly have played any but Handel's was so devoted to her father's pleasure, that she learnt all those tunes to oblige him. However, she would now and then endeavor to lead him into her own taste; and when he required the repetition of his ballads, would answer with a "nay, dear Sir"; and would often beg him to suffer her to play something else.[41]

[41] Henry Fielding, *The History of a Foundling*, IV, v.

In Fielding's novel, *Amelia*, we see the evil influence of competition enter English middle class music. This would become a plague by the nineteenth century with the brass band tradition. Here we have a young lady admit that she "never had any delight in music" and had experienced little success in her attempts to study the harpsichord. But, when a man challenged her to exceed the ability of her sister, she began to practice with great diligence.

> You have often, I believe, heard my sister Betty play on the harpsichord; she was, indeed, reputed the best performer in the whole country.
>
> I was the farthest in the world from regarding this perfection of hers with envy. In reality, perhaps, I despised all perfection of this kind; at least, as I had neither skill nor ambition to excel this way, I looked upon it as a matter of mere indifference.
>
> Hebbers first put this emulation in my head. He took great pains to persuade me, that I had much greater abilities of the musical kind than my sister; and that I might with the greatest ease, if I please, excel her; offering me, at the same time, his assistance, if I would resolve to undertake it.
>
> When he had sufficiently inflamed my ambition, in which, perhaps, he found too little difficulty, the continual praises of my sister, which before I had disregarded, became more and more nauseous in my ears; and the rather, as music being the favorite passion of my father, I became apprehensive (not without frequent hints from Hebbers of that nature) that she might gain too great a preference in his favor.

> To my harpsichord then I applied myself night and day, with such industry and attention, that I soon began to perform in a tolerable manner. I do not absolutely say I excelled my sister, for many were of a different opinion; but, indeed, there might be some partiality in all that.
>
> Hebbers, at least, declared himself on my side, and nobody could doubt his judgment. He asserted openly, that I played in the better manner of the two; and one day, when I was playing to him alone, he affected to burst into a rapture of admiration, and squeezing me gently by the hand, said, "There, Madam, I now declare you excel your sister as much in music, as," added he, in a whispering sigh, "you do her, and all the world, in every other charm."[42]

In the novels of Samuel Richardson there are a number of portraits of the young lady being asked to perform in the home. In his novel *Pamela*, for example,

> Dinner not being ready, the young ladies proposed a tune upon the spinnet. I said, I believed it was not in tune. They said, they knew it was but a few months ago. If it is, said I, I wish I had known it; though indeed, ladies, added I, since you know my story, I must own, that my mind has not been long in tune, to make use of it. So they would make me play upon it, and sing to it; which I did, a song my dear good lady made me learn, and used to be pleased with, and which she brought with her from Bath: and the ladies were much taken with the song, and were so kind as to approve my performance. And Miss Darnford was pleased to compliment me, that I had all the accomplishments of my sex.[43]

Later in this same novel we find another instance of this kind of private domestic music.

> I will only add that Miss L——, the dean's daughter, is a very modest and agreeable young lady, and a perfect mistress of music; in which the dean takes great delight also, and is a fine judge of it. The gentlemen coming in, to partake of our coffee and conversation, as they said, obtained of Miss to play several tunes on the harpsichord; and would have me play too. But really Miss L—— so very much surpassed me, that had I regarded my reputation for playing, above the desire I had (as I said, and truly said) to satisfy the good company, I ought not to have pretended to touch a key after such a mistress of it. Miss has no voice, which is a great pity; and at the request of every one, I sung to her accompaniment, twice or thrice; as did Lady Towers, whose voice exceeds her taste.[44]

[42] Henry Fielding, *Amelia*, Chapter I, vii.

[43] Samuel Richardson, *Pamela*, II, 40. The author provides the lyrics for this song.

[44] Ibid., III, 143.

A final reference to domestic performance in *Pamela* occurs after the company has had their afternoon tea service.

> Mr. B——, after tea, at which I was far from being talkative (for I could not tell what to say, though I tried as much as I could not to appear sullen), desired the countess to play one tune upon the harpsichord. She did; and sung, at his request, an Italian song to it very prettily; too prettily, I thought. I wanted to find some faults, some great faults in her: but, O madam! she has too many outward excellences! Pity she lacks a good heart!
>
> He could ask nothing that she was not ready to oblige him in! Indeed he could not!
>
> She desired me to touch the keys. I would have been excused: but could not. And the ladies commended my performance. But neither my heart to play, nor my fingers in playing, deserved their praises. Mr. B—— *said*, indeed, You play better sometimes, my dear.—Do I, sir? was all the answer I made.[45]

In Richardson's novel, *Clarissa Harlowe*, we are provided an interesting discussion of the *social* expectations of the young lady singing before private gatherings of society in early eighteenth century England.[46] A Miss Howe first describes the singing of Miss Harlowe, after commenting on her melodious voice when she read poetry.

> But if her voice was melodious when she *read*, it was all harmony when she *sung*. And the delight she gave by that, and by her skill and great compass, was heightened by the ease and gracefulness of her air and manner, and by the alacrity with which she obliged. Nevertheless, she generally chose rather to hear others sing or play, than either to play or sing herself.

Miss Howe now recalls the advice given her by Miss Harlowe on the rather complicated etiquette involved in being asked to sing.

> We form the truest judgment of persons by their behavior on the *most familiar* occasions. I will give an instance or two of the corrections she favored me with on such a one. When *very young*, I was guilty of the fault of those who want to be courted to sing. She cured me of it, at the first of our happy

[45] Ibid., IV, 110ff.

[46] Samuel Richardson, *Clarissa Harlowe*, XII, 282ff.

intimacy, by her own *example*; and by the following correctives, occasionally, yet privately enforced:

"Well, my dear, shall we take you at your word? Shall we suppose that you sing but indifferently? Is not, however, the *act of obliging* (the company so worthy!) preferable to the *talent of singing*? And shall not young ladies endeavor to make up for their defects in *one part* of education, by their excellence in *another*?"

Again, "You must convince us, by attempting to sing, that you *cannot* sing; and then we will rid you, not only of *present* but of *future* importunity." An indulgence, however, let me add, that but *tolerable* singers do not always wish to meet with.

Again, "I know you will favor us by and by; and what do you by your excuses but raise our expectations, and enhance your own difficulties?"

At another time, "Has not this accomplishment been a part of your *education*, my Nancy? How, then, for *your own* honor, can we allow of your excuses?"

And I once pleading a cold, the usual pretense of those who love to be entreated—"Sing, however, my dear, *as well as you can*. The greater the difficulty to you, the higher the compliment to the company. Do you think you are among those who know not how to make allowances? You *should* sing, my love, lest there should be anybody present who may think your excuses owing to affectation."

At another time when I had truly observed that a young lady present sung better than I; and that therefore I chose not to sing before that lady—"Fie, said she (drawing me on one side), is not this pride, my Nancy? Does it not look as if your principal motive to oblige was to obtain applause? A generous mind will not scruple to give advantage to a *person of merit*, though not always to *her own* advantage. And yet she will have a high merit in *doing that*. Supposing this excellent person absent, who, my dear, if your example spread, shall sing after you? You knew every one *else* must be but as a foil to you. Indeed I must have you as much superior to other ladies in these *smaller* points as you are in greater."

Often, as the above suggests, when we read of the young lady singing in the private home, she seems expected to resist. In Richardson's novel, *Sir Charles Grandison*, however, one young lady is always eager to sing.

They, as we do, admire her voice and her playing. They ask her for a song, for a lesson on her harpsichord. She plays, she sings, at the very first word.[47]

[47] Samuel Richardson, *Sir Charles Grandison*, XVII, 104.

In this same novel there is also a domestic music scene which touches on the important role of the accompanist. A Miss Byron describes a scene with her cousin, James.

You know and admire my grandmamma's cheerful compliances with the innocent diversions of youth. She made Lucy give us a lesson on the harpsichord, on purpose, I saw, to draw me in. We both obeyed.

I was once a little out in an Italian song. In what a sweet manner did he put me in! touching the keys himself, for a minute or two. Every one wished him to proceed; but he gave up to me, in so polite a manner, that we all were satisfied with his excuses.[48]

[48] Ibid., XVIII, 60.

And finally in this novel, a "Lady G——" relates how the battles of a married couple are reflected in their music.

He has been long careless, and now he is, at times *imperious* as well as careless. Very true! Nay, it was but yesterday that he attempted to hum a tune of contempt, upon my warbling an Italian air. An opera couple, we! Is it not charming to sing *at* (I cannot say *to*) each other, when we have a mind to be spiteful? But he has a miserable voice. He cannot sing so fine a song as I can. He should not attempt it. Besides, I can play to my song; that cannot he. Such a foe to melody, that he hates the very sight of my harpsichord. He flies out of the room, if I but move towards it.[49]

[49] Ibid., XVII, 81.

In William Congreve's novel, *Incognita*, we find a satire of the music of the lower class in the Italian's love of serenades. He refers to the serenade, by the way, as a "ridiculous entertainment."

Not a window in the streets but echoed the tuning of a lute or thrumming of a Gitarr: for, by the way, the inhabitants of Florence are strangely addicted to to the love of Musick, insomuch that scarce their children can go, before they can scratch some instrument or other. It was no unpleasing spectacle to our cavaliers to behold the diversity of figures and postures of many of these musicians. Here you should have an affected valet, who mimicked the behavior of his masters, leaning carelessly against the window, with his head on one side, in a languishing posture, whining, in a low, mournful voice, some dismal complaint; while, from his sympathizing Theorbo, issued a bass no less doleful to the hearers. In opposition to him was set up perhaps a cobbler, with the wretched skeleton of a Gitarr, battered and waxed together by his own industry, and who with three strings out of tune, and his own tearing hoarse voice, would rack attention from the neighborhood, to the great affliction of many more moderate practitioners, who, no doubt, were full as desirous to be heard.[50]

A rather extraordinary account of instrumental music is given by Swift, in his *Gulliver's Travels*, in his description to "Brobdingnag," a land of giants:

> I had learned in my youth to play a little upon the spinet; Glumdalclitch kept one in her chamber, and a master attended twice a week to teach her. I call it a spinet, because it somewhat resembled that instrument, and was played upon in the same manner. A fancy came into my head, that I would entertain the king and queen with an English tune upon this instrument. But this appeared extremely difficult, for, the spinet was nearly sixty feet long, each key being almost a foot wide; so that, with my arms extended, I could not reach to above five keys; and to press them down required a good smart stroke with my fist, which would be too great a labor, and to no purpose. The method I contrived was this. I prepared two round sticks about the bigness of common cudgels; they were thicker at one end than the other; and I covered the thicker end with a piece of a mouse skin, that by rapping on them, I might neither damage the tops of the keys, nor interrupt the sound. Before the spinet, a bench was placed about four feet below the keys, and I was put upon the bench. I ran sideling upon it that way and this, as fast as I could, banging the proper keys with my two sticks; and made a shift to play a Jig to the great satisfaction of both their majesties. But, it was the most violent exercises I ever underwent, and yet I could not strike above sixteen keys, nor, consequently, play the bass and treble together, as other artists do; which was a great disadvantage to my performance.[51]

In these essays we have argued that an indispensable element of art music is the presence of the contemplative lis-

[50] William Congreve, *Incognita*, in *The Complete Works of William Congreve* (New York: Russell & Russell, 1964). 115. William Congreve (1670–1729) is considered the best of the Restoration writers of comedy and was particularly admired by Voltaire. He studied at Trinity College, Dublin, and worked in various government offices in London.

[51] Jonathan Swift, *Gulliver's Travels*, in *The Prose Works of Jonathan Swift*, XI, 126ff.

tener, such as we find in William Congreve's novel, *Incognita*. Before the lyrics are given for a song sung by Leonora, we read "Having tuned her lute, with a voice soft as the breath of angels, she sung to it this following song." After the song, we read of the listener's reaction.

> The song ended grieved Hippolito that it was so soon ended; and in the ecstasy he was then rapt, I believe he would have been satisfied to have expired with it.[52]

[52] William Congreve, *Incognita*, 15. 148.

Another example is found in Fielding's novel, *Tom Jones*, when Jones is transfixed by the harpsichord playing of Sophia. Mrs. Honour relates:

> La! says I, Mr. Jones, what's the matter? a penny for your thoughts, says I. Why, hussy, says he, starting up from a dream, what can I be thinking of, when that angel your mistress is playing?[53]

[53] Henry Fielding, *The History of a Foundling*, IV, xiv.

A clear illustration of a non-contemplative listener is found in Fielding's novel, *The Adventures of Joseph Andrews*. For the listener, Adams, a song sung from another room is little more than background sound. He,

> had been ruminating all this time on a passage in Aeschylus, without attending in the least to the voice, though one of the most melodious that ever was heard.[54]

[54] Henry Fielding, *The Adventures of Joseph Andrews*, II, xii.

Part II

Philosophers on Music

6
Restoration Philosophers on Music

The Restoration Period in England can be viewed as an environment which somewhat limited the development of philosophy. First, the court, which in a monarchal society usually leads the culture and establishes the "Mode," when it returned from its exile in Paris brought an atmosphere to London which was hardly conducive to higher intellectual pursuits. This climate was described by Andrew Marvell, a poet in favor during both the Cromwell and Charles II periods.

> A colony of French possess the Court;
> Pimps, priests, buffoons, in privy-chamber sport.
> Such slimy monsters never approached a throne,
> Since Pharaoh's days, nor so defiled a crown.[1]

This life of the court, together with the influence of the strong Puritan movement throughout the seventeenth century, had the effect of strengthening all kinds of religious fundamentalism.[2] With this environment, philosophy was left mostly in the hands of the theologians and neither their interests nor those of the court were conducive to much discussion of the fine arts. Consequently, some of the great minds of England, men such as David Hume, came to see the battle for the Enlightenment as a battle to be fought only in the territory of the left hemisphere of the brain, and to this day it is often called "the Age of Reason."

[1] "Britannia and Raleigh," in *The Complete Works of Andrew Marvell* (New York: AMS Press, 1966), I, 326. Andrew Marvell (1621–1678) served as a secretary to Milton after the famous poet became blind.

[2] It was this period, especially in the philosophy of the Scottish Presbyterians and the Quakers, which played so great a role in the development of religious philosophy in America.

Nevertheless, a number of these very intelligent men made a few comments which might be of interest to the modern reader.

Thomas Hobbes (1588–1679)

THOMAS HOBBES was born to an Anglican clergyman of strong personality, but who left his family to be reared by his brother. After a stay at Oxford, two gifts of fate fell in the lap of Hobbes. He was hired as a secretary to Francis Bacon, which must have pointed him toward philosophy, and he was employed by the wealthy Cavendish family, who would support and protect him most of his life.

The philosophy of Hobbes was centered in mathematics, materialism and in social organization and when writing outside of those fields his comments tend to be rather superficial. According to one biographer, Hobbes was addicted to music and was a performer on the bass viol, and "at night, when he was abed, and the doors made fast, and was sure nobody heard him, he sang aloud ."[3] When living in Paris for a number of years he was a friend of Mersenne, who was unusually interested in all aspects of the philosophy of music. The fact, in spite of this, that music is hardly mentioned in the writings of Hobbes only affirms that music had ceased to be an important topic in English philosophy.

In his classic work of philosophy, *The Leviathan*, Hobbes includes a chapter in which he attempts to organize all "subjects of knowledge."[4] In this organization there are implicit value judgments. It is no surprise he finds the subject of the study of sounds to be Music. It is unexpected and revealing, however, that he regards the subject of the study of passions to be Ethics!

In another place he suggests that the listener does not find new appreciation, but rather a loss of interest in music when he hears it repeated. This may very well be, since he refers to its loss of "force," another hint that the art of improvisation was more interesting to the listener at this time than "set,"

[3] John Aubrey, *Brief Lives*, ed. O. Dick (Ann Arbor, 1957), 150ff.

[4] *Leviathan*, I, ix.

or notated, music, a point we have seen expressed by other English writers.

> The phrases of poesy, as the tunes [airs] of music, with often hearing become insipid; the reader having no more sense of their force, than our flesh is sensible of the bones that sustain it.[5]

[5] "The Answer of Mr. Hobbes to Sir William Davenant's Preface before *Gondibert*," in *The English Works of Thomas Hobbes*, IV, 455.

Hobbes regarded sound as being in the mind, not in the instrument, and he was the first to offer practical evidence. For him, the proof of this was in the echo. He believed that if the sound we hear is in the instrument which produces it, it would not be possible to "disconnect" the sound from its original source, as happens in an echo.

> Neither is sound in the thing we hear, but in ourselves. One manifest sign thereof is, that as a man may see, so he may hear double or treble, by multiplication of echoes, which echoes are sounds as well as the original; and not being in one and the same place, cannot be inherent in the body that makes them. Nothing can make anything which is not in itself; the clapper has no sound in it, but motion, and makes motion in the internal parts of the bell; so the bell has motion, and not sound, that imparts motion to the air; and the air has motion, but not sound; the air imparts motion by the ear and nerve unto the brain; and the brain has motion but not sound; from the brain, it rebounds back into the nerves outward, and thence it becomes an apparition [idea] without, which we call sound.[6]

[6] "Human Nature," II, ix.

Otherwise, when Hobbes discusses musical sounds, it is only at a rather primitive level, such as distinguishing strong and weak, high and low and clear and "hoarse."[7] Hoarse, he calls a "whispering and hissing" and he regards it as being caused by an interruption in the air column, as in singing when the air "in going out rakes the superficies of the lips."

[7] *Elements of Philosophy*, IV, xxix, 1ff.

In his only real discussion of music, the reader is struck by the disinterest Hobbes has for a subject in which he was said to be "addicted."

> Concerning the delight of hearing, it is diverse, and the organ itself not affected thereby: simple sounds please by equality, as the sound of a bell or lute: insomuch as it seems,

an equality continued by the percussion of the object upon the ear, is pleasure; the contrary is called harshness, such as is grating, and some other sounds, which do not always affect the body, but only sometime, and that with a kind of horror beginning at the teeth. Harmony, or many sounds together agreeing, please by the same reason as the unison, which is the sound of equal strings, equally stretched. Sounds that differ in any height, please by inequality and equality alternate, that is to say, the higher note strikes twice, for one stroke of the other, whereby they strike together every second time; as is well proved by Galileo, in his first dialogue concerning local motion: where he also shows, that two sounds differing a fifth, delight the ear by an equality of striking after two inequalities; for the higher note strikes the ear thrice, while the other strikes but twice. In like manner he shows wherein consists the pleasure of concord, and the displeasure of discord, in each difference of notes. There is yet another pleasure and displeasure of sounds, which consists in consequence of one note after another, diversified both by accent and measure; whereof that which pleases is called a melody; but for what reason one succession in tone and measure is a more pleasing tune than another, I confess I know not; but I conjecture the reason to be, for that some of them imitate and revive some passion which otherwise we take no notice of, and the other not; for no melody pleases but for a time, as neither does imitation.[8]

[8] "Human Nature," VIII, 2.

This last "conjecture" is actually another brilliant intuitive insight by Hobbes. Modern clinical research suggests man is born with a genetically universal repertoire of melodic fragments, which in turn appear to have emotional meaning.

John Locke (1632–1704)

JOHN LOCKE studied ancient languages, rhetoric, logic and ethics at Oxford and eventually earned a degree in medicine. He held various government positions of largely clerical nature. This experience produced a philosopher who seemed only aware of the faculties of the left hemisphere of the brain. He wrote very little on the emotions, the individual senses or any of the arts. When discussing time, for example, unlike previous philosophers, music is never mentioned.

Rarely has there been a philosopher who so completely failed to appreciate music. His most extensive explanation of his disinterest is found in his treatise on education.[9]

> Music is thought to have some affinity with dancing, and a good hand, upon some instruments, is by many people mightily valued. But it wastes so much of a young man's time, to gain but a moderate skill in it, and engages often in such odd company, that many think it much better spared: and I have, amongst men of parts and business, so seldom heard any one commended or esteemed for having an excellency in music, that amongst all those things, that ever came into the list of accomplishments, I think I may give it the last place.

He makes an identical assessment in a letter to Edward Clarke in 1686.

> Musique—I find by some mightily valued but it wastes so much of one's time to gain but a moderate skill in it and engages in such odd company that I think it much better spared. And amongst all those things that ever come into the list of accomplishments I give it next to Poetry the last place.[10]

Locke makes only one observation touching with the perception of music and again the emphasis is on the external, sound, which becomes an impression in the mind.

> Sounds also ... are modified by diversity of notes of different length put together, which make that complex idea called a melody, which a musician may have in his mind when he hears or makes no sound at all, by reflecting on the ideas of those sounds so put together silently in his own fancy.[11]

The only reference Locke makes to the purpose of music comes in his correspondence. In a letter to Lady Calverley, in 1689, Locke, in describing local activities which might be of interest to the Lady, mentions concerts [Musick meetings] which he associates with those entertainments of "pleasure and delight."[12] The only other reference to the purpose of music is found in a letter to an unknown correspondent,

[9] "Thoughts Concerning Education," in *The Works of John Locke* (London, 1823; reprinted in Aalen: Scientia Verlag, 1963), IX, 191.

[10] Quoted in E. Beer, *The Correspondence of John Locke* (Oxford: Clarendon, 1976), II, 782.

[11] "Essay on Human Understanding," II, xviii, *3.

[12] *The Correspondence of John Locke*, III, 615.

where Locke says of a lady friend that she "pleases herself with her own harmony and sings away her anger."[13]

[13] Ibid., I, 21.

The only reports of actual performances recalled by Locke were of church music. In a letter to John Strachey, written in December 1665, Locke describes church music he heard while traveling in Germany. One notes he mentions the organ, an instrument which the Puritans had destroyed by this time in English churches.

> I went to the Lutheran church, I found them all merrily singing with their hats on. So that by the posture they were in and the fashion of the building, not altogether unlike a theater, I was ready to fear that I had mistook the place. I thought they had met only to exercise their voices, for after a long stay they still continued on their melody, and I verily believe they sung the 119th psalm, nothing else could be so long, that [which] made it a little tolerable was that they sing better than we do in our churches and are assisted by an organ.[14]

[14] Ibid., I, 236.

In another letter to the same correspondent during this trip, Locke describes the music of a Christmas service in a Catholic church in Germany, the Stiftskirche in Cleves. He begins the letter describing a pageant given in the church.

> This was the show: the Musick to it was all vocal in the choir adjoining: but such as I never heard. They had strong voices, but so ill-tuned, so ill-managed, that it was their misfortune as well as ours, that they could be heard. He that could not, though he had a cold, make better Musick with *Chevy Chase* over a pot of smooth ale deserved well to pay the reckoning and go away [with] a thirst. However I think they were the most honest singing men, I ever have seen, for they endeavored to deserve their money, and earned it certainly with pains enough: for what they lacked in skill, they made up in loudness, and variety, everyone had his own tune, and the result of all was much like the noise at Parliament, where everyone endeavors to cry loudest. Besides the men there were a company of little choristers. I thought when I saw them at first, they had danced to the others Musick ... for they were jumping up and down about a good charcoal fire, that was in the middle of the Choir ... But it was not dancing, but singing they served for; when it came to their turns, away they ran to their places, and there they made as good harmony as a consort of little pigs.[15]

[15] Ibid., I, 244ff.

William Penn (1633–1718)

WILLIAM PENN, the son of the admiral who had captured Jamaica for England, attended Oxford but was expelled for refusing to attend Anglican services in 1661. Returning home, his father whipped him and threw him out of the house for good. All this contributed to his becoming one of the most strict and fervent of the Quaker preachers. His preaching led to a famous trial in 1669 in which the jury acquitted him and the judge imprisoned the jury for doing so! In 1677 he traveled to America to help bring Quakerism to the new continent and one of the states still carries his name.

In the few references to music in his sermons, Penn's view is invariably negative. He avoids entirely the innumerable instances of praise for music in the Old Testament. In a typical passage, which he based on Amos 6:4, 5, Penn warns,

> Woe unto you Protestants ... that chant to the sound of music of the viol, and invent to yourselves instruments of music ...[16]

He includes music again in a list of luxuries not appropriate to a Christian, and he considers all of them "an excessive indulgence of self in ease and pleasure ... A disease as epidemical as killing: it creeps into all stations and ranks of men."[17]

> Sumptuous apparel, rich unguents, delicate washes, stately furniture, costly cookery, and such diversions as balls, masques, concerts [music-meetings], plays, romances, etc., which are the delight and entertainment of the times, belong not to the holy path that Jesus and his true disciples and followers trod to glory ...

Later in this sermon, Penn promises condemnation for those who attend such diversions.

> There is but little need to drive away that, by foolish divertisements, which flies away so swiftly of itself; and when once gone, is never to be recalled. Plays, parks, balls, treats, romances, musics, love sonnets, and the like, will be a very

---

[16] "Truth Exalted," in *The Select Works of William Penn* (London: William Phillips, 1825), I, 122. He makes the same point in "No Cross, no Crown," Ibid., I, 456. Amos 6: 4, 5 reads,

> Woe to those who lie upon beds of ivory ...
> who sing idle songs to the sound of the harp,
> and like David invent for themselves instruments of music.

[17] Ibid., I, 454ff.

invalid plea for any other purpose than their condemnation, who are taken and delighted with them ...[18]

[18] Ibid., 469.

Needless to say, Penn never described in his publications any specific musical performance he may have heard in England. In fact, the only such description is found in a publication describing his impressions of the new world. Penn includes a brief description of the music of the American Indians, as part of what he calls their worship service.

> The other part is their cantico, performed by round dances, sometimes words, sometimes songs, then shouts, two being in the middle that begin, and by singing and drumming on a board, direct the chorus: their postures in the dance are very antic, and differing, but all keep measure. This is done with equal earnestness and labor, but great appearance of joy.[19]

[19] "A General Description of Pennsylvania," in Ibid., III, 230.

David Hume (1711–1776)

DAVID HUME, born into a Scottish Presbyterian family, studied at the University of Edinburgh, but left before graduation to pursue philosophy and indeed wrote his great *Treatise on Human Nature* at age twenty-six. He tried law briefly, but found it "nauseous." He traveled and worked at various jobs, never quite having a career although he became one of the great representatives of the Enlightenment in philosophy. He knocked the foundation out from under Christianity, not to mention traditional metaphysics, of which he said, "commit it to the flames, for it is nothing but sophistry and illusion."[20]

[20] Royce, *The Spirit of Modern Philosophy* (Boston, 1892), 98.

Hume, like other philosophers of this period in England, wrote little on the subject of music, a fact which can only be taken as a measure of how much ground music had lost, in a very brief period of time, as a relevant branch of philosophy. This is to be regretted, for there are hints in Hume's correspondence that he had an interest as a listener, at least for opera. In a letter of 1748, while visiting The Hague, he complains that he finds no opera there.[21] On a boat ride down the Danube, he finds the changing scenery reminds him of the rapid scene changes in opera.[22] And in

[21] Letter to John Home (March 3, 1748), quoted in *The Letters of David Hume*, ed. J. Greig (Oxford: Clarendon, 1932), I, 115.

[22] Ibid., 125.

another place, Hume makes this curious passing reference to the exaggerated emotional display of opera.

> Were a stranger to drop, on a sudden, into this world, I would show him, as a specimen of its ills, an hospital full of diseases, a prison crowded with malefactors and debtors, a field of battle strewed with carcasses, a fleet floundering in the ocean, a nation languishing under tyranny, famine, or pestilence. To turn the gay side of life to him, and give him a notion of its pleasures; whither should I conduct him? to a ball, to an opera, to court? He might justly think, that I was only showing him a diversity of distress and sorrow.[23]

[23] "Dialogues Concerning Natural Religion," Part X.

Hume makes only one reference, in his philosophical writings, to the perception of music. He has contended that the mind is capable of achieving correctness even though it has only an "obscure" notion of that aim, and by way of illustration he uses the musician.

> A musician finding his ear becoming every day more delicate, and correcting himself by reflection and attention, proceeds with the same act of the mind, even when the subject fails him, and entertains a notion of a complete third or octave, without being able to tell whence he derives his standard.[24]

[24] *A Treatise of Human Nature*, I, ii, ✱4.

In only two places does Hume refer to the purposes of music. The first is a rather unenthusiastic reference to the purpose of delight.

> Our sense of music, harmony, and indeed beauty of all kinds gives satisfaction, without being absolutely necessary to the preservation and propagation of the species.[25]

[25] "Dialogues Concerning Natural Religion," Part X.

In the other, music is included with other arts whose purpose includes a positive effect on the emotions of the observer.

> Nothing is so improving to the temper as the study of the beauties, either of poetry, eloquence, music, or painting. They give a certain elegance of sentiment to which the rest of mankind are strangers. The emotions which they excite are soft and tender. They draw off the mind from the hurry of business and interest; cherish reflection; dispose to tranquility; and produce an agreeable melancholy, which, of all dispositions of the mind is the best suited to love and friendship.[26]

[26] "On the Delicacy of Taste and Passion," in *David Hume, The Philosophical Works*, Ibid., III, 93.

In all the writings of Hume, there is only one description of an actual performance, his impressions of hearing the singing of psalms by Catholic Church singers. This is found in a strange report of his visit to Knittelfeld, in lower Austria.

> But as much as the country is agreeable in its wildness; as much are the inhabitants savage & deformed & monstrous in their appearance. Very many of them have ugly swelled throats: idiots & deaf people swarm in every village; and the general aspect of the people is the most shocking I ever saw. One would think, that this was the great road, through which all the barbarous nations made their irruptions into the Roman Empire, they always left here the refuse of their armies before they entered into the enemy's country; and that from thence the present inhabitants are descended. Their dress is scarce European as their figure is scarce human. There happened, however a thing today, which surprised us all. The Empress Queen, regarding this country as a little barbarous, has sent some Missionaries of the Jesuits to instruct them. They had sermons today in the street under our windows, attended with Psalms. And believe me, nothing could be more harmonious, better tuned, or more agreeable than the voices of these savages, and the chorus of a French Opera does not sing in better time.[27]

[27] Letter to John Home (April 28, 1748), in *The Letters of David Hume*, 130.

George Berkeley (1685–1753)

GEORGE BERKELEY, Ireland's contribution to philosophy of this period, became absorbed with the writings of Locke at an early age. He appears to us to have become obsessed with the growing emphasis on materialism, which as a facet of the Enlightenment distracted man's thoughts from God. His answer was *Of the Principles of Human Knowledge* which argued that no matter exists apart from its perception in the mind. Contemporaries found this concept difficult to challenge, although in a famous anecdote Samuel Johnson, discussing this with Boswell, kicked a large stone and said, "I refute it thus!"

As with all the important philosophers of the Baroque in England, we must point out again how absent is the topic of music from their consideration. This is particularly striking in the case of those who appear to have been active in attending concerts and opera. Berkeley, as a case in point, not only describes concerts in detail in his correspondence,[28] but was apparently an avid collector of instruments.

[28] Quoted in *The Works of George Berkeley, Bishop of Cloyne*, ed. A. Luce (London: Nelson, 1964), VIII, 69.

> Your care in providing the Italian psalms set to music, the four-stringed bass violin, and the antique bass viol, require our repeated thanks. We have already a bass viol made in Southwark, A.D. 1730, and reputed the best in England. And through your means we are possessed of the best in France. So we have a fair chance for having the two best in Europe.[29]

[29] Quoted in Ibid., VIII, 261.

The nearest Berkeley comes to a philosophical definition of music is one which again refers to his basic hypothesis that everything exists only in the mind.

> Though harmony and proportion are not objects of sense, yet the eye and the ear are organs which offer to the mind such materials by means whereof she may apprehend both the one and the other.[30]

[30] "Siris," in Ibid., V, 140.

In only one place does Berkeley refer to the purpose of music and it is the important observation that art music has no functional purpose. In an unpublished notebook, Berkeley observes that there are two kinds of pleasure, one which incites you to something else while the other is self-sufficient. "Thus the pleasure of eating is of the former sort, of Musick is the later sort."[31]

[31] "Notebook A," in Ibid., I, 101.

Finally, we might mention one use of music as a metaphor by Berkeley. Wishing to suggest that what is good for the mind is good for the body, Berkeley notes in passing, "For if the lute be not well tuned, the musician fails in his harmony."[32]

[32] "Siris," in Ibid., V, 31.

William Temple (1628–1699)

FOR THE MODERN READER, one finds in William Temple a style of writing so vivid, and a philosophy so perceptive, that it seems as if written in our own time. His best known work is his essay, "On Ancient and Modern Learning," which propelled his young friend Jonathan Swift into a literary career.

Temple finds the great power of poetry in its unique combination of portrait, music and eloquence. Here, in addition to acknowledging the genetic universality of music, he considers the natural power of music, which is to move the emotions.

> The powers of music are either felt or known by all men, and are allowed to work strangely upon the mind and the body, the passions and the blood; to raise joy and grief, to give pleasure and pain, to cure diseases and the mortal sting of the tarantula; to give motions to the feet as well as the heart, to compose disturbed thoughts, to assist and heighten devotion itself. We need no recourse to the fables of Orpheus or Amphion, or the force of their music upon fishes and beasts; it is enough that we find the charming of serpents, and the cure or allay of an evil spirit or possession attributed to it in [the Bible].[33]

[33] Ibid., 177.

William Wotton (1666–1727)

WILLIAM WOTTON, chaplain to the earl of Nottingham, published his *Reflections upon Ancient and Modern Learning* (1694) as a rebuttal to William Temple's essay, "Of Ancient and Modern Learning," which had suggested that little insight had been added to those of the ancient writers. Wotton first comments that it is easy to admire the ancients, "for the distance of time takes off envy."[34] Nature, he says, has nothing to do with the prominence of either the ancient or modern writers. If it has to do with Nature, he wonders,

[34] *Reflections upon Ancient and Modern Learning*, III.

> Why have we heard of no orators among the inhabitants of the Bay of Soldania, or eminent poets in Peru?

It is the twenty-fourth chapter of Wotton's book, which he calls, "Of Ancient and Modern Musick," which is of particular interest. He begins by referring to William Temple's (nearly correct) assertion that all knowledge of ancient Greek music is lost and that (incorrect) all modern music is based on the rules of church music of the Middle Ages.

> Sir William Temple having assured us that it is agreed by the learned, that the science of Musick, so admired by the ancients, is wholly lost in the world. And that what we have now is made up of certain notes that fell into the fancy of a poor Friar, in chanting his Matins.

Wotton concludes, therefore, that "it may seem improper to speak of Musick here, which ought rather to have been ranked among those sciences wherein the Moderns have ... been found to have been out-done by the Ancients." However, he adds, he is impelled to make several observations about ancient and modern music.

Like a medieval philosopher, Wotton is still thinking of music as a branch of mathematics. Therefore, he first finds it curious that while mathematicians are conversant with earlier writers, musicians are not.

> Whereas all modern mathematicians have paid a mighty deference to the ancients; and have not only used the names of *Archimedes*, *Apolonius* and *Diophantus*, and the other ancient mathematicians with great respect; but have also acknowledged, that what further advancements have since been made, are, in a manner, wholly owing to the first rudiments, formerly taught. Modern musicians have rarely made use of the writings of *Aristoxenus*, *Ptolemee*, and the rest of the ancient musicians; and, of those that have studied them, very few, unless their editors have confessed that they could understand them. Others have laid them so far aside, as useless for their purpose; that it is very probable, that many excellent composers have scarce ever heard of their names.

As the reader can see, Wotton fails to see that music has nothing to do with "rules," but is rather experiential and emotional in nature.

Nevertheless, he proposes that the essence of ancient music, insofar as its purpose, has not been entirely lost.

> Musick has still, and always will have very lasting charms. Wherefore, since the moderns have used their utmost diligence to improve whatever was improved in the writings of

all sorts of ancient authors, upon other equally difficult and very often not so delightful subjects, one can hardly imagine but that the world would, long ere now, have heard something more demonstrably proved of the comparative perfection of ancient Musick, with large harangues in the commendation of the respective inventors, if their memory had been preserved, than barely an account of the fabulous stories of *Orpheus* or *Amhion*, which either have no foundation at all, or, as Horace understood them, are allegorically to be interpreted of their reducing a wild and savage people to order and regularity. But this is not urged against Sir William Temple, who is not convinced of the extent of modern industry, sagacity and curiosity; but to other admirers of ancient Musick, who, upon hearsay, believe it to be more perfect than the modern.

The reason for this he gives in a brief, but interesting, suggestion that there are physical laws underlying music itself, which must create similarities between ancient and modern music.

Musick is a Physico-Mathematical Science, built upon fixed rules, and stated proportions; which, one would think, might have been as well improved upon the old foundations, as upon new ones, since the grounds of Musick have always been the same. And Guido's scale, as Dr. Wallis assures us, is the same for substance with the *Diagramma Veterum*.

One argument in favor of modern music which Wotton advances is that it is assumed it has the potential for more variety.

The ancients had not, in the opinion of several who are judges of the matter, so many gradations of half-notes and quarter-notes between the whole ones as are now used; which must of necessity introduce an unspeakable variety into modern Musick, more than could formerly be had. Because it is in notes, as in numbers, the more there are of them, the more variously they may be combined together.

Wotton's next topic is by far the most interesting, the general nature of the impressions of the listener. He begins by observing that on one level, all listeners appreciate certain basic qualities in music. These things he considers universal, regardless of the education of the listener.

> It is very probable that the ancient Musick had all that which still most affects common hearers. Most men are moved with an excellent voice, are pleased when time is exactly kept, and love to hear an instrument played true to a fine voice, when the one does not so far drown the other, but that they can readily understand what is sung, and can, without previous skill, perceive that the one exactly answers the other throughout; and their passions will be effectually moved with sprightly or lamentable compositions. In all which things the ancients, probably, were very perfect.

He continues by distinguishing between the "skilled" listener of music and the "common" listener. The skilled listener, according to Wotton, listens to the details, as left brain conceptual ideas, rather than on a more holistic level. Leaving no doubt, he uses the analogy of looking at a painting. The expert, he says, looks at the detail, the technique and, for all we can tell, never sees the entire painting!

> To the [ancient] men, many of our modern compositions, where several parts are sung or played at the same time, would seem confused, intricate, and unpleasant: though in such compositions, the greater this seeming confusion, the more pleasure does the skillful hearer take in unraveling every several part, and in observing how artfully those seemingly disagreeing tones join, like true-cut Tallies, one within another, to make up that united concord, which very often gives little satisfaction to common ears; and yet it is in such sort of compositions, that the Excellency of Modern Musick chiefly consists. For, in making a judgment of Musick, it is much the same thing as it is of pictures. A great judge in Painting does not gaze upon an exquisite piece so much to raise his passions, as to inform his judgment, as to approve, or to find fault. His eye runs over every part, to find out every excellency; and his pleasure lies in the reflex act of his mind, when he knows that he can judiciously tell where every beauty lies, or where the defects are discernible: which an ordinary spectator would never find out.

The "common" man, however, is interested in the theme or story of the painting and the emotions seen in it. Likewise in music, says Wotton, the common man has his "passions raised," without any contribution to his "understanding."

> The chief thing which the [common] man wants, is the story; and if that is lively represented, if the figures do not laugh when they should weep, or weep when they should appear pleased, he is satisfied. And this, perhaps, equally well, if the piece be drawn by Raphael, as by an ordinary master, who is just able to make things look like life.
>
> So likewise in Musick; He that hears a *numerous* Song, set to a very moving melody, exquisitely sung to a sweet instrument, will find this passions raised, while his understanding, possibly, may have little or no share in the business. He scarce knows, perhaps, the names of the notes, and so can be affected only with an Harmony, of which he can render no account. To this man, what is intricate, appears confused; and therefore he can make no judgment of the true excellency of those things, which seem *fiddling* to him only, for want of skill in *Musick*.

Again, for the "skilled" listener of music, the satisfaction comes not simply from the emotions of the music, but from the combination of the emotions with intellectual understanding.

> The skill or ignorance of the composer serve rather to entertain the understanding, rather than to gratify the passions of a skillful master; whose passions are then the most thoroughly raised, when his understanding received the greatest satisfaction.

Wotton's concluding thoughts are also remarkable. He concedes that ancient music better achieved than modern, the "great End of Musick, which is to please the audience." Ancient music better moved the emotions, and even changed the very nature of the listener, than modern music. And yet, he says modern music is more perfect!—to everyone except the general audience.

> Indeed, the great End of Musick, which is to please the audience, was anciently, perhaps, better answered than now; though a modern master would then have been dissatisfied, because such consorts as the ancient Symphonies properly were, in which several instruments, and perhaps voices, played and sung the same part together, cannot discover the extent and perfection of the art, which here only is to

be considered, so much as the compositions of our modern Operas.

From all this it may, perhaps, be not unreasonable to conclude, that though those charms of Musick, by which men and beasts, fishes, fowls and serpents, were so frequently enchanted, and their very natures changed, be really and irrecoverably lost; yet the art of Musick, that is to say, of singing, and playing upon harmonious instruments, is, in itself, much a more perfect thing, though, perhaps, not much more pleasant to an unskillful audience, than it ever was among the ancient Greeks and Romans.

Anthony Cooper, Earl of Shaftesbury (1671–1713)

ANTHONY COOPER, known simply as Shaftesbury, was a student of Locke, but as a wealthy and cultured gentleman, he was comfortable in discussing the arts, which was a subject rarely mentioned by Locke. While Durant perhaps exaggerates in finding that Shaftesbury "almost founded aesthetics in modern philosophy,"[35] his voice was certainly one of the few heard on this subject at this time among the upper class in England. His famous essays were published in 1711.

There are only a few comments by Shaftesbury which touch on the definition of the nature of music. In one he seems to imply that the laws of music are found in nature itself.

> Should a writer upon music, addressing himself to the students and lovers of the art, declare to them "that the measure or rule of harmony was caprice or will, humor or fashion," it is not very likely he should be heard with great attention or treated with real gravity. For harmony is harmony by nature, let men judge ever so ridiculously of music.[36]

In another place, Shaftesbury curiously includes music with architecture (and beautiful stones, woods, rivers, mountains, etc.) as belonging to the inanimate classification.[37] This strikes us as quite odd, for one of the most conspicuous

[35] Will Durant, *The Age of Louis XIV*, 590.

[36] *Characteristics of Men, Manners, Opinions, Times*, "Advice to an Author," III, iii.

[37] Ibid., "Miscellaneous Reflections," III, ii, fn.

characteristics of music in the seventeenth century was that it was invariably *live*.

On the general topic of the universality of music, Shaftesbury is not entirely consistent. In the following, he appears to argue for a genetic understanding of some elements of the musical experience.

> Nothing surely is more strongly imprinted on our minds, or more closely interwoven with our souls, than the idea or sense of order and proportion. Hence all the force of numbers, and those powerful arts founded on their management and use. What a difference there is between harmony and discord! cadency and convulsion! What a difference between composed and orderly motion, and that which is ungoverned and accidental! ...
>
> Now as this difference is immediately perceived by a plain internal sensation, so there is withal in reason this account of it, that whatever things have order, the same have unity of design, and concur in one; are parts constituent of one whole or are, in themselves, entire systems ... What else is even a tune or symphony, or any excellent piece of music, than a certain system of proportioned sounds?[38]

[38] Ibid., "The Moralists," II, iii.

The following, however, appears to argue against the importance of universality, contending that only knowledgeable people can judge.

> If a musician were cried up to the skies by a certain set of people who had no ear in music, he would surely be put to the blush, and could hardly, with a good countenance, accept the benevolence of his auditors, till they had acquired a more competent apprehension of him, and could by their own senses find out something really good in his performance. Till this were brought about, there would be little glory in the case, and the musician, though ever so vain, would have little reason to be contented.[39]

[39] Ibid., "Enthusiasm," V.

In another place, he raises a famous question first stated by Aristotle.

> If a musician performs his part well in the hardest symphonies he must necessarily know the notes and understand the rules of harmony and music. But must a man, therefore,

who has an ear, and has studied the rules of music, of necessity have a voice or hand? Can not he possibly judge a fiddle but who is himself a fiddler?[40]

In only one place does Shaftesbury touch on the subject of purpose in music, which in this case is musical therapy. He begins this discussion with a brief reference to the beginning of the arts in the ancient period.

[40] Ibid., "Miscellaneous Reflections," V, ii.

> It may be easily perceived from hence that the goddess Persuasion must have been in a manner the mother of poetry, rhetoric, music, and the other kindred arts. For it is apparent that where chief men and leaders had the strongest interest to persuade, they used the highest endeavors to please. So that in such a state or polity as has been described, not only the best order of thought and turn of fancy, but the most soft and inviting numbers, must have been employed to charm the public ear, and to incline the heart by the agreeableness of expression.
>
> Almost all the ancient masters of this sort were said to have been musicians. And tradition, which soon grew fabulous, could not better represent the first founders or establishers of these larger societies than as real songsters, who, by the power of their voice and lyre, could charm the wildest beasts, and draw the rude forests and rocks into the form of fairest cities. Nor can it be doubted that the same artists, who so industriously applied themselves to study the numbers of speech, must have made proportionable improvements in the study of mere sounds and natural harmony, which of itself must have considerably contributed towards the softening the rude manners and harsh temper of their new people.[41]

[41] Ibid., "Advice to an Author," II, ii.

Finally, Shaftesbury contends that the theorist also makes a contribution to the art of listening.

> When the persuasive arts were grown thus into repute, and the power of moving the affections became the study and emulation of the forward wits and aspiring geniuses of the times, it would necessarily happen that many geniuses of equal size and strength, though less covetous of public applause, of power, or of influence over mankind, would content themselves with the contemplation merely of these enchanting arts. These they would the better enjoy the more they refined their taste and cultivated their ear. For to all

music there must be an ear proportionable. There must be an art of hearing found ere the performing arts can have their due effect, or anything exquisite in the kind be felt or comprehended.[42]

[42] Ibid.

In another place, Shaftesbury suggests that the listener's perception of music is to some degree limited by the perspective from his own culture.

The best music of barbarians is hideous and astonishing sounds.[43]

[43] Ibid., "Advice to an Author," II, ii.

Francis Hutcheson (1694–1746)

FRANCIS HUTCHESON was born in Ireland, the son of a Presbyterian minister. He attended the university at Glasgow, where he studied the classics, philosophy and theology and from 1729 he held the chair of moral philosophy. In the field of aesthetics, he frankly acknowledged his debt to Shaftesbury. Hutcheson, in our opinion, is greatly under-recognized today. His was a far better mind than many of his more famous English Restoration philosophers.

Hutcheson's book, *An Inquiry into the Original of our Ideas of Beauty and Virtue* (1729), consists of two separate treatises, one on Beauty and one on Morals, of which we shall only be concerned with the first.

Hutcheson considers music an Original form of beauty, rather than a Comparative one, because "Harmony is not usually conceived as an imitation of anything else."[44] To his concept of "Uniformity" he associates the fact that "harmony often raises pleasure in those who know not what is the occasion of it," the concept of concord as well as order in time and tonality. Any artificial change in this "Uniformity" would result in some form of dissonance.

[44] *An Inquiry into the Original of our Ideas of Beauty*, I, II, xiii.

> This will appear, by observing the dissonance which would arise from tacking parts of different melodies together as one, although both were separately agreeable. A like Uniformity is also observable among the basses, tenors, trebles of the same tune.

But, Hutcheson was also aware that beautiful music is often filled with dissonant chords or tones. He finds the explanation for this, in part, in his other essential of beauty, "Variety."

> There is indeed observable, in the best compositions, a mysterious effect of discords. They often give as great pleasure as continued harmony; whether by refreshing the ear with Variety, or by awaking the attention, and enlivening the relish for the succeeding harmony of concords, as shades enliven and beautify pictures, or by some other means not yet known. Certain it is however that they have their place, and some good effect in our best compositions.

Hutcheson also considers the very important question of universality relative to the sense of beauty. He begins with the rhetorical question, "if there is such a thing as a sense of beauty, is there such a thing as a sense of the disagreeable?" Before giving his answer, he first defines "deformity" as "only the absence of beauty, or deficiency in the beauty expected."

> Thus *bad Musick* pleases *Rusticks* who never heard better, and the finest ear is not offended with tuning of instruments if it be not too tedious, where no harmony is expected; and yet much smaller dissonances shall offend amidst the performance, where harmony is expected.[45]

[45] Ibid., VI, i.

While on the general subject of universality, since the emotions are universal, Hutcheson pauses to pay tribute to their role in music.

> There is also another charm in Musick to various persons, which is distinct from the harmony, and is occasioned by its raising agreeable passions. The human voice is obviously varied by all the stronger passions; now when our ear discerns any resemblance between the melody of the composition [Air of a Tune], whether sung or played upon an instrument, either in its time, or modulation, or any other circumstance, to the sound of the human voice in any passion, we shall be touched by it in a very sensible manner, and have Melancholy, Joy, Gravity, Thoughtfulness excited in us by a sort of *Sympathy* or *Contagion*. This same connection is observable between the

very melody, and the Words expressing any passion which we have heard it fitted to, so that they shall both recur to us together, though but one of them affects our senses.

Now in such a diversity of pleasing or displeasing ideas which may be joined with forms of bodies, or tunes, when men are of such different dispositions, and prone to such a variety of passions, it is no wonder "that they should often disagree in their fancys of objects, even although their sense of beauty and harmony were perfectly uniform"; because many other ideas may either please or displease, according to persons tempers and past circumstances ... And this may help us in many cases to account for the diversity of fancy, without denying the Uniformity of our internal sense of beauty.[46]

[46] Ibid., VI, xii.

James Harris (1709–1780)

JAMES HARRIS was a gentleman sufficiently wealthy that he had no need to work. He studied law and held a seat in parliament as well as some minor posts in government. His *Three Treatises* on music, painting and poetry were published as a single volume in London in 1744.

The most interesting observations by Harris are all related to the role of the emotions in music, and especially in their role when music and poetry are combined. In the passage we find most valuable, Harris begins with a simple acknowledgement to the power of music to excite the emotions.

> There are various affections which may be raised by the power of music. These are sounds to make us cheerful, or sad; martial or tender; and so of almost every other affection which we feel.[47]

[47] *Three Treatises*, VI, iff.

Harris seems to have been yet another seventeenth century philosopher who intuitively understood the twin sides of our personality, the rational versus experiential and emotional, or the left versus the right hemisphere of the brain. Although he generally underestimates the affect of the emotions on man, he is quite correct, in the following, that different listeners can have different experiences listening to the same compositions, according to the circumstances under which they listen. Thus, one listening to Mozart in a cathedral, but thinking of religion, will experience functional music. Another, thinking not of God but Mozart, will hear art music. Harris is in error, however, in imagining that all depends on a reciprocal partnership between the two hemispheres of the brain, "affections and ideas," as it might more accurately be described as a choice between one or the other.

> It is also further observable that there is a reciprocal operation between our affections and our ideas, so that by a sort of natural sympathy certain ideas necessarily tend to raise in us certain affections, and those affections, by a sort of counter operation, to raise the same ideas. Thus ideas derived from funerals, tortures, murders and the like, naturally generate the affection of melancholy. And when by any physical causes that affection happens to prevail, it as naturally generates the same doleful ideas.
>
> And hence it is that ideas derived from external causes have, at different times, upon the same person so different an effect. If they happen to suit the affections which prevail within, then is their impression most sensible and their effect most lasting. If the contrary be true, then is the effect contrary. Thus for instance, a funeral will much more affect the same man if he sees it when melancholy than if he sees it when cheerful.[48]

Although Harris's pretense is an objective study of the principal arts, in reading him it is immediately evident that his real passion is poetry. Thus when he discusses poetry set to music, he is an old-fashioned sixteenth century humanist who believes the whole point must be the poetry.

> It is evident that [poetry and music] can never be so powerful singly as when they are properly united. For poetry, when alone, must be necessarily forced to waste many of its richest ideas in the mere raising of affections, when to have been properly relished, it should have found those affections in their highest energy. And music, when alone, can only raise affections, which soon languish and decay if not maintained and fed by the nutritive images of poetry. Yet must it be remembered in this union, that poetry ever have the precedence, its utility as well as dignity being by far the more considerable.[49]

[48] Ibid.

[49] Ibid., iii.

He does, interestingly enough, concede music one advantage.

> A poet, thus assisted, finds not an audience in a temper, averse to the genius of his poem, or perhaps at best under a cool indifference, but by the preludes, the symphonies and concurrent operation of the music in all its parts, roused into those very affections which [the poet] would desire ...
>
> And hence the genuine charm of music, and the wonders which it works, through its great composers: a power which consists not in imitations and the raising idea, but in the raising affections to which ideas may correspond. There are few to be found so insensible, I may even say so inhumane, as when good poetry is justly set to music, not in some degree to feel the force of so amiable a union. But to the muses' friends it is a force irresistible, and penetrates into the deepest recesses of the soul.[50]

[50] Ibid., i.

Finally, Harris acknowledges the special problem of opera and its popularity, in spite of the objections by so many critics of the theater. For the modern audience it is the music which moves, not the plot (no one would go to hear *Don Giovanni* for the story). But, for Harris it was the words, the poetry, which gave meaning to opera. In response to those who say the singing of poetry in opera lacks "probability and resemblance to nature," Harris suggests,

> To one indeed who has no musical ear this objection may have weight. It may even perplex a lover of music if it happen to surprise him in his hours of indifference. But when he is feeling the charm of poetry so accompanied, let him be angry (if he can) with that which serves only to interest him more feelingly in the subject and support him in a stronger and more earnest attention, which enforces by its aid the several ideas of the poem and gives them to his imagination with unusual strength and grandeur.[51]

[51] Ibid., ii.

7
Isaac Newton on Music

ISAAC NEWTON (1642–1727) WAS, without any doubt, the greatest mind ever born to England. He was truly a natural scientist, interested in everything which passed his eye. While all the world knows of his immense contributions to optics and gravitation, one is staggered at the thought of the time he spent on less productive efforts. The rough estimate based on one sale catalog, the Portsmouth Collection, Cambridge, indicates a million and a half words on theology and chronology; half a million words on alchemy and one hundred fifty thousand words on problems of coinage and the Mint. And he also wrote on mathematics, chemistry, astronomy and of course philosophy. It is comforting to read he was a poor student in school.

Newton's earliest scientific interest in music lay in the mathematical division of the octave, a subject which first appears in a notebook from his college days. The reader must remember that the modern system of tuning became only generally known during Newton's lifetime, replacing several tuning systems which all differed in their calculation of the whole and half-steps, as these intervals are not consistent in the overtone series. Thus in this early notebook, dating c. 1665, one finds a study of the modes, as well as a logarithmic comparison of a scale divided into twelve equal parts with an equally tempered one.

Newton mentions in a letter to John Collins in February 1670 that he had been working on a system using logarithms to express the relationships between the tones of the scale.

> In finding the aggregate of the terms of a musical progression there is one way by logarithms very obvious (by subducting the logarithm of each denominator from that of the numerator, etc.) which I supposed to be the ordinary way in practice.[1]

[1] *The Correspondence of Isaac Newton* (Cambridge: University Press, 1959), I, 24.

Less than two weeks later, he writes the same correspondent announcing that he sees yet another system of applying logarithms to the scale, "but the calculations for finding out those rules would be still more troublesome."[2]

[2] Ibid., I, 27.

Collins was also working in this direction and during the Spring had sent his system to Newton. Newton writes a diplomatic rejection in July, reading,

> Something I have yet to say and that's about your paper concerning the aggregate of the terms of a musical progression: Namely your way deduced from Mercators squaring of the Hyperbola is the same with the last of those two I had sent you together before. Only I had taken a great deal of pains to bring it to such a form as might be most convenient for practice and so had made it so intricate as to other respects that it is no wonder if you did not discern its fountain or by what method I had composed it. I beg your pardon therefore for that obscurity.[3]

[3] Ibid., I, 31.

Collins perhaps still failed to understand, for the following December, he writes to another colleague complaining of Newton:

> After I had sent him what I had to say about the musical progression he sent me word he had completed that problem, but neither promised nor has as yet communicated how.[4]

[4] Ibid., I, 55.

One of Newton's great contributions to science, and to optics in particular, was his paper of 1672, "New Theory about Light and Colors." Always hesitant to publish, this paper formulated his discovery in 1666 that sunlight is not a simple white, but a compound of red, orange, yellow, green, blue, indigo and violet, which emerge when light is passed through a prism. Always, by his own nature, looking for fundamental laws, Newton was at the same time obsessed with finding a correspondence between the rays of light and the vibrations of sound. His earliest extant, and most complete, discussion of this is found in a letter of December 7, 1675, to Henry Oldenburg, secretary of the Royal Society.[5]

[5] Ibid., I, 376ff.

> Thus much of refraction, reflection, transparency & opacity. And now to explain colors; I suppose, that as bodies of various sizes, densities, or tensions, do by percussion or other action excite sounds of various tones & consequently vibrations in the Air of various bigness so when the rays of light, by impinging on the stiff refracting superficies excite vibrations in the aether, those rays, whatever they be, as they happen to differ in magnitude, strength or vigor, excite vibrations of various bigness; the biggest, strongest or most potent rays, the largest vibrations & others shorter, according to their bigness strength or power.

After an explanation of the physical process of the eye, Newton continues,

> ...and there I suppose, affect the sense with various colors, reds & yellows; the least with the weakest, blues & violets; the middle with green, and a confusion of all, with white, much after the manner, that in the sense of hearing Nature makes use of trial vibrations of several bignesses to generate sounds of diverse tones, for the analogy of Nature is to be observed. And further, as the harmony & discord of sounds proceed from the proportions of the aereall vibrations; so may the harmony of some colors, as of a golden & blue, & the discord of others, as of red & blue proceed from the proportions of the aethereall. And possible color may be distinguished into its principal degrees, red, orange, yellow, green, blue, indigo, and deep violet, on the same ground, that sound within an eighth is graduated into tones.

With this letter, Newton enclosed a graph,[6] showing the correlation of the basic colors with relative notes of music. Regrettably, although he discusses in detail the relationships of the colors relative to this graph, he does not offer here a precise description of their correspondence to music. Nevertheless, Newton remained interested in this topic and he discusses it again in the publication of his *Opticks* in 1704.[7]

[6] Reproduced in Ibid., I, 377.

[7] See *Opticks*, Book I, Part ii, Prop. 3 and in Book II, Part i, Ops. 14, and in Part iii, Prop. 16. Newton refers to the correspondence between music and light waves again in a letter to Dr. William Briggs in April 1685. [Ibid., II, 418].

Whatever was Newton's private understanding on this subject we are left in some doubt. To his correspondents who wanted more information, he would sometimes apologize that with regard to music, "I have not so much skill in that science as to understand it well."[8]

From his studies of optics, Newton had made important discoveries relative to light waves, establishing their speed and that they moved in straight lines. We may assume that he was at least casually thinking of the correspondence of these laws with musical sound waves as well, or so a letter to John North in 1677 suggests.[9] North had sent Newton a new treatise on music by his elder brother, Francis, for review and Newton makes extensive corrections regarding the nature and direction of sound waves, as well as on the relationships between vibrating strings. At length, Newton evidently tired and signed off.

> The discourse also about breaking of tones into higher notes seems very ingenious and judicious, but I lack experience to discern whether altogether solid, & much follows about Tunes, the scale of Music, & consorts; this requiring a combination of musical & mathematical skill, & therefore I shall content myself with having thus far animadverted upon the author.

A letter to Oldenburg in June 1672 is concerned with Newton's answering objections by Robert Hooke to some of his theories. One sentence is of particular interest, as it demonstrates that Newton correctly understood that music is in the vibrations, not in the instrument—a topic still much under discussion by some writers.

> But when Mr. Hooke would insinuate a difficulty in these things by alluding to sounds in the *string* of a musical instrument before percussion, or in the *Air* of an *Organ bellows* before its arrival at the pipes, I must confess I understand it as little as if he had spoken of light in a piece of wood before it be set on fire.[10]

Newton's correspondence reveals his interest in other topics related to music and sound. An early letter of 1669 informs an unknown friend,

[8] Letter, February 1676, to Oldenburg regarding a "Mr. Berchenshaw's scale of Musick," in Ibid., I, 420.

[9] Ibid., II, 205ff. John and Francis were brothers to Roger North, whom we have treated separately.

[10] Ibid., I, 177.

Another useful instrument lately invented here, is Sir Samuel Morelands loud speaking Trumpett, of which he has written a book or history with the title *Tuba Stentorophonica*, value one shilling, by which persons may discourse at about a mile and a half distance, if not more.[11]

And in yet another letter, Newton reveals he has received a request for information about an ear-trumpet for the deaf.[12] Newton mentions such a device made "after the form of Mr. Mace's *tocoustion*," draws a picture of it, reports it comes in several sizes and that he has heard, "the biggest do ye best."

No doubt due in part to his own unsatisfactory experience in school, Newton wrote a brief treatise, "Of Educating Youth in the Universities," although the work was left unpublished during his lifetime. It is of interest to read here what an ideal university curriculum was to Newton and we take it as a testimonial to his lack of awareness of his own genius that he proposes a curriculum that probably no one else could emerge from as a graduate in four years. We also find it extraordinary to discover him still listing music as a subject to be taught by the mathematics professor!

> Undergraduate students are to be instructed by tutors in Humanities, Greek, Philosophy, Mathematics and a tutor to read Logic, Ethics, the Globes, principles of Geography and Chronology in order to understand History.
>
> The humanities and Greek lecturers are to set tasks in Latin and Greek writers once a day for the first-year students, and once a week for the rest, and to examine diligently, instruct briefly and punish by further exercises such faults as concern the lecturers.
>
> The philosophy lecturer is to read first those introductory principles of natural philosophy, time, space, body, place, motion and its laws, force, mechanical powers, gravity and its laws, hydrostatics, projectiles solid and fluid, circular motions and the forces relating to them. This is followed by natural philosophy beginning with the general system of the world and then proceeding to the particular constitution of this earth and the things therein, meteors, elements, minerals, vegetables, animals, and ending with anatomy, if he has skills therein. He is also to examine in Logic and Ethics.
>
> The mathematics lecturer is to first read easy and useful practical things, then Euclid, spheres, projections of the

[11] Ibid., I, 5. Such a megaphone was used in the French navy until well into the nineteenth century.

[12] Ibid., I, 359.

sphere, the construction of maps, trigonometry, astronomy, optics, music, algebra, etc.[13]

Newton cautions the professors to assign major reading assignments during the vacation breaks and examine the students upon their return. He also recommends that the lecturers be given only three-year appointments and that they, in turn, elect their administrators. "No regard to Seniority or anything but merit."

Regarding student life, Newton recommends that religious periods of fasting should, in so far as the students are concerned, "have a shadow of religion without any substance." Otherwise the students are forced to seek their meals outside the campus, where they will be tempted to get in trouble.

> This does great mischief by sending young students to find suppers abroad where they get into company and grow debauched.

Finally, in a recommendation which should be adopted by every university today, it was Newton's opinion that the influence of the campus should continue, even to the alumni!

> All Graduates without exception found by the Proctors in Taverns or other drinking houses, unless with travelers at their Inns, shall at least have their names given in to the Vice-Chancellor who shall summon them to answer for it before the next Consistory.

[13] Quoted in *Unpublished Scientific Papers of Isaac Newton*, ed. Rupert Hall (Cambridge: University Press, 1962), 369ff. Newton's manuscript is largely in the form of notes and incomplete sentences, which, for ease in reading, we have edited.

8
Dryden on Music

JOHN DRYDEN (1631–1700), who has been called the greatest literary man of his age,[1] was born to a Puritan family with Republican conviction and completed his university work at Cambridge. Some question his personal ethics, for eagerness to write in praise of whoever happened to be head of the government and for his conversion to Catholicism after the accession of a Catholic King. He was buried next to Chaucer in Westminster Abbey.

The thoughts which Dryden had relative to the definition of music are all expressed in context with the comparison of music with other arts. The most extensive of these is a dedication of Purcell's *The Vocal and Instrumental Musick of The Propheless*, published in 1691, which was actually written by Dryden. Evidence that this is Dryden's work includes the fact that Henry Purcell's signature at the end is in Dryden's hand.

> Music and Poetry have ever been acknowledged sisters, which walking hand in hand, support each other; as poetry is the harmony of words, so music is that of notes; and as poetry is a rise above prose and oratory, so is music the exaltation of poetry. Both of them may excel apart, but sure they are most excellent when they are joined, because nothing is then wanting to either of their perfections; for thus they appear like wit and beauty in the same person. Poetry and painting have arrived to their perfection in our country: music is yet but in its nonage, a forward child, which gives hope of what

[1] Bernard Grebanier, *English Literature* (Great Neck: Barron, 1959), 249.

it may be hereafter in England, when the masters of it shall find more encouragement. [Music is] now learning Italian, which is its best master, and studying a little of the French melody to give it somewhat more of gayety and fashion. Thus being farther from the Sun,[2] we are of later growth than our neighbor countries, and must be content to shake off our barbarity by degrees.

Painting is, indeed, another sister, being like them, an imitation of Nature. But I may venture to say she is a dumb Lady, whose charms are only to the eye: a mute actor upon the stage, who can neither be heard there nor read afterwards. Besides, that she is a single piece; to be seen only in one place, at once: but the other two, can propagate their species; and as many printed or written copies as there are of a poem or a composition of Musick, in so many several places, at the same time the poem and the Musick, may be read, and practiced and admired. Thus painting is a confined and solitary art, the other two are as it were in consort, and diffused through the world; partaking somewhat of the Nature of the Deity, which at once is in all places. This is not said in disparagement of that noble Art; but only to give the due precedence to the others, which are more noble and which are of nearer kindred to the soul.[3]

We might also mention a lovely reference to a topic still very much discussed in the seventeenth century, the Music of the Spheres, found in a poem written after the death of a young lady, who was highly talented in poetry and painting.

> That all the people of the sky
> Might know a Poetess was born on Earth.
> And then if ever, Mortal Ears
> Had heard the Musick of the Spheres![4]

On the Purpose of Music

IN THE *The Indian Emperour* (II, iii), Cortez speaks of the purpose of both feasts and music being to bring delight. The purpose of music most frequently mentioned in early literature is to soothe the player or listener, so in *The Duke of Guise* (V, ii) Malicorne cries out, "I want a Song to rouse me, my blood freezes: Musick there!" And in a poem written for the opening of a theater in Oxford, in 1681, we find,

---

[2] This is a reference to Louis XIV of France.

[3] *The Works of John Dryden*, ed. Edward Hooker (Berkeley: University of California Press, 1956), XVII, 324ff.

[4] Ibid., III, 110.

Oh! may its genius, like soft Musick move,
And tune you all to concord and to love.⁵

⁵ Ibid., II, 180.

In *The Tempest* (II, ii), off-stage music in two-parts is heard, with instrumental accompaniment. Ferdinand responds,

Where should this Musick be? in the air, or the Earth?
It wounds no more, and sure it waits upon some God
On the Island, sitting on a bank weeping against the Duke
My father's wreck. This musick hovered over me
On the waters, allaying both their fury and my passion
With charming Airs ...

Another song (III, ii) for the purpose of soothing includes dialogue ending with humor.

GONZALO. 'Tis cheerful Musick, this, unlike the first;
And seems as 'twere meant to unbend our cares,
And calm your troubled thoughts.

[*Ariel invisible Sings.*]
Dry those eyes which are overflowing,
All your storms are over-blowing ...

ALONZO. This voice speaks comfort to us.
ANTONIO. Would 'twere come; there is no Musick in a Song
To me, my stomach being empty.

The most important purpose of music is to express emotions and we have an extraordinary testimonial to this purpose in one of Dryden's most famous Odes, his "A Song for St. Cecilia's Day, 1687,"⁶ a work which was set to music by Giovanni Draghi. He begins by suggesting that the earth and man were created in harmony⁷ by God.

From Harmony, from heavenly Harmony
This universal frame began:
From Harmony to Harmony
Through all the compass of the notes it ran,
The Diapason closing full in Man.

But he quickly turns to the emotional essence of music, in a burst of enthusiasm, "What Passion cannot Musick raise

⁶ The best known ode which Dryden wrote for the celebration of St. Cecilia's Day (in 1697) carries the title "Alexander's Feast or The Power of Music." It is more celebrated as poetry, but is less valuable for our purposes as it is an allegorical work which brings to life several ancient Greek gods. We read of "flying fingers" on the lyre addressed to Jove and of trumpets, drums and hautboys in praise of Bacchus.

⁷ It is interesting that modern research is discovering relationships between music and a variety of elements of Nature and that the most recent research in physics has found that each organ of the body produces a specific pitch.

and quell!" Now he presents a remarkable survey of the emotional qualities which he associates with various musical instruments, expressed in his most vivid choice of words.

> The TRUMPETS loud clangor
> Excites us to arms
> With shrill notes of anger ...
> ......
> The double double double beat
> Of the thundering DRUM ...
> ......
> The soft complaining FLUTE
> In dying Notes discovers
> The woes of hopeless lovers,
> Whose dirge is whispered by the warbling LUTE.
> ......
> Sharp VIOLINS proclaim
> Their jealous pangs, and desperation,
> Fury, frantick indignation,
> Depth of pains, and height of passion ...
> ......
> But oh! what Art can teach
> What human voice can reach
> The sacred ORGANS praise?
> Notes inspiring holy love,
> Notes that wing their heavenly ways
> To mend the choirs above.

Dryden concludes with a reference to the music of the spheres and the trumpet of the Day of Judgment, whose "Musick shall untune the sky."[8]

[8] Ibid., III, 201ff.

A frequently mentioned purpose of music during the Renaissance was relative to its help in courting the ladies. Thus we notice in Dryden's comedy, *Secret Love* (III, i), the character, Celadon, who walks around with a string ensemble, "a whole noise of Fiddles," to be ready to court the ladies. In Act V, scene i, this ensemble is referred to as the "Queens Musick."

Genuine music therapy is called for in *The Indian Queen* (III, ii), when Ismeron calls for music for the purpose of helping Zempoalla.

You Spirits that inhabit in the Air,
With all your powerful Charms of Musick try
To bring her Soul back to its harmony.

This is followed by a stage direction reading, "Song is supposedly sung by Aerial-Spirits." The lyrics appear for a song,[9] but the intended therapy is not effective.

> ZEMPOALLA. Death on these trifles: Cannot your Art find
>   Some means to ease the passions of the mind?
>   Or if you cannot give a lover rest,
>   Can you force love into a scornful breast?
> ISMERON. It is Reason only can make passions less;
>   Art gives not new, but may the old increase;
>   Nor can it alter love in any breast
>   That is with other flames before possessed.

Of all the music mentioned in the plays by Dryden, our attention was drawn to his use of music to establish the emotional atmosphere. We find this, for example, in instances of prelude music such as *The Indian-Queen*. At the beginning the stage direction indicates, "as the Musick plays a soft Melody," which is soon followed by "when the curtain is almost up, the Musick turns into a tune expressing an alarm." *Oedipus* also begins with instrumental music intended to set an emotional tone for the beginning of the action. The stage direction reads, "The curtain rises to a plaintive tune, representing the present condition of Thebes."[10]

In other instances the music seems intended to be associated with the emotions of the characters. Ill-suited lovers in *Marriage A-La-Mode* (III, i) are instructed in the stage direction to traverse the stage, he whistling and she "singing a dull melancholy tune," the lyrics for which are not given. Perhaps a similar intent is implied in *Cleomenes* (III, ii), where the stage direction reads, "Soft Musick all the while Ptolemy and Cassandra are adoring and speaking."

All for Love (III, i) begins with a stage direction which calls for music to introduce the characters, using instruments often associated with male and female figures in ancient iconography.

[9] The lyrics for another song appear in V, i. Lyrics for songs can be found in most of Dryden's plays. Among the more unusual are a sailor's drinking song, among several others, in *The Tempest*; *Amboyna*, which includes a wedding song (which a character notes was sprightly sung) and a song describing a sea battle; and in *Love in a Nunnery* (II, iii), where the musician-servant sings a song in French

[10] One example of instrumental music at the beginning of a play seems intended to allow the audience time to reflect. At the beginning of *Secret Love*, an actor reads a prologue which deals with the rules of playwriting and then leaves the stage. Now a stage direction reads, "The Prologue goes out, and stays while a Tune is played, after which he returns again."

The entrance on both sides is prepared by Musick; the Trumpets first sounding on Antony's part: then answered by Timbrels, etc., on Cleopatra's.

One also finds in Dryden's plays examples of art song. First, however, we should remind the reader that the sixteenth century humanists were adamant that the poetry should be written first and the music composed second, to fit the words. The Baroque saw this process reverse itself, as we can see evidenced in the *Kind Keeper* (III, i) where Brainsick[11] recalls,

> ...I rose immediately in my night-gown and slippers, down I put the notes slap-dash, made words to them like lightning...

The lyric poets of ancient Greece were fond of including contests in music in their pastoral works. Such musical contests can still be found in seventeenth century pastoral poetry and it is therefore no surprise to find a humorous example in Dryden's play, *An Evening's Love* (V, i). In this case two rather combative lovers about to be married are challenged to a musical contest to decide who should "wear the breeches" in the marriage. The gentleman, Wildblood, is hesitant:

> I never sung in all my life; nor ever durst try when I was alone, for fear of braying.

The lady observes, "if we cannot sing now, we shall never have cause when we are married." They warm up with solfege, they tune and they sing a song, for which the lyrics are given. When the song is finished, we read,

> WILDBLOOD. Your judgment Gentlemen: a Man or a Maid?
> BELLAMY. If you make no better harmony after you are married then you have before, you are the miserablest couple in Christendom.

A particularly interesting incidence of an on-stage song is found in *Oedipus* (III, i). The stage is completely darkened, followed by Tiresias's lines,

---

[11] This work was written shortly after the publication of Bunyan's *Pilgrim's Progress* and the name "Brainsick" seems clearly a humorous reference to the many such names used by Bunyan.

> Must you have Musick too? then tune your voices,
> And let them have such sounds as Hell never heard
> Since Orpheus bribed the shades.

The song which follows is preceded by a very interesting stage direction. First, we are told "Musick first. Then Sing." A bracket, which appears to be associated with the word "sing," adds, "This is to be set through." Since in the literature of this period in England, the word "set," when associated with music, refers to music which is *notated*, one is forced to wonder if some of the songs in these plays, which exist on paper only in the form of the lyrics, were improvised.

In Dryden's allegorical play, *Amphitryon* (III, i) Phaedra provides a rare example of a character who does not appreciate a song accompanied by the new modern strings.

> What, with Cats-guts and Rosin! This *Sol-la* is but a lamentable, empty sound.

In *King Arthur* (II, ii) there is a song by shepherds after the style of the pastoral poetry of the ancient Greeks. In the charming lyrics of this song the shepherds observe that while the city folks are off getting killed in war, the shepherds are in their lovers' arms and playing flutes.

In Dryden's comedy, *Sir Martin Mar-all* (V, i) there is a satire on the traditional serenade. Warner explains that he will retrieve his lute from the barbers shop and play and sing in a room, in the dark, while Sir Martin pretends to play a lute under the window while making grimaces with his mouth, as if singing. A maid tells the lady, "We shall have rare Musick," while the lady herself mentions that she hears the tuning of a lute. At the conclusion of the serenade, we find this dialogue:

> SIR MARTIN. Ha! what do you say, Madam? how does your Ladyship like my Musick?
> MILLISENT. O most heavenly! just like the Harmony of the Spheres that is to be admired, and never heard.

In sixteenth and seventeenth century literature, the reader is surprised to find instances of violence associated with serenades. Sometimes this takes the form of people throwing objects at the musicians or people physically attacking the musicians. Dryden, in *An Evening's Love* (II, i), includes a serenade after which the musicians fall into fighting with other servants.

Finally, in *The Assignation; or, Love in a Nunnery*, there is a servant, Benito, who is an amateur musician. We first see him (in I, i) standing before a large dressing mirror, playing guitar and singing to himself. Another character, Aurelian, comments of him,

> He courts himself every morning in that glass at least an hour; there admires his own person ... and studies postures and grimaces ... Then the rogue has the impudence to make sonnets, as he calls them; and, which is greater impudence, he sings them too; there's not a street in all Rome which he does not nightly disquiet with this villainous serenade: with that guitar there, the younger brother of a cittern, he frights away the watch; and as for his violin, it squeaks so lewdly ... It is a mere cat-call.

When Benito begins to sing for others in this scene, Aurelian begins to kick him. The stage direction adds, "As Aurelain kicks harder, Benito sings faster."

9
English Views on Foreign Opera

ITALIAN OPERA came later to England than most countries and it took longer to overcome local prejudices. English intellectuals held opera responsible for the decay of traditional theater in England, they were hostile to French and Italian opera because of their low level of entertainment and they hated to see all those English Pounds leaving the country in the pockets of foreign singers.

Thomas Rymer (1641–1713) was born to a well to do family in the north of England and studied at Cambridge. He was not one of the great minds of seventeenth century England, but we must mention him in passing because his *The Tragedies of the Last Age* (1677) and *A Short View of Tragedy* (1692) were widely read and therefore must have touched a chord with a number of people. Both of these books are, in effect, histories of the theater and each contains lengthy descriptions of individual plays.

The only discussion of substance on the subject of music by Rymer is given to opera, a topic he includes, no doubt, because many writers during the seventeenth century had believed that the great popularity of opera had greatly diminished the fortunes of the theater. Rymer himself is quite a harsh critic of opera.

> What would Horace have said to the *French Opera* of late so much in vogue? There it is for you to bewitch your eyes, and to charm your ears. There is a Cup of Enchantment, there is

> Musick and Machine: *Circe* and *Calipso* in conspiracy against Nature and good Sense. It is a Debauch the most insinuating, and the most pernicious; none would think an Opera and Civil Reason, should be the growth of one and the same Climate ...
>
> Away with your Opera from the Theater, better had they become the Heathen Temples ...
>
> In the French, not many years before was observed the like vicious appetite, and immoderate Passion for *vers Burlesque*.
>
> They were currant in Italy an hundred years, ere they passed to this side the Alps; but when once they had their turn in France, so right to their humor, they over ran all; nothing wise or sober might stand in their way. All were possessed with the Spirit of *Burlesk*.[1]

So prevailing was the style of burlesque, claims Rymer, that in 1649 there was published in Paris a "serious treatise" with the title, *La Passion de Nostre Seigneur, En vers Burlesques* [the Passion of Jesus set in Burlesque].

Another philosopher whose specialty was the theater was Charles Gildon, best known for his, *The Life of Mr. Thomas Betterton, the Late Eminent Tragedian*. Gildon commented on the negative influence on English drama by French ballet and Italian opera.

> And while our own poets were neglected, the French dancers got estates; and this by the influence of those, who at the same expense might have made their own names and their country famous for the encouragement of the polite arts and sciences, now neglected to a degree of barbarity, greater, than most nations on this side of Lapland.
>
> I must admit, that the excuse of our leaders seems greater and more reasonable in the indulgence they show to music, in their subscriptions for Italian singers ...[2]

While Gildon believed that vocal music represented music in its highest potential, this alone did not justify opera for him.

> But although we allow the vocal the preeminence of all other sorts of music, yet we cannot without the greatest absurdities receive even that on subjects improper for it, or in a manner unnatural, that is, as it is offered to us in our

[1] *A Short View of Tragedy*, I.

[2] Charles Gildon, *The Life of Mr. Thomas Betterton, the Late Eminent Tragedian* [1710] (London: Frank Cass Reprint, 1970), 155ff.

> Opera's with which of late the Town (I mean the leading part of the audience) has been perfectly intoxicated, and in that drunken fit has thrown away more thousands of Pounds for their support, than would have furnished us with the best poetry, and the best music in the world, without declaring against common sense. Operas have been said to be the invention of modern Italy, e'er the Return of Learning, and in the midst of that barbarous ignorance, with which the inundations of Vandals, Goths, Huns and Lombards had over-whelmed it; but I think it is pretty plain, that the Romans were, before that, sunk as far from their ancient learning and sense ...

Gildon next turns to the debate regarding the aesthetic priority of French versus Italian opera, and mentions several books on this topic, although he does not name their authors. He proceeds, after mentioning one of the French books, to make his case for the excellence of the operas of Purcell.

> Although if I had any thing to do with this controversy, I should very much doubt the judgment of the Frenchman from one instance of many, where he admires the Italians for singing out of tune, that they may give the better relish to the fine harmony, that succeeds; as if a man should admire it as a perfection in another to speak nonsense first, to give the better taste to sense afterwards.
>
> I confess, I was a little surprised, to hear of and see this book with notes [music?] by Signor H... or some creature of his; for I thought they would never have ventured so far out of their depth, as to launch from mere sound into sense, from pricking musical notes, to writing; since that was the only effectual way they could take to convince the world, that we were imposed on by those, who were not content to bubble us of our money for melodies and recitatives unless they told us to our faces, that we know nothing of the matter, and music, therefore, receive whatever stuff they would be graciously pleased to bestow upon us.
>
> But this author puts a great stress on the taking of his compositions, and the miscarriage of those of others, when he had before denied, that we knew anything of the matter. But if he allow that, as a test of the excellence of his opera, that will be much stronger for Mr. Henry Purcell, whose music supported a company of young raw actors, against the best and most favored of that time, and transported

the town for several years together, as they do yet all true lovers of music. Let any master compare *twice ten hundred deities*, the music in the *Frost Scene*, several parts of the *Indian Queen*, and twenty more pieces of Henry Purcell, with all the *Arrieto's*, *Dacapo's*, *Recitativo's* of *Camilla*, *Pyrrbus*, *Clotilda*, etc. and then judge which excels. Purcell penetrates the heart, makes the blood dance through your veins, and thrill with the agreeable violence offered by his Heavenly Harmony; the *Arietto's* are pretty light Airs, which tickle the ear, but reach no further; Purcell moves the passions as he pleases, nay, *Paints in Sounds* ...

Gildon mentions that this same anonymous book has indicated that English taste has improved since the time of Purcell and that the public should no longer "relish any of these things." In answer, he suggests,

> I would therefore fain know how our taste is mended? Do the promiscuous audience know more of the art of harmony and music? No—not one in a thousand understands one single note. How shall these therefore give the preference to this new music, to that of Henry Purcell's?

Gildon now addresses himself to the purpose of opera, in particular the question, should the purpose of opera be merely to please?

> But to return from this digression, in vindication of our English music, to the absurdities of operas; I think the degeneracy of the age is but too apparent, in the setting up and encouraging so paltry a diversion, that has nothing in it either manly or noble.
> But, says a certain gentleman, the business of the stage is to *please*, and if this pleasure be found in operas, what signifies all the objected absurdities? Although this be a very ridiculous defense, and will hold of the most scandalous and dullest things in Nature; yet I have heard it urged by men of allowed wit, and indeed, who had more of that, than of Reason, and judgment, which is founded on that. But if this be really a good argument, *Clince of Barnet*, *Bartholomew-Fair* drolls, nay a *Jack-pudding* entertainment in *Moor-Fields* are noble entertainments, for all these please, and have as good a title to the stage, as operas, nay, from Reason as better, as not subject to so many absurdities ...

Would therefore a man of sense be for a diversion, which levels his understanding with that of the refuse of the Mob? Yet the following of operas does this, and insisting in their vindication, that whatever pleases deserves encouragement, since it is a scandal to be pleased with some things, as proving but a weak capacity, or a very unpolished taste.

There are some pleasures, which none but men of fine sense, and a Gust for the art, can distinguish, as in painting, engraving, etc., while the vulgar look with an equal eye on the best and the worst. A certain country squire of my acquaintance was drinking in a country alehouse, in which seeing several notable cuts, as of the *Prodigal*, *Robin Hood* and *Little John*, and some other scurvy prints, worse than ever Overton sold, he turned to the gentleman, who sat next him, and said, "Well! this painting is a noble Art." And indeed an engraving of old Vanhove's, or worse, if any worse can be, would please the vulgar, as well as one of Edlinch, Audrand, or any of the Italian cuts; and a piece of mere sign-dauber is as valuable in the eyes of a gross and common understanding, as one of Raphael's or Thornbill's. And so in music, a Taber and Pipe, a Cymbal or Horn-pipe, will ravish the mob, more than the admirable Mr. Shoar with his incomparable lute; and the Ballad Tune *Lilly Bullero* more, than a fine Sonata of Corelli. And thus in poetry, the millions will prefer Bunyan and Quarles to Milton and Dryden; and sure no gentleman of fine taste and genius in all these things, but would be ashamed to urge such an argument as pleasing, since all these, which are scandalous, please the most in number.

From the seventeenth century in England we begin to have a number of extant diaries and collections of letters which give us the views of "ordinary" people. The best known of the diaries is the one by Samuel Pepys (1633–1703) covering the years 1660 to 1669, a testimonial to his own love of music, his close attention to the musical scene and his private performance and attempts at composition. The diary is particularly valuable because it was never intended to be published, even being written in a private code, and therefore is much more candid than the publication of a gentleman could have been at this time.

The diary entry for August 2, 1664, reveals the plans of Thomas Killigrew, manager of the king's Company and of the Theater Royal, for bringing Italian opera to London. He tells Pepys,

> We shall have the best scenes and machines, the best Musique, and everything as magnificent as is in Christendome; and to that end he has sent for voices and painters and other persons from Italy.

In a lengthy account for February 12, 1667, Pepys discusses the problems in establishing opera in London. He first describes meeting with Tom Killigrew, manager of the king's Drury Lane theater, and Robert Murray, a courtier and amateur musician, and "the Italian Seignor Baptista—who has composed a play in Italian for the opera which T. Killigrew does intend to have up." The Italian composer, having only a copy of the libretto, sat at a harpsichord and played and sang a complete act of the opera.

> My great wonder is how this man does to keep in memory so perfectly the music of that whole Act, both for the voice and for the instrument too—I confess I do admire it.

Pepys was much impressed by this display of talent, but makes the argument he would often make, that no one can make any sense out of vocal music in a language they do not speak. But he says, "I was mightily pleased with the music."

Killigrew now details the improvements in the new theater, built after the fire. The stage, he says, "is now a thousand time better and more glorious than ever before." They have better candles now, for light, and everything is more civil, no longer like a "bear-garden." Instead of two or three violins, now they have nine or ten of the best. He speaks of making a number of trips to Italy to find quality music, but the London public would have none of it.

> He has ever endeavored, in the last king's time and in this, to introduce good Musique; but he never could do it, there never having been any music here better than ballads. "No," he says "*Hermit poore* and *Chevy Chase* was all the music we had—and yet no ordinary Fidlers get so much money as ours do here, which speaks of our rudeness still."

The earliest Restoration references to opera, especially Italian opera, in the correspondence and diaries of the period one sometimes senses a perplexity at the sudden popularity of the medium. In John Evelyn's report of attending the opera in 1659, for example, we read,

> I went to visit my brother in London; and, the next day, to see a new opera, after the Italian way, in recitative music and scenes, much inferior to the Italian composure and magnificence; but it was prodigious that in a time of such public consternation such a vanity should be kept up, or permitted. I, being engaged with company, could not decently resist the going to see it, though my heart smote me for it.[3]

William Wycherley, in a letter to Alexander Pope, thanks him for his help in polishing his verses, which he calls "putting my Rhymes in Tune," and adds the observation,

> since good sounds set off often ill sense, as the Italian songs, whose good [melodies], with the worst words, or meaning, make the best musick ...[4]

In a letter of March 22, 1709, to Colonel Hunter, Jonathan Swift writes relative to the founding of the paper known as the *Tatler*.

> The vogue of operas holds up wonderfully, though we have had them a year; but I design to set up a party among the wits to run them down by next winter, if true English caprice does not interpose to save us the labor.[5]

Toward the end of this period one finds specific complaints regarding the influence of opera. Jonathan Swift, in a letter of January 10, 1721, to Alexander Pope, blames politics and the introduction of opera and masquerades for the decline in the "taste for wit and sense" in the world.[6] John Gay in a letter to Jonathan Swift, of February 15, 1728, on the success of his *Beggar's Opera*, remarks on the decline of English opera.

> Lord Cobham says that I should have printed it in Italian over against the English, that the ladies might have understood what they read. The outlandish (as they call it) [normal]

---

[3] *The Diary of John Evelyn*, for May 5, 1659. The opera was probably one by William Davenant.

[4] Letter of April 11, 1710, in *The Complete Works of William Wycherley*, ed. Montague Summers (New York: Russell & Russell, 1964), 239. William Wycherley (1641–1715) studied at Oxford, joined the court in exile in France and on his return to London was imprisoned for his debts.

[5] Quoted in *The Prose Works of Jonathan Swift* (Oxford: Blackwell, 1957), II, xxv. Jonathan Swift (1667–1745) is the best known prose writer at the end of the English Baroque and shared a grandfather with Dryden. He rarely deals with artistic matters, preferring to satirize manners. Reared in Ireland, he became active in English politics until he returned to Dublin as Dean of St. Patrick's.

[6] Quoted in Ibid., IX, 27.

opera has been so thin of late that some have called that the Beggar's Opera, and if the run continues I fear I shall have remonstrances drawn up against me by the royal academy of music.[7]

Some writers are much more outspoken in their hostility towards opera in general. William Shenstone, in answer to a lady who wrote of her friends "refined taste of operas & oratorios,"

> May Heaven preserve his hearing, that he may not only hear what the *Multitude*, but what your *Ladyship* says & then I believe he need not *regret* so much as *despise* what the *Opera-Folk* sing.[8]

Chesterfield advises his son to see everything, "from opera and plays down to the Savoyards' rarée-shows." "Everything," he says, "is worth seeing once."[9] In another letter, he tells his son he does not need to write down his expenses of things unworthy of the time, such as "chair-hire, operas, etc."[10]

At the beginning of the eighteenth century, the popularity of opera had clearly begun to fade. John Vanbrugh, a playwright but better known as an architect, built an opera house in Haymarket. In a letter of 1708, he speaks of losing much money on his opera house but believes opera will yet thrive in London, especially when a period of peace comes. He indicates that the taste for opera is not yet universal in all classes.

> That though the pit and boxes did very near as well as usual, the gallery people (who hitherto had only thronged out of curiosity, not taste) were weary of the Entertainment.[11]

In a letter of 1719 he mentions that the receipts at the opera only cover approximately one-half the costs.[12]

Thomas Gray, in June 1736, reports that the audience for the opera had fallen considerably due to competition from the newly opened Vauxhall Gardens, called initially Springgarden.[13] In his early letters, Gray occasionally mentions attending the opera, but gives few details. Ironically, the most

---

[7] Quoted in *The Works of Alexander Pope* (New York: Gordian Press, 1967), VII, 115. Alexander Pope (1688–1744) was born to the family of a prosperous merchant, but as he was also born Catholic he was denied an education at any of the great universities. Thus, the greatest English poet of the eighteenth century was the product of his own education through reading. An illness as a child left him a four foot high hump-back.

[8] Letter to Lady Luxborough, May 5, 1748, in *Letters of William Shenstone* (Minneapolis: University of Minnesota Press, 1939), 104.

[9] Earl of Chesterfield, letter to his son, April 15, 1745.

[10] Earl of Chesterfield, letter to his son, January 10, 1749.

[11] Letter to the Earl of Manchester, July 27, 1708, quoted in *The Complete Works of John Vanbrugh* (London: Nonesuch Press, 1927), IV, 24. Sir John Vanbrugh (1664–1726) was not only a playwright but a celebrated architect, whose work included Blenheim Palace and the Haymarket Opera—which he also managed and which failed.

[12] Letter to Jacob Tonson, December 31, 1719, quoted in Ibid., IV, 124.

[13] Letter to Walpole, June 11, 1736, in *Correspondence of Thomas Gray* (Oxford: Clarendon Press, 1971). Thomas Gray (1716–1771) spent the greater part of his adult life in academic seclusion in Cambridge.

information is found in an outline for a proposed, but never written, book, the fourth chapter of which would have been devoted to opera. Following are the subjects he apparently intended to discuss.

> Goes to the Opera; grand Orchestra of Humstrums, Bagpipes, Salt-boxes, Tabours, & Pipes. Anatomy of a French Ear, showing the formation of it to be entirely different from that of an English one, & that sounds have a directly contrary effect upon one & the other. Farinelli at Paris said to have a fine manner, but no voice. Grand Ballet, in which there is no seeing the dance for Petticoats. Old Women with flowers & jewels stuck in the curls of their gray hair; red-heeled shoes & roll-ups innumerable, hoops & Paniers immeasurable, paint unspeakable. Tables, wherein is calculated with the utmost exactness, the several degrees of red, now in use ... [14]

[14] Quoted in Ibid., I, 139.

We also read of the extreme measures taken in an attempt to make opera once again popular. In London, in May 1742, Gray reports attending Pergolesi's opera, *Olimpiade*, which turned out to be a pasticcio, with some of Pergolesi's music being replaced by that of other composers.

Finally, the correspondence and diaries of this period make reference to performances of opera in foreign lands. The *Diary* of John Evelyn reports his hearing an opera in Venice in 1645.

> This night, having with my Lord Bruce taken our places before, we went to the Opera, where comedies and other plays are represented in recitative music, by the most excellent musicians, vocal and instrumental, with variety of scenes painted and contrived with no less art of perspective, and machines for flying in the air, and other wonderful notions; taken together, it is one of the most magnificent and expensive diversions the wit of man can invent. The history was, Hercules in Lydia; the scenes changed thirteen times. The famous voices, Anna Rencia, a Roman, and reputed the best treble of women; but there was an eunuch who, in my opinion, surpassed her; also a Genoese that sung an incomparable bass. This held us by the eyes and ears till two in the morning.[15]

[15] *The Diary of John Evelyn*, in a long entry for May 21, 1645.

Thomas Gray reports hearing a "fine concert of music" in Venice, which included, among the rest two eunuchs' voices, that were a perfect feast to ears that had heard nothing but French operas for a year.[16]

The playwright, James Thomson, in a letter written in Paris in 1732, offers his impressions of Italian music and of French opera.

> The language and music in Italy are enchanting. Being but an infant in the language I ought not to pretend to judge of it, yet cannot I help thinking it not only very harmonious, and expressive, but even not at all incapable of manly graces. As for their music, it is a sort of charming malady that quite dissolves them in softness, and greatly heightens in them that universal indolence men naturally fall into when they can receive little or no advantage from their industry. They talk of the Tarantula in Italy, for whose bite music is a cure. That Tarantula must, I fancy, mean the bad government, for whose oppression music if not a cure is at least some relief, by gently lulling them into a sweet forgetfulness of misery. Now that I mention music, one cannot, I believe, have a stronger instance of the power of custom with regard to taste than one meets with here [in Paris] in the French opera. While they themselves die away in rapture at what they call their beaux morceaux, others whose taste is formed by the Italian music would rather hear the Screech-owl than their screaming heroines. Their excessive vanity has led them into this difference of taste of their own, although to have it they must forsake Nature.[17]

The wide public interest in opera at this time helps explain why this also became a topic for poets and writers of fiction. On the subject of opera, the Restoration poets were almost invariably hostile. Among the more tame examples, Shenstone was probably thinking of Italian opera when he wrote of the songs of birds,

> My doubt subsides—'tis no Italian song,
> Nor senseless ditty, cheers the vernal tree ... [18]

After Dryden converted to Catholicism in 1686, Charles Sackville wrote an anti-Catholic commentary, recommending that Dryden use the Catholic fables as material for new operas.

[16] Letter to Richard West, November 21, 1739, in *Correspondence of Thomas Gray*. In December 1739, while in Vienna, Gray observes that everyone is hoping for a safe delivery by Maria Theresa of a child, for then there will be balls and operas, which otherwise would not be given until Carnival.

[17] Letter to Lady Hertford, October 10, 1732, in *James Thomson, Letters and Documents* (Lawrence: University of Kansas Press, 1958), 82. James Thomson (1700–1748) was highly respected by both Voltaire and Lessing, but has never been esteemed by his own countrymen.

[18] William Shenstone, "Elegy VI," in *The Poetical Works of William Shenstone*, (Edinburgh: James Nichol, 1854), 10.

> Thy mind, disused to truth, must entertain
> With tales more monstrous, fanciful, and vain
> Than even thy poetry could ever feign.
> Or sing the lives of thy own fellow saints—
> 'Tis a large field and thy assistance wants.
> Thence copy out new operas for the stage
> And with their miracles divert the age.[19]

[19] *The Poems of Charles Sackville* (New York: Garland, 1979), 19. Charles Sackville, Earl of Dorset (1638–1706), was the recipient of the dedication of Dryden's "Essay of Dramatic Poesie."

Turning to the more outspoken poets, Richard Steele was one who was adamantly opposed to Italian opera. We can see this in the Epilogue he wrote for the play, *The Tender Husband*, whose lines include,

> Britons, who constant war, with factious rage,
> For liberty against each other wage,
> From foreign insult save this English stage.
> No more the Italian squalling Tribe admit,
> In tongues unknown; it is Popery in wit.
> The songs (their selves confess) from Rome they bring;
> And 'tis High Mass, for ought you know, they sing.
> Husbands take care, the danger may come nigher,
> The women say their eunuch is a Friar.

Steele has also written an intentionally insipid little poem called "Lyric for Italian Music," of which he sarcastically comments that his poem will not "disturb the head, but merely serves to be added to sounds proper for the syllables." He even wrote a poem to celebrate the departure of the famous Italian singer, Nicolino Grimaldi, who left England to return to Italy in 1712. Among other insults, he reminds the reader that the singer was a castrato.

> Begone, our nation's pleasure and reproach!
> *Britain* no more with idle trills debauch;
> Back to thy own unmanly *Venice* sail,
> Where luxury and loose desires prevail;
> There thy emasculating voice employ,
> And raise the triumphs of the wanton boy.[20]

[20] "On Nicolini's leaving the Stage."

Joseph Addison laments the decline in British drama caused by the popularity of Italian opera.

> Long has a race of heroes filled the stage,
> That rant by note, and through the gamut rage;
> In songs and airs express their martial fire,
> Combat in trills, and in a fugue expire.
> While, lulled by sound, and undisturbed by wit,
> Calm and serene you indolently sit,
> And, from the dull fatigue of thinking free,
> Hear the facetious fiddle's repartee.
> Our home-spun authors must forsake the field,
> And Shakespeare to the soft Scarlatti yield.[21]

In his "Epistle III," John Gay satirizes French opera through a character who has returned to tell of life in Paris.[22] He finds there that "Opera claims the foremost place" and in a discussion of the *Toilette* mentions "Madame today puts on her Opera face." Eventually, we get an interesting view of French opera, seen through English eyes, followed by a stated preference for Italian music. The extraordinary thing for the modern reader here, customs described in French sources as well, is the participation of the audience, including crowding onto the stage itself!

> Adieu, Monsieur—The Opera hour draws near,
> Not see the Opera! all the world is there;
> Where on the stage the embroidered youth of France
> In bright array attract the female glance:
> This languishes, this struts, to show his mien,
> And not a gold-clocked stocking moves unseen.
> But hark! the full Orchestra strike the strings;
> The Hero struts, and the whole audience sings.
>
> My jarring ear harsh grating murmurs wound,
> Hoarse and confused, like *Babel's* mingled sound.
> Hard chance had placed me near a noisy throat,
> That in rough quavers bellowed every note.
> Pray, Sir, says I, suspend awhile your song,
> The Opera's drowned; your lungs are wondrous strong;
> I wish to hear your *Roland's* ranting strain,
> While he with rooted forfeits strows the plain.
> Sudden he shrugs surprise, and answers quick,
> *Monsieur apparemment n'aime pas la musique.*
> Then turning round, he joined the ungrateful noise;
> And the loud Chorus thundered with his voice.

[21] "Prologue to Smith's Phaedra and Hippolitus," lines 1ff.

[22] "Epistle III," in *The Works of John Gay* (London: Edward Jeffery, 1745), III, 20ff. John Gay (1685–1732) was born of humble stock and worked for a while as a silk merchant. He became one of the most beloved of English literary figures.

> O soothe me with some soft Italian air,
> Let harmony compose my tortured ear!
> When Anastatia's voice commands the strain,
> The melting warble thrills through every vain;
> Thought stands suspense, and silence pleased attends,
> While in her notes the heavenly Choir descends.

> But you'll imagine I'm a *Frenchman* grown,
> Pleased and content with nothing but my own,
> So strongly with this prejudice possessed,
> He thinks *French* musick and *French* painting best.
> Mention the force of learned *Corelli's* notes,
> Some scraping fiddler of their Ball he quotes;
> Talk of the spirit *Raphael's* pencil gives,
> Yet warm with life whose speaking picture lives;
> Yes, Sir, says he, in color and design,
> *Rigaut* and *Raphael* are extremely fine!

Gay makes his personal prejudice quite clear in the final lines of this poem.

> Should I let Satire loose on English ground,
> There fools of various character abound;
> But here my verse is to one race confined,
> All Frenchmen are of *Petit-maitre* kind.

Finally, we might mention an elegy by Gay on the death of a performer.

> But bear me faintly through the lonely grove;
> No more these hands shall over the spinnet bound,
> And from the sleeping strings call forth the sound;
> Musick adieu, farewell Italian airs![23]

[23] "Araminta," in Ibid., III, 124.

Among the anti-Italian opera reflections by Swift is a rather nasty poem of 1731 called "Apollo." Someone had apparently become obsessed with the observation that, among the Greek gods, Apollo never married a female god. Swift offers to solve this "problem" by contending that Apollo, like the famous Italian singer known in London as "Nicolini," was a castrato.

> Yet, with his beauty, wealth, and parts,
> Enough to win ten thousand hearts,

> No vulgar deity above
> Was so unfortunate in love.
> Three weighty causes were assigned,
> That moved the nymphs to be unkind.
> Nine Muses always waiting round him,
> He left them virgins as he found them.
> His singing was another fault;
> For he could reach to B in *alt*:
> And, by the sentiments of Pliny,
> Such singers are like Nicolini.
> At last, the point was fully cleared;
> In short, Apollo had no beard.

Alexander Pope was also inevitably critical of opera, as in this reference to the court's preference to Italian opera:

> Get place and wealth—if possible with grace;
> If not, by any means, get wealth and place.
> For what? to have a box where eunuchs sing,
> And foremost in the circle eye a king.[24]

In the same work, Pope makes a similar comment and in a footnote he indicates he was thinking of *The Siege of Rhodes*, by William Davenant, the first opera sung in England.

> No wonder then, when all was love and sport,
> The willing Muses were debauched at Court:
> On each enervate string they taught the note
> To pant, or tremble through an eunuch's throat.[25]

In his curious attack on literary charlatanism, *The Dunciad*, Pope finds,

> Already Opera prepares the way,
> The sure fore-runner of her gentle sway:
> Let her thy heart, next Drabs and Dice, engage,
> The third mad passion of thy doting age.
> Teach thou the warbling Polypheme to roar,
> And scream thyself as none ever screamed before![26]

Pope intends his most famous "Epigram on the Feuds about Handel and Bononcini," as an expression of his boredom with the discussion of opera in the press.

> Strange! all this difference should be
> 'Twixt Tweedle-*dum* and Tweedle-*dee*![27]

[24] "Imitations of Horace," Book I, Epistle I, in *The Works of Alexander Pope*. Ibid., III, 338.

[25] Ibid., Book II, Epistle I, lines 151ff.

[26] *The Dunciad*, Book III, lines 301ff, in Ibid., IV, 182.

[27] Quoted in Ibid., IV, 445.

In the English fiction of the Baroque one also finds rather derogatory remarks about opera. Defoe, in discussing the entertainments of the colosseum of ancient Rome, comments in passing,

> ... the cutting in pieces forty or fifty slaves, and the seeing twenty or thirty miserable creatures thrown to the lions and tigers, was no less pleasant to them than the going to see an opera, a masquerade, or a puppet-show is to us.[28]

In Henry Fielding's novel, *The Adventures of Joseph Andrews*, a Frenchman commenting on the poor dress at English opera observes, "I positively assure you, at the first opera I saw since I came over, I mistook the English ladies for chambermaids!"[29] In Richardson's novel, *Clarissa Harlowe*, a line mentions in passing that a young lady and her mother never missed being present at the opera, which is referred to as a mere "diversion."[30]

In his novel, *Pamela*, Richardson devotes a lengthy passage to opera, which is rich in its insights to the English gentleman's perspective of Italian opera at this time.[31] This passage is contained in a fictional letter written by a Mrs. B—- to Lady Davers. Mrs. B—- begins by writing that she will relate her opinion of an opera she attended the previous evening. At the beginning she recites arguments that had been used in ancient literature against music, in particular that it is transitory, exists in the air and does not last and therefore is, in itself, insignificant and also that it is effeminate. Next she mentions an argument frequently used against opera, that it inappropriate for great characters to sing, rather than speak.

> But what can I say when I have mentioned what you so well know, the fine scenes, the genteel and splendid company, the charming voices, and delightful music!
>
> If, madam, one were all ear, and lost to every sense but that of harmony, surely the Italian opera would be a transporting thing!—But when one finds good sense, and instruction, and propriety, sacrificed to the charms of sound, what an unedifying, what a mere temporary delight does it afford! For what does one carry home, but the remembrance of having been pleased so many hours by the mere vibration of air,

[28] Daniel Defoe, "Robinson Crusoe," (Garden City: Doubleday, n.d.), III, 120.

[29] Henry Fielding, *The Adventures of Joseph Andrews*, II, iv.

[30] Samuel Richardson, *Clarissa Harlowe* (New York: AMS Press Reprint, 1972), XII, 335. Samuel Richardson (1689–1761) was reared in the company of spinsters and his novels are considered to reflect unusual knowledge of female psychology.

[31] Samuel Richardson, *Pamela*, IV, 48ff.

> which being but sound, you cannot bring away with you: and must therefore enter the time passed in such a diversion, into the account of those blank hours from which one has not reaped so much as one improving lesson?
>
> I speak this with regard to myself, who know nothing of the Italian language: But yet I may not be very unhappy that I do not, if I may form my opinion of the sentiments by the enervating softness of the sound, and the unmanly attitudes and gestures made use of to express the passions of the men performers, and from the amorous complainings of the women; as visible in the soft, too-soft, action of each.
>
> Then, though I cannot but say that the music is most melodious, yet to see a hero, as an Alexander, or a Julius Caesar, warbling out his achievements in war, his military conquests, as well as his love, in a song, it seems to be to be making a jest of both.

Another point she makes is very curious. She argues for national isolationism and condemns music for the fact that it is *universal*.

> Every nation, Mr. B—- says, has its peculiar excellence: The French taste is comedy and harlequinery; the Italian, music and opera; the English, masculine and nervous sense, whether in tragedy or comedy—why can't one, methinks, keep to one's own particular national excellence, and let others retain theirs? For Mr. B—- observes, that when once sound is preferred to sense, we shall depart from all our own worthiness, and at best, be but the apes, yea, the dupes, of those whom we may strive to imitate; but never can reach, much less excel.

At the end of her letter, she returns to the idea that music is merely air. One must point out that she reflects here the long, and misdirected university concept of "speculative" music, in which music is defined only as physical sound. It not only misses the point, but misleads, for the real essence of music is the communication of *feeling*.

> But what have I said, what can I say, of an Italian opera? Only, little to the purpose as it is, I wonder how I have been able to say so much: for who can describe sound? Or what words shall be found to embody air?—And when we return, and are asked our opinion of what we have seen or heard, we are only able to answer, as I hinted above, the scenery is fine; the

company splendid and genteel; the music charming for the time; the action not extraordinary; the language unintelligible; and for all these reasons—the instruction none at all.

Mr. B—- himself now enters the room. Mrs. B—- shows him her comments on opera, asks his opinion and quotes his observations. His first remarks center on the problem of doing opera in translation, all of which, of course, is only a reflection of the attitude advanced that the words are more important than the music.

> Operas, said he, are very sad things in England, to what they are in Italy; and the translations given of them abominable: and indeed our language will not do them justice.
> Every nation, as you take notice, has its excellencies; and you say well, that ours should not quit the manly nervous sense, which is the distinction of the English drama. One play of our celebrated Shakespeare will give infinitely more pleasure to a sensible mind, than a dozen English-Italian operas. But, my dear in Italy they are quite another thing: and the sense is not, as here, sacrificed so much to the sound, but that they are both very compatible.

Mrs. B—- now asks Mr. B—- to add a sheet himself to this letter and he does so. His portion concentrates on the emphasis of words above music, claiming in fact that in Italy the story was always more important than the music. Surely any rational person today would conclude that if this were intended by the late sixteenth century persons involved in the first opera, there would have been no need or purpose achieved in creating opera. They would have been far more effective in producing another Italian play. Now, Mr. B—-'s letter is quoted.

> In Italy, judges of operas are so far from thinking the drama, or poetical part of their operas, nonsense, as the unskilled in Italian rashly conclude in England, that if the Libretto, as they call it, is not approved, the opera, notwithstanding the excellence of the music, will be condemned. For the Italians justly determine, that the very music of an opera cannot be complete and pleasing, if the drama be incongruous, as I may call it, in its composition; because, in order to please, it must have the necessary contrast of the grave and the light; that

is, the diverting, equally blended through the whole. If there be too much of the first, let the music be composed ever so masterly in that style, it will become heavy and tiresome; if the latter prevail, it will surfeit with its levity: Wherefore, it is the poet's business to adapt the words for this agreeable mixture: for the music is but secondary, and subservient to the words; and if there be an artful contrast in the drama, there will be the same in the music, supposing the composer to be a skillful master.

Now, since in England the practice has been to mutilate, curtail and patch up a drama in Italian, in order to introduce favorite arias, selected from different authors, the contrast has always been broken thereby, and the opera damned, without every one's knowing the reason: And since ignorant, mercenary prompters, though Italians, have been employed in the hotch-potch, and in translating our dramas from Italian into English, how could such operas appear any other than incongruous nonsense?

Mr. B—- concludes by defining "Recitativos."

To avoid the natural dissonance and irregularity in common speech, recitativos in music, and dramatical performances were invented; and although the time in pronouncing the words contained in them, is scarce longer than in common conversation; yet the harmony of the chords of the thorough-bass, which then accompanies the voice, delights the ears of discerning judges: Wherefore recitative is a regular way of speaking musically, as I may say, in order to avoid and correct the irregularities of speech often found in nature, and to express the variety of the passions, without offense to the ear.

10
Dryden on Opera

JOHN DRYDEN (1631–1700), who has been called the greatest literary man of his age,[1] was born to a Puritan family with Republican conviction and completed his university work at Cambridge.

[1] Bernard Grebanier, *English Literature* (Great Neck: Barron, 1959), 249.

The play, *The State of Innocence*, was intended to be a libretto for an opera, but as Dryden admits in the preface to its publication, the work never made it to the stage. In the play, nevertheless, one finds a few clues to the prospective music which Dryden envisioned. In Act I, scene one, a stage direction calls for a song of rather epic nature:

> ...and a Song expressing the change of their condition; what they enjoyed before; and how they fell bravely in Battel, having deserved Victory by their Valor; and what they would have done if they had conquered.

At the end of II, ii, a stage direction reads "soft Musick and a Song is sung,' and "soft Music" is called for again in V, iv, together with "a Song and Chorus."

Dryden called his play *King Arthur* a "dramatic opera," and in fact it was set to music by Purcell. In the dedication, Dryden compliments Purcell and then appears compelled to explain that he has had to alter his poetry in some places to fit the requirements of the music.

> There is nothing better than what I intended, but the music; which has since arrived to a greater perfection in England

than ever formerly; especially passing through the artful hands of Mr. Purcell, who has composed it with so great a genius, that he has nothing to fear but an ignorant, ill-judging audience. But the numbers of poetry and vocal music are sometimes so contrary, that, in many places, I have been obliged to cramp my verses, and make them rugged to the reader, that they may be harmonious to the hearer; of which I have no reason to repent me, because these sorts of entertainments are principally designed for the ear and eye; and therefore, in reason, my art, on this occasion, ought to be subservient to his. And, besides, I flatter myself with an imagination, that a judicious audience will easily distinguish betwixt the songs wherein I have complied with him, and those in which I have followed the rules of poetry, in the sound and cadence of the words.[2]

[2] *The Works of John Dryden*, ed. Walter Scott (London: William Miller, 1808), VIII, 119.

As for this libretto itself, there are much greater numbers of musicians mentioned in the stage directions and they are much more specific. For example, one stage direction (IV, i) reads "A Bass and two Trebles sing the following Song to a Minuet." There are also unusual references in the stage directions to instrumental music, such as in V, i, "A concert of Trumpets within," and later "a Warlike Concert."

Dryden's most extensive discussion of opera is found in the preface to his libretto for the opera, *Albion and Albanius*.[3] The music for this opera was composed by Louis Grabu, a Frenchman who became Composer-in-ordinary to Charles II. Dryden, who had worked with Purcell, saw no less ability in Grabu, pointing in particular to,

[3] *The Works of John Dryden*, ed. Edward Hooker (Berkeley: University of California Press, 1956), XV, 3ff.

his extraordinary talent, in diversifying the Recitative, the lyrical part, and the Chorus. In all which ... the best judges, and those too of the best quality, who have honored his rehearsals with their presence, have no less commended the happiness of his genius than his skill. And let me have the liberty to add one thing; that he has so exactly expressed my sense, in all places, where I intended to move the passions, that he seems to have entered into my thoughts, and to have been the poet as well as the composer. This I say, not to flatter him, but to do him right; because because amongst some English musicians, and their scholars ... the imputation of being a French-man, is enough to make a [political] Party [against him], who maliciously endeavor to decry him. But the knowledge of Latin and Italian poets, both which he possesses, besides his skill in Musick, and his being acquainted with all the performances of the French operas, adding to these the good sense to which he is born, have raised him to a degree above any man, who shall pretend to be his rival on our stage. When any of our countrymen excel him, I shall be glad, for the sake of old England, to be shown my error.

Next, Dryden offers this definition of opera.

An Opera is a poetical tale or fiction, represented by vocal and instrumental Musick, adorned with scenes, machines and dancing. The supposed persons of this musical Drama, are generally supernatural, as Gods and Goddesses, and Heroes, which at least are descended from them, and are in due time, to be adopted into their number. The subject therefore being extended beyond the limits of human nature, admits of that sort of marvelous and surprising conduct, which is rejected in other plays.

The essential problem in opera is one of right (music) versus left (story) hemispheres of the brain, for they are not particularly well adapted to work equally in a simultaneous mode. Dryden is quite correct, therefore, when he observes that while beauty of expression is important,

the Songish part [musical accompaniment] must abound in the softness and variety of numbers: its principal intention, being to please the hearing, rather than to gratify the understanding.

Dryden admits he has been unable to determine the origin of opera, which he now several times calls "Dramatique Musical Entertainment,"[4] and his best guess is incorrect, that its origin was among the entertainment music of the Spanish Moors. Nevertheless, he suggests that anyone interested today in writing opera should study the Italians who have brought this form into perfection.

[4] Ibid., 5.

But however it began (for the above is only conjectural), we know that for some centuries, the knowledge of Musick has flourished principally in Italy, the Mother of learning and the arts; that poetry and painting have been restored there, and so cultivated by Italian masters, that all Europe has been enriched out of their treasury: and the other parts of it in relation to those delightful arts, are still as much provincial to Italy, as they were in the time of the Roman Empire.

Although, as he has indicated above, the principal roles are given to gods and heroes, he adds that it is still appropriate to admit shepherds,

> by reason of the spare time they had, in their almost idle employment, had most leisure to make verses, and to be in love; without somewhat of which passion, no opera can possible subsist.

He finds the Italians have a distinct advantage in opera due to the very nature of their language.

> It is the softest, the sweetest, the most harmonious, not only of any modern tongue, but even beyond any of the learned [Greek and Latin]. It seems indeed to have been invented for the sake of poetry and Musick: the vowels are so abounding in all words, especially in the termination of them, that excepting some few monosyllables, the whole language ends in them. Then the pronunciation is so manly and so sonorous, that their very speaking has more of Musick in it, than [German] poetry and song.

The French, he maintains, "who now cast a longing eye to [Italy], are not less ambitious to achieve elegance in poetry and Musick." However, he finds them restricted by nature.

> But after all, as nothing can be improved beyond its own species, or farther than its original nature will allow (as an ill voice, though never so thoroughly instructed in the rules of Musick, can ever be brought to sing harmoniously ...), so neither can the natural harshness of the French, or their perpetual ill accent, be ever refined into perfect harmony like the Italian.

The English, he finds, are hampered by "effeminacy of our pronunciation," which he suggests was inherited from the Danes, and by a scarcity of female rhymes.

Dryden now offers several rules for the poet who would write for an opera. The first necessity, he says, is "double rhythms, and ordering of the words and numbers for the sweetness of the voice." These, he says, are,

> the main hinges, on which an opera must move; and both of these are without the compass of any Art to teach another to perform; unless Nature in the first place has done her part, by enduing the poet with that nicety of hearing, that the discord of sounds in words shall as much offend him, as a seventh in Musick would a good composer.

Next in importance for Dryden, is choice of vocabulary.

> The chief secret is in the choice of words; and by this choice I do not here mean elegancy of expression, but propriety of sound to be varied according to the Nature of the subject.

Under this subject, Dryden again turns to the inherent problems of the English language. He says that in writing for song he has had to actually invent new words and it is in this context that he mentions the objections which all earlier poets had expressed, that they had to alter their words for the sake of the composer and his music. Dryden adamantly promises he will never do this again.

> I am often forced to coin new words, revive some that are antiquated, and botch others; as if I had not served out my time in poetry, but was bound an apprentice to some doggerel Rhymer, who makes songs to tunes, and sings them for a lively-hood. It is true, I have not been often put to this drudgery; but where I have, the words will sufficiently show, that I was then a slave to the composition, which I will never be again. It is my part to invent, and the musicians to humor that invention.

Dryden makes an extraordinary observation later, when he returns to his concern that the efforts of the composer, Grabu, will be accepted by the English composers and critics. Of the public he is not concerned, because he seems aware of the fact that music is both universally and genetically understood by all men.

> For the greatest part of an audience is always unimpressed, though seldom knowing; and if the Musick be well composed,

and well performed, they who find themselves pleased, will be so wise as not to be imposed upon and fooled out of their satisfaction.

Dryden offers an observation on the French versus the English with respect to opera.

When operas were first set up in France, they were not followed over eagerly; but they gained daily upon their hearers, till they grew to that height of reputation, which they now enjoy. The English I confess, are not altogether so musical as the French.

Later, in the prologue, he attributes the development of musical sophistication by the French to the former court of Louis XIV.

In France, the oldest man is always young,
Sees opera's daily, learns the tunes so long,
Till foot, hand, head, keep time with every song.
Each sings his part, echoing from pit and box
With his hoarse voice, half harmony, half pox.
Le plus grand Roy du Monde is always ringing;
They show themselves good subjects by their singing.[5]

[5] Ibid., 15.

We might add that in the stage directions for this libretto, Dryden mentions a much broader range of instruments than are usually found in his plays. He mentions by name such instruments as "Base Voil," trumpet, harp and "Ho-boys." He also includes a number of "symphonies," which appear to mean a brief instrumental work, often for the purpose of allowing the appearance or movement of stage machinery. One of these precedes a song (III, i), another is a "Sinphony of Fluts-Doux"

Finally, in his poem in honor of the painter, Sir Godfrey Kneller, Dryden speaks of the fact that the taste of the present age discourages the artist from striving for the highest, most exalted, in art. In this context, he briefly reflects in passing a lower artistic level for opera, as compared to the theater.

For what a Song, or senseless Opera
Is to the Living Labor of a Play ...[6]

[6] Ibid., IV, 465ff.

The most important English musician in history is honored in a Dryden poem called, "An Ode, on the Death of Mr. Henry Purcell," which was later set to music by John Blow. Dryden begins by mentioning the singing of birds, an inevitable topic for poets, but contends their music is no challenge to Purcell.

> So ceased the rival Crew when Purcell came,
> They sung no more, or only sung his fame,
> Struck dumb they all admired the God-like Man ...

Dryden concludes by crediting Heaven for Purcell's music.

> The Heavenly Choir, who heard his notes from high,
> Let down the Scale of Musick from the sky:
> They handed him along,
> And all the way He taught, and all the way they sung.[7]

[7] Ibid., IV, 468ff.

11
Restoration Journals on Opera

JOURNALS AND NEWSPAPERS were not new to this period, but the extensive coverage of music and manners was. Richard Steele began the *Tatler* on April 12, 1709, writing primarily under the name Isaac Bickerstaff, as a paper designed for the conversation of the coffee house crowd. These journals are valuable in part for their presentation of this class, much of it middle-class, which is virtually absent in traditional political biographies and histories.

Steele and Joseph Addison created the *Spectator* with the issue of March 1, 1711. For the first year its actual circulation was small, rarely more than four thousand issues, but its influence became much larger as bound volumes were sold at the rate of nine thousand each year.

These journals are filled with references to music, musical humor and musical instruments, however, we present below only those passages which offer the modern reader insight into the contemporary views of opera.

In the very first issue of the *Tatler*, for April 12, 1709, Richard Steele mentions a complaint frequently made during this period, that the popularity of Italian opera had caused the decline of theater in England.[1]

> It is not now doubted but plays will revive, and take their usual place in the opinion of persons of wit and merit, notwithstanding their late apostacy in favor of dress and sound.

[1] Regarding the popularity of Italian opera, the *Tatler* for April 27, 1710, carries a fictional advertisement for an opera in which the composer "hopes he has pretensions to the favor of all Lovers of Musick, who can get over the prejudice of his being their Countryman."

In an issue the same month, for April 19, 1709, Steele is somewhat more outspoken in his attack on opera.

> Letters from the Hay-market inform us, that on Saturday night last the opera of *Pyrrhus and Demetrius* was performed with great applause. This intelligence is not very acceptable to us friends of the theater; for the stage being an entertainment of the Reason and all our faculties, this way of being pleased with the suspense of them for three hours together, and being given up to the shallow satisfaction of the eyes and ears only, seems to arise rather from the degeneracy of our understanding, than an improvement of our diversion. That the understanding has no part in the pleasure is evident, from what these letters very positively assert, to wit, that a great part of the performance was done in Italian.

The issue of May 7, 1709, continues arguments of this kind and attacks for the first time the Italian singers who were castrati.

> When the seat of wit was thus mortgaged, without equity of redemption, an architect arose, who has built the Muse a new palace, but secured her no retinue; so that instead of action there, we have been put off by song and dance. This latter help of sound has also began to fail for want of voices; therefore the palace has since been put into the hands of a surgeon, who cuts any foreign fellow into an Eunuch, and passes him upon us for a singer of Italy.

The burial of the most famous English actor of the seventeenth century, Thomas Betterton, inspired the *Tatler* to once again attack opera. An argument used against it here is a very ancient one, that music is of only brief duration and then disappears.

> I extremely lament the little relish the Gentry of this nation have at present for the just and noble representations in some of our Tragedies. The Operas, which are of late introduced, can leave no trace behind them that can be of service beyond the present moment. To sing and to dance are accomplishments very few have any thoughts of practicing.[2]

The *Tatler* for January 3, 1710, reports a small audience at the opera, which it attributes to the fact that the tumbler was

[2] *Tatler*, May 4, 1710. An earlier issue, for January 10, 1710, had also mentioned in passing "the Gentry's immoderate frequenting the Operas." The issue of March 14, 1710, complains that the Gentry at the opera is occupied in looking around at the people in the audience "without any manner of regard to the stage."

not scheduled to appear. This issue does comment, however, on the acting ability of the famous singer, Nicolini.

> Every limb, and every finger, contributes to the part he acts, insomuch that a deaf man might go along with him in the sense of it. There is scarce a beautiful posture in an old statue which he does not plant himself in, as the different circumstances of the story give occasion for it.

The most famous article in the early eighteenth century journals on the subject of opera was written by Addison for the *Spectator* issue of March 21, 1711.

> It is my design in this paper to deliver down to posterity a faithful account of the *Italian* Opera, and of the gradual progress which it has made upon the *English* stage: for there is no question but our great grand-children will be very curious to know the reason why their forefathers used to sit together like an audience of foreigners in their own country, and to hear whole plays acted before them in a tongue which they did not understand.
>
> *Arsinoe* was the first opera that gave us a taste of *Italian* musick. The great success this opera met with, produced some attempts of forming pieces upon *Italian* plans, which should give a more natural and reasonable entertainment than what can be met with in the elaborate trifles of that nation. This alarmed the poetasters and fidlers of the town, who were used to deal in a more ordinary kind of ware; and therefore laid down an established rule, which is received as such to this day, *That nothing is capable of being well set to Musick, that is not Nonsense.*

Addison next discusses the frequent errors he has heard in attempting to translate the Italian into English, resulting in the placement of words against music which is consequently inappropriate. This proving unsuccessful, he describes the next alternative.

> The next step to our refinement, was the introducing of Italian actors into our opera; who sung their parts in their own language, at the same time that our countrymen performed theirs in our native tongue. The king or hero of the play generally spoke in Italian, and his slaves answered him in English. The lover frequently made his court and gained

the heart of his princess in a language which she did not understand ...

At length the audience grew tired of understanding half the opera, and therefore to ease themselves entirely of the fatigue of thinking, have so ordered it at present that the whole opera is performed in an unknown tongue. We no longer understand the language of our own stage ...

One scarce knows how to be serious in the confutation of an absurdity that shows itself at the first sight. It does not want any great measure of sense to see the ridicule of this monstrous practice; but what makes it the more astonishing, it is not the taste of the rabble, but of persons of the greatest politeness, which has established it.

He concludes by suggesting, as others had done, that even if "the Italians have a genius for Musick above the English," it is nevertheless to be regretted that opera had caused the public to lose interest in English theater. As he continues, he questions even the importance of music itself.

Musick is certainly a very agreeable entertainment, but if it would take the entire possession of our ears, if it would make us incapable of hearing sense, it would exclude Arts that have a much greater tendency to the refinement of human nature ...

At present, our notions of Musick are so very uncertain, that we do not know what it is we like; only, in general, we are transported with anything that is not English. So it be of a foreign growth, let it be Italian, French, or [German], it is the same thing. In short, our English Musick is quite rooted out, and nothing yet planted in its stead.

Addison, in the *Spectator* for April 3, 1711, comments on the general absurdity of sung plays.

There is nothing that has more startled our *English* audience, that the *Italian Recitativo* at its first entrance upon the stage. People were wonderfully surprised to hear generals singing the word of command, and ladies delivering messages in Musick. Our countrymen could not forbear laughing when they heard a lover chanting out a Billet-doux, and even the superscription of a letter set to a tune.

In a satire on singing in Italian, Addison, in the April 5, 1711, issue of *Spectator*, writes of a fictitious plan for an opera in Greek.

> The only difficulty that remained, was, how to get performers, unless we could persuade some gentlemen of the universities to learn to sing, in order to qualify themselves for the stage.

Further issues of the *Spectator* contain continual demeaning characterizations of opera by Addison. In the issue for March 15, 1711, he refers to the "forced thoughts, cold conceits and unnatural expressions of Italian opera," and in the issue for December 11, 1711, he calls attending the opera "throwing away your time."

In the *Spectator* for March 6, 1711, Addison even criticizes opera stage sets, which he generally finds designed only "to gratify the senses and keep up an indolent attention in the audience." Among the interesting examples he provides is the release of sparrows on stage, with a consort of "flagellet" players off-stage to supply the birds' song. Addison also mentions that opera, such as Handel's *Rinaldo*, had brought indoors "thunder, lightning, illuminations and fireworks," which people could now enjoy without catching cold outdoors. Also regarding sets, a fictitious advertisement appeared in the *Spectator* for March 16, 1711, which read,

> On the first of April will be performed at the Play-house in the Hay-market an opera called *The Cruelty of Arteus*. N.B. The scene wherein Thyestes eats his own children, is to be performed by the famous Mr. Psalmanazar, lately arrived from Formosa: The whole Supper being set to Kettle-drums.

Of these writers, it was Steele who described the audiences who attend opera. When he first addresses this topic, he seems to blame the stage itself for the subsequent behavior of the audience. He writes in the *Spectator* for March 26, 1711,

> The word *Spectator* being most usually understood as one of the audience at public representations in our theaters, I seldom fail of many letters relating to plays and operas. But indeed there are such monstrous things done in both, that if one had not been an eye-witness of them, one could not

believe that such matters had really been exhibited. There is very little which concerns human life, or is a picture of nature, that is regarded by the greater part of the company. The understanding is dismissed from our entertainments. Our mirth is the laughter of fools, and our admiration the wonder of idiots; else such improbable, monstrous, and incoherent dreams could not go off as they do, not only without the utmost scorn and contempt, but even with the loudest applause and approbation.

A fictitious letter to the editor of the *Spectator* for September 12, 1711, addresses the "Impertinencies" which occur when the individual becomes part of a crowd, such as at an opera.

Sometimes you have a set of whisperers, who lay their heads together in order to sacrifice every body within their observation; sometimes a set of laughers, that keep up an insipid mirth in their own corner, and by their noise and gestures show they have no respect for the rest of the company. You frequently meet with these sets at the opera.[3]

Steele, in his *Spectator* issue for July 29, 1712, again turns his attention to the uncultured nature of English audiences at the opera. He publishes a fictitious letter supposedly written by an English opera singer now performing in Italy.

[3] In the issue of June 20, 1711, Steele mentions one listener who sat in the gallery, beating time with a cudgel.

I little thought in the green years of my life, that I should ever call it an happiness to be out of dear England; but as I grew to woman, I found myself less acceptable in proportion to the increase of my merit. Their ears in Italy are so differently formed from the make of yours in England, that I never come upon the stage, but a general satisfaction appears in every countenance of the whole people. When I dwell upon a note, I behold all the men accompanying me with heads inclining, and falling of their persons on one side, as dying away with me. The women too do justice to my merit, and no ill-natured worthless creature cries, "the vain thing," when I am wrapped up in the performance of my part, and sensibly touched with the effect my voice has upon all who hear me. I live here distinguished, as one whom Nature has been liberal to in a graceful person, an exalted mien, and heavenly voice. These particularities in this strange country, are arguments for respect and generosity to her who is possessed of them.

> The Italians see a thousand beauties I am sensible I have no pretense to, and abundantly make up to me the injustice I received in my own country, of disallowing me what I really had. The humor of hissing, which you have among you, I do not know anything of; and their applauses are uttered in sighs, and bearing a part at the cadences of voice with the persons who are performing ...
>
> The whole city of Venice is as still when I am singing, as this polite hearer was to Mrs. Hunt. But when they break that silence, did you know the pleasure I am in, when every man utters applause, by calling me aloud the "Dear Creature," the "Angel," the "Venus"; "What Attitude she moves with!—Hush, she sings again!" We have no boisterous wits who dare disturb an audience, and break the public peace merely to show they dare. Mr. Spectator, I write this to you ... to tell you I am very much at ease here, that I know nothing but joy; and I will not return, but leave you in England to hiss all merit of your own growth off the stage.

Regarding the influence of opera on individual patrons, Steele reveals how familiar some members of the audience had become with some Italian operas in his recalling, in the *Spectator* of August 20, 1711, of a citizen who entered a tavern, with an opera score under his arm and "practiced his Airs to the full house who were turned upon him." In his issue of February 8, 1712, he complains that women have been so taken by Italian opera that they have taken on a new interest in Latin, thinking of it as an earlier Italian language. Budgell, in the Spectator for April 29, 1712, was so concerned for the influence of opera on women that he recommends "the Puppet-show much safer for them than the Opera."

A decade later, the journals seem more light-hearted on the subject of opera, or perhaps they had found humor to be the best vehicle for criticism. Jonathan Swift, writing in Irish journal, the *Intelligencer* [Number III, 1728], in an essay in which he defends and praises Gay's *Beggars Opera,* reflects back over the first controversial period of Italian opera in London and offers this summary.

> This comedy likewise exposes with great justice that unnatural taste for Italian Musick among us, which is wholly unsuitable to our Northern Climate, and the genius of the

people, whereby we are overrun with Italian-Effeminacy, and Italian Nonsense. An old Gentleman said to me, that many years ago, when the practice of an unnatural vice grew so frequent in London that many were prosecuted for it, he was sure it would be the Fore-runner of Italian Operas and Singers; and then we should lack nothing but stabbing or poisoning, to make us perfect Italians.

Mary Wortley Montagu contributed a letter to the editor of the journal *The Nonsense of Common-Sense*[4] [Number III, for January 3, 1738], under the fictitious name of "Balducci." The writer claimed to be an authority in "the business of statuary and machinery," and, having noticed the great sums of money spent by the English on singers from his country, Italy, he proposes to invent mechanical singers which could make possible financial savings.

[4] Only nine issues, from December 16, 1737, to March 14, 1738, of this weekly newspaper are extant.

By my Art, I have found out a method of making a statue imitate so exactly the voice of any *Singer* that ever did, or ever can appear upon the stage, that I'll defy the ravished listener to distinguish the one from the other. Nay, what is more, this statue shall sing any *Opera* Air the audience pleases to call for, and shall chant it over again and again, as long as they please to cry, *Ancora*, which is an honor, I presume, they will as often confer upon my artificial machines, as ever they did upon any of the natural machines of Italy; and to add to the astonishment of all persons of polite taste, it shall perform at first sight any of the most difficult pieces of Musick the learned Mr. H[ande]l can compose. Then, Sir, by the help of my wonderful art in machinery, I can make my statue walk about, and tread the stage with as good a grace, and look upon the pit with as much contempt, as ever did the famous *Senesino*;[5] by which means it will be able to perform its part in the *Recitativo*, and shall rage with fury, die away in raptures, or stare with amazement and surprise, in as natural a manner, and with as true a taste, as any actor that ever trod the stage.

[5] Francesco Bernardi (1680–1750), known as Senesino, was a famous castrato.

Balducci offers additional advantages for such a mechanical singer: it could immediately absorb all instructions from the music critics, it would rescue the Academy of Musick from spending all its time trying to pacify fighting singers and it would make composers such as Handel happy, as their music would be sung as written and not be subject to improvisation by live singers. He recommends that as English nobles tour Italy and hear "some new singer just blazed out at Venice, Naples or Rome," he will immediately go there and bring the singer back in effigy, charging the noble only for his trip and expenses. Since, he observes, England has already assembled great collections of Italian pictures, statues, busts and antiques, his mechanical singers will make it possible to add famous singers to its collections as well.

> However, I do not propose to diminish the price of an *Opera ticket*, or that any of my singers shall perform in private for a *less mighty Purse* than the proudest of our late performers; for this, I know, would spoil all; nothing can be fit for persons of an elegant taste that can be had at a small price. Yet I am not so avaricious as to propose to take all the profits to myself. On the contrary, I shall be satisfied with my net charges, and a very moderate salary. As for the residue of the profits, which will certainly amount to a large sum yearly, the disposal of it shall be left to the great wisdom of the directors of the *Academy of Musick*; in which case I would humbly propose, it should be distributed yearly by way of charity, for the subsistence of those antiquated *Beaus* and *Belles*, who in their younger years had ruined themselves by attending *Operas, Masquerades*, etc.

By the 1730s there were two opera companies in London, but by 1738 one of them, the "Opera of the Nobility," had apparently closed. It was in reference to this that Lord Chesterfield contributed an article, "Close of the Opera," to the October 14, 1738, issue of *Common Sense*.

> Such is the uncertainty and unstability of the things of this world, that there is scarce any event which ought to surprise us, or anything new to be said upon it ...
> I confess this happened to me lately, when I heard that Operas were no more, and that too at a time when the vigor and success, with which a subscription was carried on, both by the great and the fair, seemed to promise them in their fullest luster.

In attempting to decide if the closing of the opera represents a national loss or a national advantage, Chesterfield first reviews the role of music reflected in ancient Greek literature. He mentions in particular the stories of the aulos performing the Pyrrhic melodies which so inspired the Greek armies.

> This tune, by the way, must have infinitely exceeded our best modern marches, which, by what I have been able to observe in Hyde Park, rather sets our army a-dancing than a-fighting. I ascribe this difference wholly to the unskillfulness of our modern composers; for I will never believe that my countrymen have not as much potential courage in them as the Greeks, if properly excited.

After retelling the tale about Pythagoras causing a lust-filled youth to cool down by playing a certain kind of music, he observes,

> Our Operas have not been known to occasion any attempts of this violent nature; which I likewise impute to the effects of the composition, and not to any degree of insensibility or modesty in our youth, who, it must be owned, give a fair hearing to music, and whose short bobs seem admirably contrived for the better reception of sounds.

Lord Chesterfield, after citing the incident in which music caused an apparent change in personality in Alexander the Great, provides some interesting contemporary anecdotes involving music.

> I am apt to believe that in music, as in many other arts and sciences, we fall infinitely short of the ancients. For I take it for granted, that we should be open to the same impressions, if our composers had but the skill to make them. However, though music does not now cause those surprising effects which it did formerly, it still retains power enough over men's passions to make it worth our care: and I heard some persons, equally skilled in music and politics, assert that King James was sung and fiddled out of this kingdom by the Protestant tune of Lillybullero; and that somebody else would have been fiddled into it again, if a certain treasonable Jacobite tune had not been timely silenced by the unwearied pains and diligence of the administration...
>
> The Swiss, who are not a people of the quickest sensations, have at this time a tune, which, when played upon their fifes,

inspires them with such a love of their country, that they run home as fast as they can: which tune is therefore, under severe penalties, forbidden to be played, when their regiments are on service, because they would instantly desert.

Regarding this last anecdote, Chesterfield suggests that he can think of some situations in London, such as court or legislative functions, when it would be valuable to have such a tune played which would cause everyone to immediately run home.

> I would therefore most earnestly recommend it to the learned Dr. Green, to turn his thoughts that way. It is not from the least distrust of Mr. Handel's ability, that I address myself preferably to Dr. Green: but Mr. Handel, having the advantage to be by birth a German, might probably, even without intending it, mix some modulations in his composition, which might give a German tendency to the mind, and therefore greatly lessen the national benefit I propose by it.

Finally, Chesterfield returns to his original question, regarding the significance of the closing of the opera.

> How far the polite part of the world is affected by the cessation of Operas, I am no judge myself; but I asked a young gentleman of wit and pleasure about town, whether he did not apprehend that he should be a sufferer by it in his way of business, for that I presumed those soft and tender sounds soothed and melted the fairest breasts, and fitted them to receive impressions? He answered me very frankly, that, as far as he could judge, the loss would be but inconsiderable to their profession; that some years ago, indeed, the taste of music, being expressive and pathetic, had inspired tender sentiments, and softened stubborn virtue; but the fashion being of late for both the composers and the performers only to show what tricks they could play, had rather taught the ladies to play tricks too, than made the proper impressions upon them, and that he oftener found them tired than softened at the end of an Opera. But he confessed that they might happen to miss the Opera books a little, because, as most of his profession could make a shift to read the English version at least, they found, in those incomparable dramas, sentiments proper for all situations, which might not otherwise have occurred to them, and which, by emphatical signs and looks,

they could apply to the proper objects; insomuch that he had often known very pretty sentimental conversations carried on through a whole opera by these references to the book.

Having thus shown the power and effects of music both among the ancients and the moderns, and the good and ill uses which may be made of it, I shall submit it to persons wiser than myself, what is to be done in this important crisis. I look upon Operas to have been the great national establishment of music, and I am persuaded that innumerable sects will rise from their ruins, and break into various conventicles of vocal and instrumental, which, if not attended to, may prove of ill consequence.

Several years later, after Italian opera had been restored in London, Lord Chesterfield contributed a humorous article to the November 14, 1754, issue of *The World*.

I am sensible that Italian Operas have frequently been the objects of the ridicule of many of our greatest wits, and viewed in one light only, perhaps not without some reason. But as I consider all public diversions singly with regard to the effects which they may have upon the morals and manners of the public, I confess I respect the Italian Operas as the most innocent of any.

For one thing, he suggests, humorously bringing up the old objection which was seriously argued forty years earlier, no one understands the words anyway.

Were what is called the poetry of it intelligible in itself, it would not be understood by one in fifty of a British audience; but I believe that even an Italian of common candor will confess, that he does not understand one word of it. It is not the intention of the thing, for should the ingenious author of the words, by mistake, put any meaning into them, he would, to a certain degree, check and cramp the genius of the composer of the music, who perhaps might think himself obliged to adapt his sounds to the sense: whereas now he is at liberty to scatter indiscriminately, among the Kings, Queens, heroes, and heroines, his Adagios, his Allegros, his Pathetics, his Chromatics, and his Jigs. It would also have been a restraint upon the actors and actresses, who might possibly have attempted to form their action upon the meaning of their parts; but as it is, if they do but seem, by turns to be angry and sorry in the two first acts, and very merry in the last scene of the last, they are sure to meet with the deserved applause.

Signor Metastasio attempted some time ago a very dangerous innovation. He tried gently to throw some sense into his Operas, but it did not take: the consequences were obvious, and nobody knew where they would stop.

Another virtue of Italian opera which Chesterfield advances, is that by the time it is over, everyone is so tired they go home to bed and avoid getting into trouble.

The most delightful portion of Chesterfield's article is his discussion of the Italian singers, their manners and their impositions on English society.

Having thus rescued these excellent musical dramas from the unjust ridicule which some people of vulgar and illiberal tastes have endeavored to throw upon them, I must proceed, and do justice to the Virtuosos and Virtuosas who perform them. But I believe it will be necessary for me to premise, for the sake of many of my English readers, that VIRTU among the modern Italians signifies nothing less than what VIRTUS did among the ancient ones, or what VIRTUE signifies among us; on the contrary, I might say that it signifies almost everything else. Consequently those respectable titles of Virtuoso and Virtuosa have not the least relation to the moral characters of the parties. They mean only that those persons, endowed some by nature, and some by art, with good voices, have from their infancy devoted their time and labor to the various combinations of seven notes, a study that must unquestionably have formed their minds, enlarged their notions, and have rendered them most agreeable and instructive companions, and as such, I observe that they are justly solicited, received, and cherished by people of the first distinction.

As these illustrious personages come over here with no sordid view of profit, but merely *per far piacer a la nobilita Inglese,* that is, to oblige the English nobility, they are exceedingly good and condescending to such of the said English nobility, and even gentry, as are desirous to contract an intimacy with them. They will, for a word's speaking, dine, sup, or pass the whole day with people of a certain condition, and perhaps sing or play, if civilly requested. Nay, I have known many of them so good as to pass two or three months of the summer at the country-seats of some of their noble friends, and thereby mitigate the horrors of the country and mansion-house, to my lady and her daughters. I have been assured by many of their chief patrons and patronesses, that they are all the best creatures in the world; and from the time of Signor Nicolini down to this day, I have constantly heard the several great performers, such as Farinelli, Carestini, Monticelli, Gaffarielli, as well as the Signore Cuzzoni, Faustina, etc., much more praised for their affability, the gentleness of their manners, and all the good qualities of the head and heart, than for either their musical skill or execution.[6] I have even known these, their social virtues, lay their protectors and protectresses under great difficulties, how to reward such distinguished merit. But benefit-nights luckily came in to their assistance, and gave them an opportunity of insinuating, with all due regard, into the hands of the performer, in lieu of a ticket, a considerable bank-bill, a gold snuff-box, a diamond-ring, or some such trifle. It is to be hoped, that the illustrious Signor Farinelli has not yet forgot the many instances he experienced of British munificence, for it is certain that many private families *still remember them*.

[6] On the contrary, of course, these two ladies were infamous for their fights on stage before the audience.

He closes with a common objection that the Italian singers take all this money home to Italy,

Some of them, when they have got ten or fifteen thousand pounds here, unkindly withdraw themselves, and purchase estates in land in their own countries.

Part III

The Public and Music

12
Civic Music on the English Baroque

PUBLIC CONCERTS IN ENGLAND, other than band concerts, began after the Restoration as privately sponsored events. However humble the occasion, there was nevertheless the crucial distinction that it was music to be listened to. An interesting definition in this regard is given by Hawkins.

> But a concert, properly so called, was a sober recreation; persons were drawn to it, not by an affectation of admiring what they could not taste, but by a genuine pleasure which they took in the entertainment.[1]

The best known of these privately sponsored concerts is first mentioned in a December 30, 1672, issue of the London Gazette.

> This is to give notice, that at Mr. John Banister's house (now called the Musick-school) over against the George tavern in White Fryers, this present Monday, will be musick performed by excellent masters, beginning precisely at 4 of the clock in the afternoon, and every afternoon for the future, precisely at the same hour.

Future issues of the paper advertise a great variety of vocal and instrumental performances, such as a "rare concert of four Trumpets Marine, never heard of before in England."

One of the most curious hosts of these kinds of concerts was a poor coal supplier in Clerkenwell, named Thomas

[1] John Hawkins, *A General History of the Science and Practice of Music* [1776] (New York: Dover Reprint, 1963), II, 762.

Britton. Aside from the concerts he began in 1678, this self-educated music lover acquired an extensive library of books and music.[2] Britton organized his concerts in a room above that in which he stored his coal, entered by stairs outside the building. In spite of the despicable house, in a poor area of London, these concerts drew even members of the aristocracy. A prior wrote the following lines in honor of this poor coal dealer.

> Tho' doom'd to small-coal, yet to arts ally'd,
> Rich without wealth, and famous without pride;
> Musick's best patron, judge of books and man,
> Belov'd and honour'd by Apollo's train;
> In Greece or Rome sure never did appear
> So bright a genius in so dark a sphere.[3]

By the end of the century newspaper advertisements suggest a wider public concert activity, now often held in the York Buildings and Stationers' Hall. Many concerts lasted up to two hours and seem to have been characterized by great variety. In 1697 the concept of a continuing series of concerts appears for the first time.

In 1656 one William Davenant persuaded the Protectorate government to allow him to reopen a theater, under the promise that he would produce not a play but an opera. While his first effort, *First Dayes Entertainment*, was an opera in name only, and while further obstacles remained, nevertheless opera, and opera for the public, was firmly established in England by the early years of the eighteenth century.

But it was Italian opera which swept up the public, not English opera, and we can see in an advertisement of 1705, by Thomas Clayton (1673–1725), some sense of concern that this new medium would be understood by the English public.

> The Design of this Entertainment being to introduce the *Italian* manner of Musick on the *English* stage, which has not been before attempted: I was oblig'd to have an *Italian* Opera translated ... The Musick being Recitative, may not, at first, meet with that general Acceptation as is to be hop'd for, from the Audience's being better acquainted with it: but if this

[2] A catalog of these hundreds of books and scores is quoted in Ibid., II, 792ff.

[3] Quoted in Ibid, II, 790. Britton's death was as curious as his life. A locally famous ventriloquist, making his voice appear from far away, informed Britton that he would die in a few hours. Britton returned to his house, where he took to his bed and died within a few days.

Attempt shall be a means of bringing this manner of Musick to be us'd in my Native country, I shall think all my Study and Pains very well employ'd.[4]

But soon it was genuine Italian opera, sung in Italian, which won over the public. Addison, for one, was confused.

Our great-grandchildren will be very curious to know the reason why their forefathers used to sit together like an audience of foreigners in their own country, to hear whole plays acted before them in a tongue which they did not understand.[5]

During the 1730s a genuine English medium became popular in the broadest sense of the word. This was, of course, the Oratorio, and it brought concerts with great numbers of performers as well as listeners.

Perhaps we should acknowledge at this point that the contribution made to English musical life by large numbers of foreign musicians, who had begun coming to England for political reasons during the sixteenth century, continued. Among them were numerous talented Germans, foremost of which was Handel. The question which no English-speaking person wants to face is, What would eighteenth century English music be without the foreign-born composers? The greatest English-born composer who ever lived, Purcell, saw this clearly in 1690. "English music," he said, "is yet but in its nonage, a forward child, which gives hope of what it may be hereafter ... when the masters of it shall find more encouragement."[6]

At the end of the seventeenth century the Hautboisten band arrived in England—from France, in spite of its Germanized name. The preference for the Hautboisten band instrumentation during the early eighteenth century, apparently led to an expansion of oboe and bassoon players in London. This seems to be inferred by several accounts of concerts which included works for bassoon ensembles. One of these was a concert given at Stationers' Hall, in 1713, which included "an uncommon piece of Musick by Bassoons only."[7] Even more extraordinary is an advertisement for a concert at Lincoln's Inn Theater in 1744, which promised a,

[4] Quoted in Ibid., 358.

[5] *The Spectator*, Nr. 18.

[6] Quoted in Charles Burney, *General History of Music* (New York, 1957), II, 399.

[7] John Ashton, *Social Life in the Reign of Queen Anne* (London, 1911), 277.

new concerto grosso of 24 bassoons, accompanied by Signor Caporale on the violoncello, intermixed with Duettos by 4 doublebassoons, accompanied by a German flute, the whole blended with numbers of violins, hautboys, fifes, tombany's, French horns, trumpets, drums and kettle-drums.[8]

[8] London, *General Advertiser* (October 21, 1744).

During the seventeenth century a great wave of involvement in music performance swept the middle class in England. One wonders if it were a private retreat from the grim public face of the civil war and the Puritans. Pepys, in his famous *Diary*, observed every third boat on the Thames contained virginals and he gives the impression that everyone he knew performs music and sings.[9] Indeed, a great explosion of popular song ensued and credit must be given to Charles II who brought back from Paris a lighter mood in music. The great public response confirmed what the music theorists had failed to see for one thousand years: music is not mathematics.

[9] Pepys, *Diary*, for September 2, 1666, and January 16, 1660.

This broad interest by the middle class in actually performing music can be documented by a profusion of publications which began to appear in the first decade of the seventeenth century. Soon great quantities of music, including songs and works for lute, viol and virginal were in circulation, both in print and in manuscript.[10]

More difficult to document, but nevertheless evident, was an equally broad participation in music making by the lower classes. One form of music which does survive are the so-called "broadside ballads," popular songs printed for this facet of society. One source of music which was apparently frequently heard by members of the lower class was the local barber shop. Barbershops were often equipped with instruments, upon which the waiting customer could perform. The barbers as well are often mentioned in literature as engaging in performance as an outside source of income. While there is little extant documentation about the actual music making of these barber musicians, we do find some interesting details in a poem written in honor of John Est, who apparently had a certain reputation for his performance in London. We also

[10] Peter Walls, "London, 1603–49," in *The Early Baroque Era* (Englewood Cliffs: Prentice Hall, 1994), 288ff, provides a fine summary of this activity.

read here the titles of seven popular songs as presumably representative of the repertoire of the barbers.

> In former time 't hath been upbrayded thus,
> That barber's musick was most barbarous,
> For that the cittern was confin'd unto
> The Ladies Fall, or John come kiss me now,
> Green Sleeves, and Puddng Pyes, with Nell's delight,
> Winning of Bolloigne, Essex' last good night.
> But, since reduc'd to this conformity,
> And company became society,
> Each barber writes himself, in strictest rules,
> Master, or bachelor i' th' musick schools,
> How they the mere musitians do out-go,
> These one, but they have two strings to their bow.
> Barber musitians who are excellent,
> As well at chest, as the case instrument,
> Henceforth each steward shall invite his guest
> Unto the barber's and musitian's feast,
> Where sit ye merry, whilst we joy to see
> Art thus embrac'd by ingenuity.

In Jacobean prose one finds a number of interesting references to music occurring in civic life. One of these, by Thomas Dekker, is relative to the plague of 1603.

> I was amazed to remember what dead Marches were made of three thousand trooping together; husbands, wives & children being led as ordinarily to one grave, as if they had gone to one bed.[11]

In another place he mentions the Lord Mayor's Parade.

> ...demanded of his Waterman why there was such drumming, and piping, and trumpetting, and wherefore all those Barges (like so many Water-pageants)...[12]

John Earle presents a portrait of a musician frequently seen in both civic and court duties, the trumpeter.

> A trumpeter is the elephant with the great trunk, for he eats nothing but what comes through this way. His profession is not so worthy as to occasion insolence, and yet no man so much puffed up. His face is as brazen as his trumpet, and (which is worse) as a fiddler's, from whom he differs only in

[11] Thomas Dekker, "The Wonderfull Yeare of 1603," in Grosart, *The Non-Dramatic Works of Thomas Dekker* (New York, Russell & Russell, 1963), I, 112. Thomas Dekker (b. 1570) was a very fluent writer, producing plays of his own and in collaboration with others, in addition to "entertainments" and pamphlets on a variety of subjects. It has been said that no writer gave a more vivid picture of London at this time. He, however, failed to earn a living and was often in prison—once for three years. Nothing is known of him after the 1630s.
[12] Thomas Dekker, "Jests to Make you Merrie" (1607), Ibid., II, 287.

this, that his impudence costs you more. The sea of drink and much wind make a storm perpetually in his cheeks, and his look is like his noise, blustering and tempestuous ... He is the common attendant of glittering folks, whether in the court or stage, where he is always the prologue's prologue.[13] He is somewhat in the nature of a hogshead, shrillest when he is empty; when his belly is full he is quiet enough.[14]

Thomas Overbury, in his description of the professional "tinker," which appears to have included the blacksmith craft, mentions the old myth about Pythagoras and the blacksmith.

> From his Art was Musicke first invented, and therefore is he always furnished with a song: to which his hammer keeping tune, proves that he was the first founder of the Kettle-drumme. Note that where the best Ale is, there stands his musick most upon crotchets.[15]

In the Jacobean drama literature there are several references to dance and music. Most references to wedding music in the Jacobean plays deal with dancing and it is usually the lowly fiddler who plays.[16] In Dekker's *Satiromastix* (I, i) we find a humorous lack of appreciation for this musician.

> ...and last of all in cursing the poore nodding fidlers, for keeping Mistress Bride so long up from sweeter Revels...

There are also occasional references to actual wedding songs.[17] In Marston's *The Tragedy of Sophonisba* (I, ii) the stage direction calls for four boys, dressed as cupid and dancing "a fantastic measure" to the music of cornetts. Soon a larger ensemble sings a wedding song.

> *Chorus, with cornets, organ and voices. Io to Hymen!*

There are many references of incidental music for dancing in this literature and often specific dances are mentioned. In Middleton's *Women Beware Women* (III, ii) we find a humorous review of the dances associated with various levels of society.

---

[13] Since the fifteenth century, at least, three trumpet signals indicated the play was about to begin.

[14] John Earle, *Microcosmography* [1628] (St. Clair Shores: Scholarly Press, 1971), 79ff. John Earle (1600–1665) was a chaplain to Charles II, during the King's exile, and a Dean of Westminster during the Restoration.

[15] The "Conceited Newes" of Sir Thomas Overbury and His Friends, 124. In *Sir Thomas Browne's Works*, ed. Simon Wilkin (London: Pickering, 1836), IV, 191, one will find a treatise called "Of Cymbals, etc.," which reviews references to this instrument in early literature.

[16] See Beaumont and Fletcher's *The Maid in the Mill* (V, ii) for a reference to hiring "Fidlers" for dance music for a wedding. In Marston's *The Dutch Courtezan* (II, iii) there is a reference to dance music being performed by an ensemble of six flutes.

[17] For the lyrics for a wedding song, see John Ford's *The Broken Heart* (III, v).

> Plain men dance the measures, the sinquapace [galliard] the
>   gay;
> Cuckolds dance the hornpipe, and farmers dance the hay;
> Your soldiers dance the round, and maidens that grow big;
> Your drunkards, the canaries; your whore and bawd, the jig.
> Here's your eight kind of dancers; he that finds
> The ninth let him pay the minstrels.

In another Middleton play, *Mayor of Queenborough* (II, ii), the stage directions call for the cornetts to "sound a lavolta," for dancing. In Marston's *The Malcontent* (IV, i) a call goes out for music for dancing the branle, but the characters indicate they have forgotten the steps. Guerrino reviews the dance as follows:

> Why, it is but two singles on the left, two on the right, three doubles forward, a traverse of six round: do this twice, three singles side, galliard trick-of-twenty, coranto-pace; a figure of eight, three singles broken down, come up, meet, two doubles, fall back, and then honor.

As for the music, Aurelia calls out,

> Music, sound high, as in our heart! sound high!

Finally, in Dekker's *Old Fortunatus* (III, i), on observing the music is playing but no one is dancing, Athelstane says "Here's Musicke spent in vaine, Lords, fall to dancing."

We should perhaps also add here two comments about dance from among Lord Chesterfield's letters to his son in which he again finds dancing demeaning and of value only for posture development.

> Dancing is in itself a very trifling, silly thing; but it is one of those established follies to which people of sense are sometimes obliged to conform.[18]
>
> ......
>
> You must dance well, in order to sit, stand, and walk well; and you must do all these well, in order to please.[19]

---

[18] Earl of Chesterfield, letter to his son, November 19, 1745.

[19] Earl of Chesterfield, letter to his son, January 3, 1751.

The Wait Bands

BY THE END of the sixteenth century the civic wind band tradition in England had begun to decline and consequently accounts of their quality vary considerably. It is for this reason that we have such a variety of comments about civic bands in Samuel Pepys' famous *Diary*. On October 9, 1667, he hears the Cambridge "town musique" and makes the curious comment, "Lord, what sad music they made—however, I was pleased with them." On October 11, 1667, he hears the Huntington civic music and finds them better than that of Cambridge. On June 13, 1668, he hears some civic musicians at the spa at Bath and finds them as good as anything he had ever heard in London. At Marlborough, however, he hears music of which he only comments that their "innocence pleases me."[20] In Reading, on June 17, 1668, he hears the "worst music we have had."

One reason for the decline lay in the fact that the wind instrument was no longer the exclusive instrument of the professional musician. The demands for wider choices of musical expression forced the civic musicians to obtain wider skills, which must have tended to lower their abilities on all, as is clear in a description of the Norwich Waits in 1600.

> Passing the gate ... where ... stood the City Waits ... such Waits few Cities in our Realm have the like, none better; who beside their excellency in wind instruments, their rare cunning on the Viol and Violin, their voices be admirable, every one of them able to serve in any Cathedral Church in Christendom.[21]

Apart from this demand for more diverse skills was the severe influence of the Puritans who were little interested in music. During the seventeenth century entire civic wind bands were being disbanded, including Leicester (1602), Manchester (1620), Coventry (1635), Canterbury (1640, for "disorders and misbehaviour"[22]) and Durham (1684, for "indecent expression" toward the mayor[23]). The famous Norwich Waits, so praised above in 1600, were discharged

[20] Pepys *Diary*, June 15, 1668.

[21] Quoted in Bridges, "Town Waits and their Tunes," in *Proceedings of the Musical Association* (London, 1927–1928), 85.

[22] Ibid., 73.

[23] Ibid., 72.

in 1622. A civic order implementing this order includes an interesting survey of the city owned instruments.

> The Waytes discharged and desired to deliver their instruments several of which they had sold, but delivered as follows: Three Sackbuts, four Hoboyes and an old one broken, two tenor Cornetts, one Treble recorder, two Counter-Tenor Recorders, five Chaynes and five Flaggs.[24]

[24] Ibid., 79.

In 1612, curiously, the entire civic wind band of Chester disappeared without a trace.

> George Musitian exhibiteth his petician desiring that he and his fellow musitians may be admitted Waytes of this Cittie instead of the waytes now absent, finding instruments of his own charge to perform the service; which is deferred to be graunted untill it may be understode what are become of the ould waytes.[25]

[25] Ibid., 73.

Even the distinguished London Waits appear to have suffered this demise, as an 1625 edict by the civic government suggests.

> ...through the contentions and ill dispositions of some particular persons of this society [of waits] the whole company suffereth often in their credits and reputations by uncivil and retorting of bitter and unsavory jests and calumnious aspersions upon one or other of them; which only nourish the discord and confusion amongst them with continual quarreling and heartburning yea especially in the times of their service to his honorable city.[26]

[26] Walter L. Woodfill, *Manners in English Society from Elizabeth to Charles I* (Princeton: Princeton University Press, 1953), 43ff.

By the eighteenth century the proud London Waits had declined sufficiently as to become the object of cruel humor in contemporary literature.

> We blundered on in pursuit of our felicity, but scarce had walked the length of a horse's tether, ere we heard a noise so dreadful and surprising, that we thought the devil was riding on hunting through the City, with a pack of deep-mouthed hell-hounds, to catch a brace of tallymen for breakfast ...
> One was armed, as I thought, with a faggot-bat, and the rest with strange wooden weapons in their hands in the shape of clyster pipes, but as long, almost, as speaking-trumpets. Of

a sudden they raised them to their mouths, and made such a frightful yelling, that I thought the world had been dissolving and the terrible sounds of the last trumpet to be within an inch of my ears.

Under these amazing apprehensions I asked my friend what was the meaning of this infernal outcry? "Prithee," says he, "what's the matter with thee? Why these are the City Waits, who play every winter's night through the streets."

"Lord bless me!" said I, "I am very glad it's no worse. Prithee let us make haste out of the hearing of them."

At this my friend laughed at me. "Why, what," says he, "don't you love music? These are the topping tooters of the town, and have gowns, silver chains, and salaries, for playing *Lillabolaro* to my Lord Mayor's Horse through the City."

"Marry," said I, "if his horse liked their music no better than I do, he would soon fling his rider for hiring such bugbears to affront his ambleship."[27]

[27] Ned Ward, *The London Spy*, ed. Arthur Hayward (New York: Doran), 29ff.

For those wait bands who managed to continue on the numerous records of their activity includes the ancient duty of watch musicians. A contract for two new civic musicians in Rochester in 1640 reads in part, "they do promise ... to play through the Citty every morning upon their lowde musicke."[28] In the city of Aberdeen, the city fathers once decided to save money by replacing such watch musicians with a bagpipe player. This quickly resulted in unhappy citizens:

[28] Bridges, "Town Waits," 74.

The common piper of all going through the town at nycht, or in the morning, in tyme coming, with his pype - it being an incivill forme to be usit withing sic a famous burghe, and being often found fault with, als weill by sundrie nichbouris of the toune as by strangers.[29]

[29] Francis Collinson, *The Bagpipe* (London, 1975), 98.

Of course, like civic bands from the most ancient times, these civic bands were involved in welcoming ceremonies for visiting nobles. But one eyewitness account, of a water procession welcoming the king's return from Richmond in 1610, suggests that we should not assume such occasions consisted only of ceremonial music. On this occasion there were ceremonial instruments present, of course, but also a wind band [noyse],

...bardges upon the water, with their streamers and ensigns gloriously displayed, drommes, trumpets, fifes, and other musikes attending on them, to awaite the Lord Maior and the Aldermen's coming. No sooner had his honor and the rest taken bardge, but on they rowed, with such chearefull noyse of harmonie... as made the beholders and hearers not meanly delighted.[30]

Civic wind bands also performed for a variety of university celebrations. On the occasion of the laying of the cornerstone of the Bodleian Library, in Oxford in 1634, one reads of "the University Musicians who stood upon the leads at the west end of the Library sounded a lesson on their wind music." The use of "lesson" here as a synonym for a composition reminds us of a report of the Queen's visit to Bath in 1613, which speaks of a student wind band of sorts.

...of which Ferebe having timely notice, he composed a song in four parts, and instructed his scholars to sing it very perfectly, as also to play a lesson or two (which he had composed) on their wind instruments.

Among the more artistic appearances by these civic bands was their employment in the theater. It was no doubt one of these bands which was honored by the testimonial of Samuel Pepys to the power of their music. After he had attended a play, *The Virgin Martyr,* in 1668, he wrote in his famous diary,

But that which did please me beyond any thing in the whole world was the wind-musique when the angel comes down, which is so sweet that it ravished me, and indeed, in a word, did wrap up my soul so that it made me really sick, just as I have formerly been when in love with my wife; that neither then, nor all the evening going home, and at home, I was able to think of any thing, but remained all night transported, so as I could not believe that ever any musick hath that real command over the soul of a man as this did upon me: and makes me resolve to practice wind-musique, and to make my wife do the like.[31]

It is also important to remind the reader that these civic wind bands continued to perform concerts before the public. We know that both the Norwich and London wait bands gave

[30] John Nichols, *The Progresses of King James The First* (London 1828), 318.

[31] *The Diary of Samuel Pepys* (London, 1924), VII, 319ff, for February 25–27, 1668.

regular performances of a concert nature.[32] In London these were given every Sunday evening, between seven and eight o'clock, from a turret of the Royal Exchange. Woodfill is one of the very few scholars who has recognized the role of these civic wind bands in the development of concerts as we know them today.

[32] Woodfill, *Manners in English Society from Elizabeth to Charles I,* 81 and Mary Ede, *Arts and Society in England under William and Mary* (London: Stainer and Bell), 94ff.

> It places the earliest public concerts in England a century before the concerts begun by John Banister in 1672, the accepted date for the first public concerts in England. Banister's concerts stand as the first commercial venture of the kind in London, but take second place to the waits' concerts for antiquity and continuity of existence.[33]

[33] Woodfill, *Manners in English Society from Elizabeth to Charles I,* 50.

Indeed, an edict by the London Court of Aldermen in 1625 indicates the long tradition of such concerts. It renewed the demand for concerts from the turret of the Royal Exchange, "upon such days and at such times as have been anciently observed."[34]

[34] Ibid.

But, there was a very broad range of possible performance opportunities for these civic musicians, ranging from serenade duty,

> ...as the custom prevails at present, there is scarce a young man of any fashion in a Corporation who does not make love with the town music; the waits often help him through his courtship.[35]

[35] Bridges, "Town Waits,", 66.

to duty on the river,

> At the Thames they beate drums, to direct the Watermen to make the shore, no lights being bright enough to penetrate the fogg.[36]

[36] *The Diary of John Evelyn* (Oxford, 1955), V, 363, for November 5, 1699.

An account in one of the famous journals, the *Spectator* for November 8, 1714, gives a similar reference to the use of drums to direct people.

> The celebration of this night's solemnity was opened by the obstreperous joy of drummers, who, with their parchment thunder, gave a signal for the appearance of the mob under their several classes and denominations.

Finally, we should note that an icon on the border of a writing sampler, issued by James Cole in 1742 illustrating "The Procession of the Lord Mayor," shows the "City Musick" now playing as an Hautboisten ensemble with three oboes and two bassoons.[37]

[37] The engraving is reproduced in Edward Croft-Murray, "The Wind-Band in England, 1540–1840," in *Music and Civilisation* (London, 1980), plate 109.

The Minstrels

IN THE SIXTEENTH CENTURY there occurred the formation of the unique independent minstrel guild in London, which was an attempt to preserve casual performance rights for resident musicians of London against the remaining wandering musicians. This guild, ever attempting to strengthen its authority, acquired a new charter from the city in 1604, now changing its name to "Master Wardens and Commonality of the Art or Science of the Musicians of London."[38] Among the usual regulations concerning weddings, etc., two attract the attention of the modern reader. One reflects the rapidly changing preference for strings by stating that any consort of Violins must include at least four wind players. Another regulation forbids members from walking through the city with "an instrument uncased or uncovered," which must have been aimed at identifying the resident musician from those poorer vagrants who did not own cases.

[38] See H. A. F. Crewdson, *The Worshipful Company of Musicians* (London: Charles Knight), 40.

Unfortunately the renewed zeal of this guild alarmed the royal musicians, who set out in 1634 to deliberately destroy the independent guild—and they succeeded. The true wandering minstrel continued to be the object of various civic and national government edicts. During a debate in Parliament in 1656 on the topic of rouges, vagabonds and beggars, one member asked that,

> fiddlers and minstrels be included, as they did corrupt the manners of the people and inflame their debauchery by lewd and obscene songs.[39]

[39] Bridges, "Town Waits," 67ff.

Another member hastened to plea that the London Waits not be included.

We may assume such edicts had little effect, as indeed is reflected in yet another of 1677, which worried that,

> foreign musicians, Swiss fiddlers, pipers, waits and others do frequently play up and down in all parts of this City, expressly contrary to divers good orders of the Common Council. On this the Court ordered and strictly enjoined that no manner of person or persons not being free of this city do use or exercise singing or playing upon any instrument in any common Hall, Tavern, Inn, Alehouse, or any other like place within this City.[40]

[40] Crewdson, *The Worshipful Company of Musicians,* 168.

13
Music and English Manners

HERE WE CONSIDER a few literary works specifically addressed to manners, together with observations in individual diaries and correspondence which reflect privately on music and manners of Restoration England. Before looking at comments on music specifically, there are some areas of discussion in this literature in which the reader may find some insights regarding the environment for music making in England.

The most frequently discussed subject regarding the emotions during the English Baroque was that emotion known as Melancholy. Shenstone offers an interesting observation on this subject, regarding some elegies he has written.

> They are written rather with the spirit of *Melancholy* than that of Poetry; if Melancholy may be said to be fraught with any spirit at all as I believe it *may*; for I believe a pretty *Spirit* may be distilled from *Tears*.[1]

In his discussion of the emotions in general, Shenstone reflects, and rejects, the Puritan attitude toward the subduing of the emotions.

> While we labor to subdue our passions, we should take care not to extinguish them. Subduing our passions, is disengaging ourselves from the world; to which, however, whilst we reside in it, we must always bear relation; and we may detach ourselves to such a degree as to pass an useless and insipid

[1] Letter to Lady Luxborough, June 1, 1748, in *Letters of William Shenstone* (Minneapolis: University of Minnesota Press, 1939), 106.

life, which we were not meant to do. Our existence here is at least one part of a system.[2]

Putting aside the question of the struggle between Reason and the emotions, and the control of the latter, Shenstone nevertheless found a strong relationship between the emotions and the most sensitive and talented persons.

> People of real genius have strong passions; people of strong passions have great partialities.[3]
>
> ......
>
> People of the finest and most lively genius have the greatest sensibility, of consequence the most lively passion.[4]

Shenstone was the only writer of this period in England to write extensively on the subject of Taste. In his *Men and Manners*,[5] as an illustration of the difficulties of making final definitions of taste, he imagines a discussion between a citizen, a courtier and a professor. The citizen maintains that the basic principles of art are universal, only the technicalities are left to the "experts."

> I am told continually of taste, refinement, and politeness; but I think the vulgar and illiterate generally approve the same productions with the connoisseurs. One rarely finds a landskip, a building, or a play, that has charms for the critic exclusive of the mechanic. But, on the other hand, one readily remarks students who labor to be dull, depraving their native relish by the very means they use to refine it. The vulgar may not indeed be capable of giving the reasons why a composition pleases them. That mechanical distinction they leave to the connoisseur.

The courtier says no this is not true, pointing out that poetry, for example, depends on such things as metaphor and allusion, the subtleties of which are beyond the citizen. The professor, of course, points out that while the citizen can understand art on some level, with instruction can appreciate it even more.

> All ranks and stations have their different spheres of judging. That a clown of native taste enough to relish Handel's Messiah, might unquestionably be so instructed as to relish it yet more.

[2] William Shenstone, *Men and Manners* (Boston: Houghton Mifflin, 1927), 53.

[3] Ibid., 79. William Shenstone (1714–1763) attended Oxford, but did not finish. He was one of the minor figures in English literature of the early eighteenth century, but was possessed of a perceptive intelligence.

[4] Ibid., 60.

[5] Ibid., 2ff.

The professor adds that the artist must never actually aim his work at the level of the common citizen.

> Let a writer then in his first performances neglect the idea of profit, and the vulgar's applause entirely. Let him address them to the judicious few, and then profit and the mob will follow. His first appearance on the stage of letters will engross the politer compliments; and his latter will partake of the irrational huzza.

Shenstone offers several other interesting generalizations on the subject of taste.

> We say, he is a man of sense who acknowledges the same truths that we do; that he is a man of taste who allows the same beauties. We consider him as a person of better sense and finer taste, who discerns more truths and more beauties in conjunction with ourselves. But we allow neither appellation to the man who differs from us.[6]

......

> Virtue should be considered as a part of taste (and perhaps it is so more in this age, than in any preceding one) and should as much avoid deceit or sinister meanings in discourse, as they would do puns, bad language or false grammar.[7]

......

> Wherever there is a lack of taste, we generally observe a love of money, and cunning: and wherever taste prevails, a want of prudence, and an utter disregard to money ...
>
> The person of a good taste requires real beauty in the object of his passion; and the person of bad taste requires something which he substitutes in the place of beauty ...
>
> Persons of fine taste are men of the strongest sensual appetites.[8]

We find particularly interesting a little summary of Shenstone's conclusions resulting from his contemplation on the subject of taste as found in the general population. He proposes that out of one hundred persons one might expect to find taste in the following proportions:[9]

[6] Ibid., 59.

[7] Ibid., 60.

[8] Ibid., 92.

[9] Ibid., 90.

Pedants	15
Persons of common sense	40
Wits	15
Fools	15
Persons of a wild uncultivated taste	10
Persons of original taste, improved by art	5

One cannot help but noticing his view here that Wits and Fools are equally lacking in Taste and that neither Pedants nor amateurs are improved much by education. Today we might arrive at somewhat different proportions! After all this, Shenstone concludes,

> I am sick of the word *taste*; but I think the *thing* itself the only proper *ambition*, and the *specific pleasure* of all who have any share in the faculty of imagination.[10]

[10] Letter to Richard Graves, February 16, 1751, in *Letters of William Shenstone*, 215.

In our essays on sixteenth century England we drew the reader's attention to, and explained the cause for, the revolution in manners through which musical performance became no longer appropriate to the gentleman and became the province of the "slave." In Margaret Cavendish's *Sociable Letters*, dating from the mid-seventeenth century, we find music still listed as an important study for the gentleman.

> For proper and fit sciences for noble persons to be learned and known, as fortification, navigation, astronomy, cosmography, architecture, Musick, and history; and for Wit, as scenes, songs, poems, and the like.[11]

Curiously, however, for women, she finds music not appreciated for its own sake, but merely for its use in dance.

> Neither does our sex take much pleasure in harmonious Musick, only in violins to tread a measure.[12]

[11] Margaret Cavendish, *Sociable Letters* [1664] (Menston: The Scholar Press, 1969), Letter XVIII. Margaret Cavendish (1624–1673), Duchess of Newcastle, wrote plays, essays, poetry and philosophy. Contemporary reaction to the present work was mixed. Charles Lamb thought it a jewel of a book; Pepys thought she was insane and conceited.

[12] Ibid., Letter XXI.

We might also add that Cavendish also complains that everyone is obsessed with following the "Mode." But the just and wise will disapprove of an activity if the only purpose is to thus follow the fashion. Among a large number of examples, she includes music.

> Neither do they affect Mode-Songs or Sounds, because they are in the fashion to be sung or played, but because they are well-set tunes, or well-composed Musick, or witty songs, and well sung by good voices, or well played on instruments ...[13]

[13] Ibid., Letter LXIII.

Nearly a century later, in the letters of Lord Chesterfield, we find a dramatic revolution in manners has occurred. Now, as he writes to his son in Venice, he argues that the gentleman is not to actually perform music himself.

> There are liberal and illiberal pleasures as well as liberal and illiberal arts ... As you are now in the musical country, where singing, fiddling and piping are not only the common topics of conversation, but almost the principal objects of attention; I cannot help cautioning against giving into those (I will call them illiberal) pleasures (though music is commonly reckoned one of the liberal arts), to the degree that most of your countrymen do when they travel in Italy. If you love music, hear it; go to operas, concerts, and pay fiddlers to play to you; but I insist upon your neither piping nor fiddling yourself. It puts a gentleman in a very frivolous, contemptible light; brings him into a great deal of bad company; and takes up a great deal of time, which might be better employed. Few things would mortify me more, than to see you bearing a part in a concert, with a fiddle under your chin, or [an instrument] in your mouth.[14]

[14] Earl of Chesterfield, letter to his son, April 19, 1749.

In a letter of June 22, 1749, Chesterfield adds that inasmuch as the Italians now value music above painting and sculpture, he regards it as "a proof of the decline of that country."

On the Perception of Music

WILLIAM SHENSTONE devotes attention to several aspects regarding the perception of music. One comment reminds us of Aristotle's curiosity over why we prefer music which is familiar to us, rather than new music. Shenstone's observation is somewhat different and we wish he had supplied more information with respect to his conclusion.

> There seems a pretty exact analogy between the objects and the senses. Some tunes, some tastes, some visible objects, please at first, and that only; others only by degrees, and then long.[15]

[15] William Shenstone, *Men and Manners*, 91.

Another interesting observation deals with the universality of musical materials, apart from any personal preferences.

> It is evident enough to me, that persons often occur, who may be said to have an ear to music, and an eye for proportions in visible objects, who nevertheless can hardly be said to have a relish or taste for either. I mean, that a person may distinguish notes and tones to a nicety, and yet not give a discerning choice to what is preferable in music. The same, in objects of sight.
> On the other hand, they cannot have a proper feeling of beauty or harmony, without a power of discrimination for those notes and proportions on which harmony and beauty so fully depend.[16]

[16] Ibid., 95.

In one very interesting discussion, Shenstone touches on the fact we know today that non-musicians listen to music with the left ear (right hemisphere of the brain), while musicians who also tend to listen to conceptual detail in music listen with the right ear (left hemisphere, where the notation of music dwells). This has led to some suggesting that one result to modern music school training is to ruin the students as listeners! Shenstone struggles with this problem in the following:

> I have heard it claimed by adepts in music, that the pleasure it imparts to a natural ear, which owes little or nothing to cultivation, is by no means to be compared to what they feel themselves from the most perfect composition—The state of the question may be best explained by a recourse to objects that are analogous—Is a country fellow less struck with beauty than a philosopher or an anatomist, who knows how that beauty is produced? Surely no. On the other hand, an attention to the cause may somewhat interfere with the attention to the effect—They may, indeed, feel a pleasure of another sort—The faculty of reason may obtain some kind of balance, for what the more sensible faculty of the imagination loses.[17]

[17] Ibid., 96.

All philologists today believe that music preceded speech and that speech began as a development of simple emotional utterances, varying only in pitch and melodic pattern, in early man. We carry much of this in our genes yet today, as the right hemisphere of the brain adds emotional color to give meaning to our speech and in the melodic contour found in each sentence we speak. William Shenstone provides a fascinating discussion of the importance of a writer having a musical ear. His comments, which are also very relevant to the issue of the separate hemispheres of the brain, make us wonder if, instead of saying speech developed after music, we should perhaps say speech is a form of music.

> It may in some measure account for the difference of taste in the reading of books, to consider the difference of our ears for music. One is not pleased without a perfect melody of style, be the sense what it will. Another, of no ear for music, gives to sense its full weight without any deduction on account of harshness.
>
> Harmony of period and melody of style have greater weight than is generally imagined in the judgment we pass upon writing and writers. As proof of this, let us reflect, what texts of scripture, what lines in poetry, or what periods we most remember and quote, either in verse or prose, and we shall find them to be only musical ones.[18]

In this regard he adds later,

> I have sometimes thought Virgil so remarkably musical, that were his lines read to a musician, wholly ignorant of the language, by a person of capacity to give each word its proper accent, he would not fail to distinguish in it all the graces of harmony.[19]

Finally, Shenstone contributes this curious thought,

> One reason why the sound is sometimes an echo to the sense, is that the pleasantest objects have often the most harmonious names annexed to them.[20]

[18] Ibid., 49.

[19] Ibid., 73.

[20] Ibid.

On the Purpose of Music

SHENSTONE EMPHASIZES the purpose of pleasure in music, as he advises a friend,

> I would recommend some musical instrument that is most agreeable to you. I have often looked upon music as my dernier resort, if I should ever discard the world, and turn eremite entirely. Consider what other amusement can make an equal impression in old age.[21]

[21] Letter to Richard Graves, September 23, 1741, in *Letters of William Shenstone*, 27.

Chesterfield touches on the communication of emotions, but conditions this on the accuracy of the performance.

> The best compositions of Corelli, if ill executed and played out of tune, instead of touching, as they do when well performed, would only excite the indignation of the hearers, when murdered by an unskilled performer.[22]

[22] Earl of Chesterfield, letter to his son, July 9, 1750.

In his discussion of emotions versus Reason, Samuel Butler, perhaps from too much association with Puritans, reverts back to the ancient notion that music has no real value because it disappears and no longer exists when the performance concludes.

> Is his own Siren, that turns himself into a beast with musick of his own making. His perpetual study to raise *passion* has utterly debased his *reason*; and as music is wont to set false values upon things, the constant use of it has rendered him a stranger to all true ones … This puts him into the condition of a traitor, whom men hate but love the treason; so they delight in music, but have no kindness for a musician. The scale of music is like the ladder that Jacob saw in a dream, reaching to heaven with angels ascending and descending; for there is no art in the world that can raise the man higher, but it is but in a dream, and when the music is done, the mind wakes and comes to itself again. And therefore a musician, that makes it his constant employment, is like one that does nothing but make love, that is half mad, fantastic and ridiculous to those that are unconcerned. Cupid strings his bow with the strings of an instrument, and wounds hearts through the ear.[23]

[23] Samuel Butler, *Characters*, "A Musitian."

Margaret Cavendish, after hearing art songs performed in a private home, concludes that music's value is only a secondary one.

> The other day, at Mrs. D. U's house, I heard harmonious and melodious musick, both instruments and voices, but in my opinion, there is no musick so sweet, and powerful as oratory, for sweet words are better than a sweet sound, and when they are joined together, it ravishes the soul; wherefore lyric poetry has advantage of all other poetry, because both sound and sense are harmonious, wherefore the ancients had both their epic poems, and comedies, and tragedies, in verse, and tunes set to them, and sung, both in their theaters of war and peace, as in the fields and stages ... [24]

[24] Margaret Cavendish, *Sociable Letters*, Letter CXVII.

She also offers (in a *very* long sentence!) her perception of the distinctions between art song and the popular ballads. It is interesting that she associates improvisation with art song rather than with popular song.

> The last week your sister Katherine and your sister Frances were to visit me, and so well pleased I was with their neighborly and friendly visit, as their good company put me into a frolic humor, and for a pastime I sung to them some pieces of old Ballads; whereupon they desired me to sing one of the songs my Lord made, your brother set [to music], and you were pleased to sing; I told them first, I could not sing any of those songs, but if I could, I prayed them to pardon me, for neither my voice, nor my skill, was proper or fit for them, and neither having skill nor voice, if I should offer to sing any of them, I should so much disadvantage my Lord's poetical wit, and your brother's musical composition, as the fancy would be obscured in the one, and the art in the other, nay, instead of Musick, I should make discord, and instead of wit, sing nonsense, knowing not how to humor the words, nor relish the notes, whereas your harmonious voice give their works both grace and pleasure, and invites and draws the soul from all other parts of the body, with all the loving and amorous passions, to sit in the hollow cavern of the ear, as in a vaulted room, wherein it listens with delight, and is ravished with admiration; wherefore their works and your voice are only fit for the notice of souls, and not to be sung to dull, unlistening ears, whereas my voice and those songs, would be as disagreeing to your voice and old Ballads, for the vulgar and

plainer a voice is, the better it is for an old Ballad; for a sweet voice, with quavers, and Trilloes, and the like, would be as improper for an old Ballad, as ... diamond buckles on clouted or cobled shoes, or a feather on a monk's hood; neither should old Ballads be sung so much in a tune as in a tone, which tone is between speaking and singing, for the sound is more than plain speaking, and less than clear singing, and the rumming or humming of a wheel should be the Musick to that tone, for the hummings is the noise the wheel makes in the turning round, which is not like the Musick of the Spheres; and Ballads are only proper to be sung by spinsters, and that only in cold Winter nights, when a company of good housewives are drawing a thread of flax; but as they draw threads of flax, so time draws their threads of life, as their web makes them smocks, so times web makes them death's shirts, to which, as to death, afterwards those good housewives are married, and lie in the bed of earth, their house being the grave, and their dwelling in the region of oblivion; and this is the fate of poor spinners, and ballad-singers, whereas such a singer as you, such a composer as your brother, such a poet as my Lord, are clothed with renown, marry fame, and live in eternity ... [25]

[25] Ibid., Letter CCII.

The Diary of John Evelyn records a number of artists he heard perform in London, among them a locally famous freak, "the hairy woman," whom he met in 1657 and whom he reports "played well on the harpsichord."[26] Two other diary entries for 1674 are quite interesting in their detail of actual performances.

[26] *The Diary of John Evelyn*, for September 15, 1657. John Evelyn (1620–1706) began his famous diary in 1640.

> [November 19] I heard that stupendous violin, Signor Nicholao (with other rare musicians), whom I never heard mortal man exceed on that instrument. He had a stroke so sweet, and made it speak like the voice of a man, and, when he pleased, like a concert of several instruments. He did wonders upon a note, and was an excellent composer. Here was also that rare lutanist, Dr. Wallgrave; but nothing approached the violin in Nicholao's hand. He played such ravishing things as astonished us all.
>
> [December 2] At Mr. Slingsby's, Master of the Mint, my worthy friend, a great lover of music. Heard Signor Francisco on the harpsichord, esteemed one of the most excellent masters in Europe on that instrument; then, came Nicholao with his violin, and struck all mute, but Mrs. Knight, who sung incomparably, and doubtless has the greatest reach of

any English woman; she had been lately roaming in Italy, and was much improved in that quality.

Evelyn also reflects on the singing of his own daughter, on the day of her death:

> She had an excellent voice, to which she played a thorough-bass on the harpsichord, in both which she arrived to that perfection, that of the scholars of those two famous masters, Signors Pietro and Bartholomeo, she was esteemed the best; for the sweetness of her voice and management of it added such an agreeableness to her countenance, without any constraint or concern, that when she sung, it was as charming to the eye as to the ear.[27]

Of particular interest, among the entries in Evelyn's diary, are descriptions of concerts performed in private homes. He mentions, for example, having dinner at a gentleman's home, in 1672, which was followed by "a concert of music."[28] A similar entry for September 23, 1680, describes hearing in his own home a recital by Signor Pietro,

> ...a famous musician, who had been long in Sweden in Queen Christina's court; he sung admirably to a guitar, and had a perfect good tenor and bass.[29]

An entry for July 25, 1684, describes a dinner at the home of Lord Falkland, Treasurer of the Navy, after which,

> We had rare music, there being amongst others, Signor Pietro Reggio, and Signor John Baptist, both famous, one for his voice, the other for playing on the harpsichord, few if any in Europe exceeding him. There was also a Frenchman who sung an admirable bass.

Similarly, in 1685 Evelyn had dinner at Lord Sunderland's,

> being invited to hear that celebrated voice of Mr. Pordage, newly come from Rome; his singing was after the Venetian recitative [manner], as masterly as could be, and with an excellent voice both treble and bass; Dr. Walgrave accompanied it with this theorbo lute, on which he performed beyond imagination, and is doubtless one of the greatest masters in Europe on that charming instrument.[30]

[27] Ibid., for March 10, 1685.

[28] Ibid., for December 23, 1672.

[29] In this entry, Evelyn briefly alludes to a murder committed by Queen Christina, something we have not read of elsewhere.

[30] *The Diary of John Evelyn*, for January 27, 1685.

Evelyn heard the singer Pordage the following day at a dinner at the home of Lord Arundel, who had just been released from the Tower. On this occasion he again heard "that excellent and stupendous artist," Signor John Baptist, on the harpsichord.

In the correspondence of this period one finds additional references to personal music making. In several letters, the poet Thomas Gray speaks of his activity as a musician. On July 3, 1735, for example, he writes,

> I have composed a hymn about it mighty moving and [play] it perpetually, for I have changed my harp into a harpsichord and am as melodious, as the day is long.[31]

Alexander Pope, in a letter of August 15, 1731, to Lord Oxford, relates,

> The said Faustina, alias Mrs. Hasse, has sent to Lady Cobham divers notes of music and new tunes, which those that can play and sing shall communicate to the less deserving who are mere auditors and auditoresses.[32]

[31] Letter to Walpole, July 3, 1735, in *Correspondence of Thomas Gray* (Oxford, Clarendon Press, 1971). Thomas Gray (1716–1771) spent the greater part of his adult life in academic seclusion in Cambridge.

[32] Quoted in *The Works of Alexander Pope* (New York: Gordian Press, 1967), VIII, 288. Alexander Pope (1688–1744) was born to the family of a prosperous merchant, but as he was also born Catholic he was denied an education at any of the great universities. Thus, the greatest English poet of the eighteenth century was the product of his own education through reading. An illness as a child left him a four foot high hump-back. Faustina Bordoni, a famous opera singer, married the composer Hasse in 1730.

14
Pepys on Music

SAMUEL PEPYS (1633–1703) was a notable exception to the trend which began in sixteenth century England, in which gentlemen disassociated themselves from personally performing of music. His famous diary, covering the years 1660 to 1669, is a testimonial to his own love of music, his close attention to the musical scene, his private performance and attempts at composition. The diary is particularly valuable because it was never intended to be published, even being written in a private code, and therefore is much more candid than the publication of a gentleman could have been at this time.

He served as a kind of Minister of the Navy under James II, during which time he introduced important economies into the Navy—and managed to improve his own economy immensely. Later he served in the House of Commons and was elected President of the Royal Society.

As mentioned above, this man's diary reflects not only a love, but almost an obsession for music. In 1663 Pepys comments that he is fearful "of being too much taken with musique, for fear of returning to my old dotage thereon and so neglect my business as I used to."[1] In his diary entry for March 9, 1666, he again fears he will neglect business for his love of music, concluding,

> However, music and women I cannot but give way to, whatever my business is.

[1] Pepys *Diary*, February 17, 1663.

Indeed, on July 30, 1666, he reports his wife is angry because he has been spending too much time with a young singer, but he apologizes again that "music is the thing of the world that I love most." The following February 12, 1667, Pepys, eager to compare an Italian choir with one under Cooke, again reveals how much music means to him.

> I do consider that [music] is all the pleasure I live for in the world, and the greatest I can ever expect in the best of my life.

For November 16, 1667, Pepys describes going to Whitehall to hear a performance under Pelham Humfrey,[2] but apparently Humfrey and his musicians did not show up. Instead Pepys goes to another room where,

> I did hear the best and the smallest organ that ever I saw in my life, and such a one as, by the grace of God, I will have the next year if I continue in this condition, whatever it cost me. I never was so pleased in my life.

Pepys' most philosophical comments on music come in a letter of November 5, 1700, after the period covered by the famous diary. A correspondent had sent Pepys a proposal for a new method of teaching mathematics, written by Dr. David Gregory, the Savilian Professor of Astronomy at Oxford. It is evident that Pepys, following the ancient Roman Church's invention, was still thinking of music as a branch of mathematics, for he wrote to the professor pointing out that his proposal had omitted music. In the course of his offering his views on the nature and purpose of music, we also see a reflection of his long experienced frustration that none of his composer friends would offer him a simple, effective set of rules for composition. It is quite nice to read that nothing has changed: the composers point to the official rules and then ignore them in the interest of art.

> I would now recommend to your giving the same regard to ... Musick, a science peculiarly productive of a pleasure that no state of life, public or private, secular or sacred; no difference of age or season; no temper of mind or condition of health exempt from present anguish; nor, lastly, distinction of quality,

[2] Humfrey (1647–1674) from childhood was associated with court music in England.

renders either improper, untimely, or unentertaining. Witness the universal gusto we see it followed with, wherever to be found, by all whose leisure and purse can bear it. While the same might to much better effect, both for variety and delight to themselves and friends, be ever to be had within their own walls, and of their own composures too as well as others, were the doctrine of it brought within the simplicity, perspicuity, and certainty common to all other parts of mathematical knowledge, and of which I take this to be equally capable with any of them, in lieu of that fruitless jargon of obsolete terms and other unnecessary perplexities and obscurities wherewith it has been ever hitherto delivered, and from which, as I know of nothing eminent, or even tolerable, left us by the Ancients, so neither have I met with one modern Master (foreign or domestic) owning the least obligation to it for any their now nobler compositions; but on the contrary charging all (and justly too) upon the happiness of their own genius only, joined with the drudgery of a long and unassisted practice. A condition not to be looked for from the more generous and elevated spirits of those we are here concerned for; and therefore most deserving, as well as most needing, the abilities and application of our present most learned Professor to remedy.[3]

[3] *Private Correspondence of Samuel Pepys*, ed. J. Tanner (London: Bell and Sons, 1926), II, 109.

Far from being absorbed only with the conceptual nature of music, Pepys' great love of music was expressed more directly through his own performance. He owned his own instruments and performed on flute, lute, theorbo, violin and viol and on one occasion even considered taking lessons in whistling.[4] He had an insatiable curiosity about everything regarding music and his diary is filled with references to various instruments, individual musicians and an extensive number of actual compositions. In many of his observations on music, one can see his views were shaped by his own experience. For example, Pepys enjoyed private, amateur music making, but apparently felt uncomfortable if a professional musician was present on such an occasion. He describes a performance of music in a home on July 29, 1664, adding,

[4] Pepys *Diary*, May 17, 1661.

> But I begin to be weary of having a master with us, for it spoils methinks the ingenuity of our practice.

As a private listener Pepys preferred simple compositions which communicated directly without the complexities enjoyed by the "experts." An entry of July 22, 1664, describes hearing,

> the best piece of musique, counted of all hands in the world, made by Seignor Carissimi, the famous master in Rome. Fine it was indeed, and too fine for me to judge of.

For the same reason he found little enjoyment in contrapuntal music. On September 15, 1667, he observes in his diary,

> I am more and more confirmed that singing with many voices is not singing, but a sort of instrumental music, the sense of the words being lost by not being heard, and especially as they set them with fugues of words, one after another; whereas singing properly, I think, should be but with one or two voices at most, and that counterpoint.

It is this view which is reflected in an entry of December, 1666. Here Pepys refers to a visit the court organist, John Hingston,[5] to get him to either write, or rewrite, one of Pepys' songs.

> I took him to the Dogg tavern and got him to set me a bass to my "It is decreed," which I think will go well; but he commends the song, not knowing the words, but says the ayre [melody] is good, and believes the words are plainly expressed. He is of my mind, against having [many] eighth-notes necessarily in composition. This did all please me mightily.[6]

On December 10, 1667, Pepys again mentions that he runs into Hingston and attempts to question him about composition, but is disappointed with the response.

> I do find that he can no more give an intelligible answer to a man that is not a great master in his art than another man—and this confirms me that it is only want of an ingenious man that is master in Musique, to bring music to a certainty and ease in composition.

[5] John Hingston (1612–1683) was also in charge of tuning and repairing the court keyboards.

[6] Pepys *Diary*, December 19, 1666.

Pepys becomes obsessed with discovering a simpler process of composition. In his diary he writes on March 20, 1668,

> At my chamber all the evening, writing down some things and trying some conclusions upon my viol, in order to the inventing a better theory of Musique than has yet been abroad; and I think verily I shall do it.

Three days later he writes he is thinking of acquiring a harpsichord,

> to confirm and help me in my music notions, which my head is nowadays full of, and I do believe will come to something that is very good.

On March 29, 1668, he reports that he had the opportunity to discuss composition with John Banister.[7]

> I had very good discourse with him about music, so confirming some of my new notions about music that it puts me upon a resolution to go on and make a Scheme and Theory of music, not yet ever made in the world.

Other than the fact that the surviving compositions of Pepys are in the nature of elementary songs, we are inclined, on the basis of the following, to think his new method of composition must also have been a simple one. He reports attempting to have a discussion with Hooke, who evidently brushed him off,

> so the reason of Concords and Discords in music—which they say is from the aequality of the vibrations; but I am not satisfied in it, but will at my leisure think of it more and see how far that does go to explain it.[8]

Apparently nothing ever came of this new system of composition and the last we read of it is on January 11, 1669.

> So home; and there at home all the evening, and made Tom to write down some little conceits and notions of mine in Musique, which does mightily encourage me to spend some more thoughts about it; for I fancy, upon good reason, that I am in the right way of unfolding the mystery of this matter better than ever yet.

[7] John Banister (1625–1679), born the son of a member of the London Waits, became proficient on numerous instruments. It was he who was displaced by the Frenchman, Grabu, as head of court music. He went on to organize concerts in the private sector.

[8] Pepys *Diary*, April 2, 1668.

On Music of the Court

THE EARLY DIARY REFERENCES to the music of the court are often centered on the presence of French influence, beginning with this curious notice of 1660.

> The king did put a great affront upon Singleton's Musique, he bidding them to stop and bade the French Musique play—which my Lord says does much out-do ours.[9]

[9] Ibid., November 20, 1660.

In 1665 a French musician, Louis Grabu,[10] was appointed "composer to his Majesty's musique." The resentment among the English did not die quickly, for we read in an entry of 1667,

[10] Grabu (d. 1694) was a French composer, however of Spanish origin. Dismissed from the court in 1674, he remained active in London.

> Here they talk also how the king's violin, Bannister, is mad that the king has a Frenchman [Louis Grabu] come to be chief of some part of the king's music—at which the duke of York made great mirth.[11]

[11] Pepys *Diary*, February 20, 1667.

Pepys himself heard a large scale polyphonic work for chorus and orchestra conducted by Grabu, in this same year, and was not impressed.

> ... to White-hall and there ... to hear the music which the king is presented this night by Monsieur Grebus, the master of his music—both instrumental (I think 24 violins) and vocal, an English song upon peace; but God forgive me, I was never so little pleased with a consort of music in my life—the manner of setting of words and repeating them out of order, and that with a number of voices, makes me sick, the whole design of vocal music being lost by it ... I did not see many pleased with it; only, the instrumental music he had brought by practice to play very just.[12]

[12] Ibid., October 1, 1667.

The following year, however, he attends a rehearsal and reports,

> to the fiddling concert and heard a practice mighty good of Grebus.[13]

[13] Ibid., April 15, 1668.

To give some credit to Grabu, he worked during a difficult time for court music. Pepys reports a conversation with the court organist, Hingston, when the latter informed him that the king's musicians were on the verge of starvation, being five years behind in their wages.

> Nay, Evens, the famous man upon the harp, having not his equal in the world, did the other day die for mere want, and was fain to be buried at the alms of the parish—and carried to his grave in the dark at night.[14]

[14] Ibid., December 19, 1666.

The tone of Pepys' comments on court music change with the return of Humfrey from France. A musician Pepys evidently did not like, he finds him upon his return much affected with French manners, "an absolute Monsieur, full of form and confidence and vanity." Pepys also objects that Humfrey is criticizing everyone's skill but his own.

> The truth is, everyone says he is very able; but to hear how he laughs at all the king's music here ... that they cannot keep time nor tune nor understand anything, and that Grebus the Frenchman, the king's Master of the Musique, how he understands nothing nor can play on any instrument and so cannot compose, and that he will give him a lift out of his place, and that he and the king are mighty great, and that he has already spoke to the king about Grebus, would make a man piss.[15]

[15] Ibid., November 15, 1667.

In a similar mood, Pepys finds no particular enjoyment in the music of Humfrey.

> I to White hall and there got into the Theater-room and there heard both the vocal and instrumental music, where the little fellow [Pelham Humfrey] stood keeping time; but for my part, I see no great matter, but quite the contrary, in both sorts of music. The composition I believe is very good, but no more of delightfulness to the ear or understanding but what is very ordinary.[16]

[16] Ibid., November 16, 1667.

On Music of the Theater

THE DIARY ENTRIES by Pepys on the music he heard used in the theater are among the few eyewitness account of the music which is otherwise known to us only in the form of lyrics in published plays. Pepys, always interested primarily in the music, complains in his diary entry for February 6, 1668, that the theater was so crowded that he could "see but little and hear not at all." Therefore, when he attended a performance of *The Faithful Shepherdess* on February 26, 1669, which was poorly attended, he observed,

> The emptiness of the house took away our pleasure a great deal, though I liked it the better; for that I plainly discern the music is the better, by how much the House is the emptier.

He had first discussed theater acoustics in his diary entry of May 8, 1663, speaking of the Theater Royal and its early example of an orchestral pit.

> The house is made with extraordinary good contrivance; and yet has some faults, as the narrowness of the passages in and out of the pit, and the distance from the stage to the boxes, which I am confident cannot hear. But for all other things it is well. Only, above all, the Musique being below, and most of it sounding under the very stage, there is no hearing of the basses at all, nor very well of the trebles, which sure must be mended.

In general, Pepys liked what he heard and one finds such entries as that for April 19, 1667, where he reports hearing a musical adaptation of *Macbeth* by Davenant and finds the "variety of dancing and music the best I ever saw." Most of his diary entries, however, are simple comments on one or another singer which he either did or did not like. A typical example follows his attending a performance of *The Faithful Shepherdess* on October 14, 1668, when he mentions that the singing of a French eunuch was beyond all he had ever heard.

Judging by one entry in the diary of Pepys, it would appear that some of the music heard in the plays was produced at the last moment. In the entry for May 7, 1668, Pepys comments on his enjoyment in seeing several actors all dressed in their costumes, and privately complains that these mere actors become so confident in their talk when they come off the stage. Then he adds a note about a song which would be used in *The Mulberry Garden*, which premiered the following day.

> Here took up Knepp into our coach and all of us with her to her lodging, and hither comes Bannester with a song of hers that he has set in Sir Charles Sidly's play for her, which is I think but very meanly set; but this he did before us, teach her; and it being but a slight, silly, short ayre, she learnt it presently. But I did here get him to prick me down [notate] the notes of the Echo Song in *The Tempest*, which pleases me mightily.

In so far as the quality of the music Pepys heard in these dramatic plays, he was by far his most enthusiastic over a composition for wind ensemble in the *Virgin Martyr* by Dekker, which he describes on February 27, 1668.

> What did please me beyond anything in the whole world was the wind-musique when the Angel comes down, which is so sweet that it ravished me; and indeed, in a word, did wrap up my soul so that it make me really sick, just as I have formerly been when in love with my wife; that neither then, nor all the evening going home and at home, I was able to think of anything, but remained all night transported, so as I could not believe that ever any music has that real command over the soul of a man as this did upon me; and makes me resolve to practice wind-music and to make my wife do the same.

He attends this play again on March 2, 1668, and this music has the same effect.

> ...above all the Musique at the coming down of the Angel which at this hearing the second time does so still command me as nothing ever did, and the other music is nothing [compared] to it.

Two months later he sees the play again and mentions that he "heard the music that I like so well."[17]

[17] Ibid., May 6, 1668.

We may assume the individual songs from these plays were made available for the public for amateur performance. Indeed in Pepys' diary for August 23, 1667, he tells of a visitor bringing two "flagelettes" and some music used at the king's playhouse, which they played together and which Pepys looks forward to playing later with his wife.

The sixteenth century humanists in Italy and France argued extensively for the principle that in sung poetry, it is the words which carry meaning and emotion. It is the very nature of music itself, however, which made their position untenable. Pepys, for reasons of his rather simple approach to music, was of the "old school." He found hearing an art song in a language he did not speak failed to move him. In the following, he is speaking not only of the meaning of the words, in order to judge the composer's choice of music to go with them, but even such subtleties as accents peculiar to that language. On one occasion in 1667, he was invited to the home of Lord Brouncker to hear a private concert by visiting musicians from Italy.

> By and by [came] the music, that is to say, Seignor Vincentio, who is the master composer, and six more [musicians], of which two were eunuchs and one woman, very well dressed and handsome enough but would not be kissed, as Mr. Killigrew, who brought the company in, did acquaint us. They sent two harpsichords before; and by and by, after tuning them, they began; and I confess, very good music they made; that is, the composition exceeding good, but yet not at all more pleasing to me than what I have heard in English by Mrs. Knipp, Captain Cooke and others. Nor do I dote on the eunuchs; they sing indeed pretty high and have a mellow kind of sound, but yet I have been as well satisfied with several women's voices, and men also ... The woman sung well, but that which distinguishes all is this: that in singing, the words are to be considered and how they are fitted with notes, and then the common accent of the country is to be known and understood by the listener, or he will never be a good judge of the vocal music of another country. So that I was not taken with this at all, neither understanding the first nor by practice reconciled to the latter, so that their motions and risings and fallings, though it may be pleasing to an Italian or one that understands that tongue, yet to me it did not. [I] do from my heart believe that I could set words in English, and make music of the, more agreeable to any Englishman's ear (even the most judicious) than any Italian music set for the voice and performed before the same man, unless he be acquainted with the Italian accent of speech. The composition as to the instrumental part [the Musique part] was exceeding good, and

their justness in keeping time by practice much before any that we have, unless it be a good band of practiced fiddlers.[18]

An interesting insight to a rather practical form of this question, the struggle between poet and composer, we find in a diary entry for February 13, 1667. In addition, we find here interesting references to improvisation, both in the "humoring" of individual notes and in the cadences.

> Discourse most about plays and the opera; where among other vanities, Captain Cooke had the arrogance to say that he was fain to direct Sir W. Davenant in the breaking of his verses into such and such lengths, according as would be fit for music, and how he used to swear at Davenant and command him that way when W. Davenant would be angry, and find fault with this or that note; but a vain coxcomb I perceive he is, though he sings and composes so well ... After dinner, Captain Cooke and two of his boys to sing; but it was indeed, both in performance and composition, most plainly below what I heard last night, which I could not have believed. Besides, overlooking the words when he sung, I find them not at all humored as they ought to be, and as I believed he had done all [as] he had notated—though he himself does indeed sing in a manner, as to voice and manner, the best I ever hard yet; and a strange mastery he has in the making of extraordinary surprising cadenzas [cadences], that are mighty pretty; but his bragging that he does understand tones and sounds as well as any man in the world, and better than Devenant or anybody else, I do not like by no means ...

Although Pepys himself played a variety of instruments, as a listener he generally prefered vocal music. A typical diary entry describes his going to a public building to hear a private instrumental concert.

> I must confess, whether it be that I hear it but seldom, or that really voices is better, but so it is, that I found no pleasure at all in it, and methought two voices were worth twenty of it.[19]

[18] Ibid., February 16, 1667.

[19] Ibid., August 10, 1664.

15
Restoration Journals on Music

JOURNALS AND NEWSPAPERS were not new to this period, but the extensive coverage of music and manners was. Richard Steele began the *Tatler* on April 12, 1709, writing primarily under the name Isaac Bickerstaff, as a paper designed for the conversation of the coffee house crowd. These journals are valuable in part for their presentation of this class, much of it middle-class, which is virtually absent in traditional political biographies and histories. Some have also pointed to these issues as the birthplace of modern short stories.

Steele and Joseph Addison created the *Spectator* with the issue of March 1, 1711. For the first year its actual circulation was small, rarely more than four thousand issues, but its influence became much larger as bound volumes were sold at the rate of nine thousand each year.

These journals are filled with references to music, musical humor and musical instruments, however we present below only those passages which offer the modern reader insight into aesthetics, manners or taste relative to music of this period.

In the *Tatler* for August 15, 1710, Addison lists "Eloquence, Musick, and Poetry," as "those things which refine our lives." In the *Spectator* for June 16, 1711, in discussing the "Diversions of Life," Addison observes,

> A man that has a taste of Musick, Painting, or Architecture, is like one that has another sense, when compared with such as have no relish in those arts.

Several issues of these journals suggest that music was an important hallmark of the cultured lady, as we see, for example, in the *Spectator* for March 17, 1712, where Steele publishes a fictitious letter by a man praising his "virtuous lovely woman," and mentions as part of her "good breeding and polite education," that she "sings, dances, plays on the lute and harpsichord." Ladies with similar accomplishments are mentioned in the issues for August 5 and November 1, 1712.

On the other hand, some contributors cast doubt on the general appreciation of music by the English society at this time. Jonathan Swift, writing in Irish journal, the *Intelligencer* [Number III, 1728], in an essay in which he defends and praises Gay's *Beggars Opera*, quotes the Addison definition given above, but doubts whether the average man has any independent basis for judgment of those arts.

> As to Poetry, Eloquence and Musick, which are said to have most power over the minds of men, it is certain that very few have a taste or judgment of the excellencies of the two former; and if a man succeeds in either, it is upon the authority of those few judges, that lend their taste to the bulk of readers, who have none of their own. I am told there are as few good judges in Musick, and that among those who crowd in operas, nine in ten to hither merely out of curiosity, fashion or affectation.

On the Perception of Music

LOOKING AT THIS LITERATURE as a whole, one has clear reason to doubt whether either Steele or Addison themselves had much depth in their understanding of music. Steele, for example, writing on the supremacy of sight among the senses, in the *Spectator* of September 1, 1712, suggests that it is the addition of *sight* to hearing which gives significance to music, by which he means the addition of Reason to hearing, or as we would say today, the left hemisphere of the brain giving meaning to the right. In any case, this is only new language for the old misinformed conclusion that music has no meaning unless it is a rational concept, a view, we might add, which has not entirely died in academic circles.

> The *sight* informs the statuary's chisel with power to give breath to lifeless brass and marble, and the painter's pencil to swell the flat canvas with moving figures actuated by imaginary souls. Musick indeed may plead another original, since Jubal by the different falls of his hammer on the anvil, discovered by the ear the first rude Musick that pleased the Antediluvian fathers; but then the *sight* has not only reduced those wilder sounds into artful Order and Harmony, but [through notation] conveys that Harmony to the most distant parts of the world without the help of sound.

Among other journals which deal with the perception of music, Addison, in the *Tatler* for February 14, 1710, writes an essay on Silence. In commenting on the power of silence, he uses music as an illustration.

> I have my self been wonderfully delighted with a Master-Piece of Musick, when in the very tumult and ferment of their harmony, all the voices and instruments have stopped short on a sudden, and after a little pause recovered themselves again as it were, and renewed the concert in all its parts. Methoughts this short interval of silence has had more Musick in it than any the same Space of Time before or after it.

What is really being discussed here is the *emotional* power of silence. It can be equally powerful in that moment between the final note of a performance and the applause.

In the *Tatler* for April 1, 1710, Addison mentions a painting, *The Consort of Musick,* by Zampieri, which pictured famous painters, each holding an instrument which corresponded to their character. Addison then speculates how the various instruments might also serve as metaphors for styles of conversation, in the process offering his view of the individual character of the various instruments. The percussion, for example, he finds are like "Blusterers in Conversation," with lots of noise but "seldom any wit, humor, or good breeding." Nevertheless they are appropriate to the ignorant and to ladies of little taste. The lute he considers the opposite to the percussion, having a soft sound, "exquisitely sweet, and very low, easily drowned in a multitude of instruments." The lute, then, corresponds to "men of fine genius, uncommon reflection, great affability ... and good taste."

The trumpet, an instrument he finds of "no compass of Musick, or variety of sound," having only four or five notes, although it is pleasing enough, he equates with the gentleman of fashionable education and breeding, yet who are shallow, with weak judgment and little understanding.

Regarding the violin, it is interesting that Addison first thinks of its use in improvisation.

> Violins are the lively, forward, importunate wits, that distinguish themselves by the flourishes of imagination, sharpness of repartee, glances of satyr, and bear away the upper part in every consort. I cannot however but observe, That when a man is not disposed to hear Musick, there is not a more disagreeable sound in harmony than that of a violin.

Addison associates every sensible, "true-born Britain" with the Bass-Viol, as "Men of rough sense, and unpolished parts ... but who sometimes break out with an agreeable bluntness, unexpected wit, and surly pleasantry." Musically, he finds this instrument one which "grumbles in the bottom of the consort, with a surly masculine sound, strengthens the harmony, and tempers the sweetness of the several instruments that play along with it."

The "Rural Wits," which he associates with horns and which he is not quite sure should be permitted in polite society. The bagpipe, with its perpetual repetition of a few notes over a drone, he associates with the "dull, heavy, tedious story-tellers."

These comments, Addison admits, are concerned only with "male instruments," the female ones he promises to discuss in a later issue. In the meantime, however, he warns the reader to, make a narrow search into his life and conversation, and upon his leaving any company, to examine himself seriously, whether he has behaved himself in it like a drum or trumpet, a violin or a Bass-Viol; and accordingly endeavor to mend his Musick for the future.

As he promised, Addison discusses the "female" instruments in his issue of April 11, 1710. The flute he finds an instrument with small compass, sweet and soft, which lulls and soothes the ear and raises "a most agreeable passion between transport and indolence." This reminds him of the conversation of a "mild and amiable woman, that has nothing in it very elevated, or at the same time anything mean or trivial." The flageolet, on the other hand, is like a young lady "entertaining the company with tart ill-natured observations, pert fancies, and little turns which she imagined to be full of life and spirit." Curiously, Addison also considers the oboe to be part of the flute family.

> I must here observe that the Hautboy is the most perfect of the flute-species, which, with all the sweetness of the sound, has a greater strength and variety of notes; though at the same time I must observe, that the hautboy in one sex is as scarce as the harpsichord in the other.

The "Prude," characterized by "the gravity of her censures and composure of her voice," he associates with the "ancient serious matron-like instrument the Virginal." The "Romantic instrument called a Dulcimer," he finds a pleasant rural instrument, as is also the hornpipe, while the Welsh harp is a "Female Historian." It is interesting that he includes among the female instruments, the timpani.

> But the most sonorous part of our consort was a She-Drum, or (as the vulgar call it) a Kettle-Drum, who accompanied her discourse with motions of the body, tosses of the head, and brandishes of the fan. Her Musick was loud, bold and masculine. Every thump she gave alarmed the company, and very often set somebody or other in it a blushing.

Some interesting remarks on the nature of program music are made by Addison in the *Spectator* for June 27, 1712.

It is certain there may be confused, imperfect notions of this nature raised in the imagination by an artificial composition of notes; and we find that great masters in the art are able, sometimes, to set their hearers in the heat and hurry of a battle, to overcast their minds with melancholy scenes and apprehensions of deaths and funerals, or to lull them into pleasing dreams of groves and Elisiums.

In all these instances, this secondary pleasure of the imagination proceeds from that action of the mind, which compares the ideas arising from the original objects, with the ideas we receive from the statue, picture, description, or sound that represents them. It is impossible for us to give the necessary reason why this operation of the mind is attended with so much pleasure, as I have before observed[1]; but we find a great variety of entertainments derived from this single principle.

[1] He refers here to a discussion in the issue of June 24, 1712, in which he had quoted Locke as contending that light and colors are creations of the imagination and have no material basis.

On Emotions in Music

ADDISON, in a discussion of opera in the *Spectator* of April 3, 1711, makes a fundamental error regarding the perception of music, in view of which the reader must question his basic understanding of music and many of his subsequent comments on it. He did not understand that what music *really* communicates is emotion and that this emotional understanding is universal and genetic. Because of the close affinity of emotions and music in the right hemisphere of the brain, and especially the genetic musical information which modern clinical research suggests is carried into birth, it appears the old saying that "music is the international language" is in fact true.[2] But this expression relates to the emotions expressed through music and has nothing to do with words or any other rational concepts.

It is most curious that Addison seems unaware of his own fundamental contradiction, in this regard. On one hand, in the *Spectator* for March 21, 1711, he objects strongly that the English people are listening to opera in a language they do not understand. Yet, in this issue of April 3, he builds his case that the source of the emotions are the words.

[2] Addison later associates music in this regard with architecture, painting, poetry and oratory, but he is again incorrect. There is nothing universal or genetic in painting, architecture, poetry or oratory.

The physiological truth is that words may be sung, but the emotions are in the music!

In this April issue, he understands the music of opera to be something which expressed the *words*, thus his great concern here with the inevitable problems in translating libretti. It follows that since each language has a different form of tone and accent, Addison thought music should be therefore fundamentally different in each country. Addison's conclusion which follows is incorrect and cannot be supported by either common practice or medical research.

> For this reason the Italian artists cannot agree with our English musicians, in admiring Purcell's compositions, and thinking his tunes so wonderfully adapted to his words, because both nations do not always express the same passions by the same sounds ...
>
> A composer should fit his Musick to the genius of the people, and consider that the delicacy of hearing, and taste of harmony, has been formed upon those sounds which every country abounds with: In short, that Musick is of a relative nature, and what is harmony to one ear, may be dissonance to another.

Addison apparently based his concept that music should be fundamentally different in each country in part on the basis of his perceived distinction between French and Italian opera. In his discussion of this we find the curious information that the audience in Paris participated, and, according to some sources, even went upon the stage.

> Signor Baptist Lully acted like a man of sense in this particular. He found the French Musick extremely defective, and very often barbarous. However, knowing the genius of the people, the humor of their language, and the prejudiced ears he had to deal with, he did not pretend to extirpate the French musick, and plant the Italian in its stead; but only to cultivate and civilize it with innumerable graces and modulations which he borrowed from the Italian. By this means the French Musick is now perfect in its kind; and when you say it is not so good as the Italian, you only mean that it does not please you so well, for there is scarce a Frenchman who would not wonder to hear you give the Italian such a preference. The Musick of

> the French is indeed very properly adapted to their pronunciation and accent, as their whole opera wonderfully favors the genius of such a gay airy people. The Chorus in which that opera abounds, gives the Parterre frequent opportunities of joining in consort with the stage. This inclination of the audience to sing along with the actors, so prevail with them, that I have sometimes known the performer on the stage do no more in a celebrated song, than the clerk of a parish church, who serves only to raise the psalm, and is afterwards drowned in the Musick of the congregation.

In all fairness to Addison, we must acknowledge that there were others at this time who apparently misunderstood the true role of music in opera. The *Spectator* for December 26, 1711, for example, carries a letter to the editor signed by Thomas Clayton, Nicolino Haym and Charles Dieupart, three men who figured in the development of opera in England in the early years of the eighteenth century, in which the argument is again made that emotion is found in the words, not in the music.

> We conceive hopes of your favor from the speculations on the mistakes which the town run into with regard to their pleasure of this kind; and believing your method of judging is, that you consider Musick only valuable as it is agreeable to and heightens the purpose of poetry, we consent that That is not only the true way of relishing that pleasure, but also that without it a composition of Musick is the same thing as a poem where all the rules of poetical numbers are observed, but the words of no sense or meaning; to say it shortly, mere musical sounds are in our Art no other than nonsense verses are in poetry. Musick therefore is to aggravate what is intended by poetry; it must always have some passion or sentiment to express, or else violins, voices, or any other organs of sound, afford an entertainment very little above the rattles of children.

Curiously, Addison discovered in common ballads the universality of emotion in music which he failed to find in Italian opera. In his first discussion of this, in the *Spectator* issue for May 21, 1711, he begins with an anecdote about Molière which argues for the universality of emotions.

Molière, as we are told by Monsieur Boileau,³ used to read all his comedies to an old woman who was his house-keeper, as she sat with him at her work by the chimney-corner; and could foretell the success of his play in the theater, from the reception it met at his fire-side ...

So ... an ordinary song or ballad that is the delight of the common people cannot fail to please all such readers as are not unqualified for the entertainment by their affectation or ignorance; and the reason is plain, because the same paintings of nature which recommend it to the most ordinary reader, will appear beautiful to the most refined.

In this passage, Addison again appears to be thinking of emotion only in terms of the words, even though he is discussing ballads set to music. In the issue of May 25, 1711, he discusses the most popular of all ballads, "Chevy Chase," and here he comes closer to associating the emotions with the music.

> Had this old song been filled with epigrammatical turns and points of wit, it might perhaps have pleased the wrong taste of some readers; but it would never have become the delight of the common people, nor have warmed the heart of Sir Philip Sidney "like the sound of a trumpet"; it is only Nature that can have this effect, and please those tastes which are the most unprejudiced or the most refined.

In discussing another often mentioned ballad, "Children of the Wood," Addison, in the issue of June 7, 1711, once again seems to place his understanding of the emotions on the words. We believe modern clinical research would suggest that he is asking more of language, in this regard, than is possible.

> This song is a plain simple Copy of Nature, destitute of all the helps and ornaments of Art. The tale of it is a pretty tragic story, and pleases for no other reason, but because it is a Copy of Nature. There is even a despicable simplicity in the verse; and yet, because the sentiments appear genuine and unaffected, they are able to move the mind of the most polite reader with inward meltings of humanity and compassion.

The problem is, when he says "the sentiments ... move the mind," he is thinking of language, being unaware that

---

³ The original, in the *Works of Boileau* (1711–1712), II, 89,

> Molière has often shown me an old maid of his, to whom, he told me, he read his Comedies; assuring me, that when any part of the pleasantry did not strike her, he corrected it; because he frequently found at his theater, that those very places did not succeed.

In our own days as a member of a touring concert organization, we knew a conductor who, not being impressed with the acclamation of audiences of thousands of persons, would invariably request the opinion of a local stage hand at the end of the concert.

the "sentiments" are in a different hemisphere of the brain [together with music] than those of language.

More accurate is Steele, in the *Spectator* for September 24, 1712, who notes in a fictitious letter, "A loose trivial song gains the affections, when a wise Homily is not attended to." That is, it is the music, not the words, which carry emotion.

Art Music

IN THE *Tatler* for September 9, 1710, Addison,[4] having been unable to sleep the previous night due to a serenade, devotes himself to this topic. He notes that in London the civic musicians are often hired by young men to sing their serenades for them.

[4] The paper is ascribed to Steele, but scholars believe it to be by Addison.

> For as the custom prevails at present, there is scarce a young man of any fashion in a Corporation who does not make Love with the Town-Musick. The Waits often help him through his courtship.

Addison states that "authors of all countries are unanimous" in believing that the tradition of the evening serenade began in Italy, adding in an indirect jab at Italian opera, that it was the castrati who began this tradition. That it was Italy in which this custom began, seems evident to Addison because of the mild climate there. To sing outdoors at night in colder England—well, one might as well serenade in Greenland! Indeed, he maintains that the trills he has heard in London serenades were caused by the cold weather.

Secondly, he points to the fact that everyone in Italy is so musical by nature, a fact which he regards as another clue to the origin of the serenade.

> Nothing is more frequent in that country, than to hear a cobbler working to an opera tune ... There is not a laborer, or handicraftsman, that in the cool of the evening does not relieve himself with solos and sonatas.
>
> The Italian soothes his Mistress with a plaintive voice, and bewails himself in such melting Musick, that the whole neighborhood sympathizes with him in his sorrow ...

> On the contrary, our honest countrymen have so little an inclination to Musick, that they seldom begin to sing till they are drunk, which also is usually the time when they are most disposed to serenade.

A fictional letter, written by Steele, in the *Spectator* of April 28, 1712, reports the objection of a bridegroom to an intended humorous tradition of serenading newly married couples on the following morning with percussion.

> ...to my surprise I was awakened the next morning by the thunder of a set of drums. These warlike sounds are very improper in a marriage consort, and give great offense; they seem to insinuate, that the joys of this state are short, and that jars and discord soon ensue. I fear they have been ominous in many matches, and sometimes proved a prelude to a battle in the Honeymoon.

These journals are also valuable for their inclusion of announcements of private concerts in and around London, which add to our understanding of the concert life in that city at this time. The *Spectator* for May 1, 1711, for example, carries mention of a forthcoming "Consort of Musick" to be held in the Haberdashers-hall. The *Spectator* for January 18, 1712, carries an advertisement for a series of concerts organized by three men previously associated with opera, Thomas Clayton, Nicolino Haym and Charles Dieupart. Curiously, it was these same three writers who had earlier argued that emotion is found only in the words, who now apparently find emotion elsewhere.

> We think it a groundless imputation that we should set up against the Opera in it self. What we pretend to assert is, that the songs of different authors injudiciously put together, and a foreign tone and manner which are expected in every thing now performed amongst us, has put Musick it self to a stand; insomuch that the ears of the people cannot now be entertained with any thing but what has an impertinent gaiety, without any just Spirit; or a Languishment of Notes, without any Passion or common sense.

Some announcements are rather unusual, as in the case of the *Spectator* for April 7, 1712, which carries the announcement of a vocal and instrumental concert for the benefit of one, "Mr. Edward Keen, the father of twenty children." This must have been a regular *raison d'etre* for Keen's concerts for a similar advertisement can be found in 1707, and in fact another as early as 1699.[5] The *Spectator* for July 21, 1714, reports music made by the master of a tavern on a variety of kitchen objects, in a repertoire that included arias from Italian operas.

[5] See *The Spectator*, ed. Donald Bond (Oxford: Clarendon Press, 1965), III, 291, fn. 3.

Bibliography

1 Music in the English Restoration Court

Bryant, Sir Arthur. *King Charles II*. London, 1955.

Burrows, Donald. "London: Commercial Wealth and Cultural Expansion." In *The Late Baroque Era*. Englewood Cliffs: Prentice Hall, 1994.

Evelyn, John. *The Diary of John Evelyn*. Oxford, 1955.

Grove, George, ed. *Dictionary of Music* (1980).

Holman, Peter. "London: Commonwealth and Restoration." In *The Early Baroque Era*. Englewood Cliffs: Prentice Hall, 1994.

Lord Chamberlain Accounts, London.

Magalotti, Lorenzo. *Relazione d'Inghilterra* [1668].

McGrady, Richard. "The Court Trumpeters of Charles I and Charles II." In *The Music Review* (1974).

Ogilby, John. *The Relation of His Majestic's Entertainment passing through the City of London to His Coronation*. London, 1661.

Pepys, Samuel. *The Diary of Samuel Pepys*. London, 1924.

Pope, Alexander. *The Works of Alexander Pope*. New York: Gordian Press, 1967.

Sévigné, Madame de. *Letters of Madame de Sévigné*. Edited by Richard Aldington. London: Routledge, 1937.

Standford, Francis. *The History of the Coronation of ... James II*. London, 1687.

Wilson, John. *Roger North on Music*. London: Novello, 1959.

2 Music in the Restoration Church

Ashmole, Elias. *The Autobiographical Notes of Elias Ashmole*. Edited by C. H. Josten. Oxford, 1966.

Avison, Charles. *An Essay on Musical Expression* [London, 1753]. New York: Broude Reprint, 1967.

Bunyan, John. *The Works of John Bunyan*. Edited by George Offor. London: Blackie and Son, 1853.

Butler, Charles. *Principles of Musick* [1636].

Crashaw, Richard. *The Complete Poetry of Richard Crashaw*. Edited by George Williams. New York: New York University Press, 1972.

Defoe, Daniel. *Robinson Crusoe*. Garden City: Doubleday.

De Lafontaine, Henry. *The King's Musick*. London, 1909.

Dryden, John. *The Works of John Dryden*. Edited by Edward Hooker. Berkeley: University of California Press, 1956.

Earle, John. *Microcosmography* [1628]. St. Clair Shores: Scholarly Press, 1971.

Herbert, George. *The Poems of George Herbert*. Edited by Ernest Rhys. London: Walter Scott, 1885.

Herrick, Robert. *The Poetical Works of Robert Herrick*. Oxford: Clarendon Press, 1963.

Holman, Peter. "London: Commonwealth and Restoration." In *The Early Baroque Era*. Englewood Cliffs: Prentice Hall, 1994.

Lord Chamberlain Accounts, London.

MacDermott, K. H. *The Old Church Gallery Minstrels*. London, 1948.

Mace, Thomas. *Musick's Monument* [1676]. Paris: Editions du Centre National de la Recherche Scientifique, 1966.

Milton, John. *The Works of John Milton*. Edited by Frank Paterson. New York: Columbia University Press, 1931–1938.

North, Roger. *The Musicall Gramarian*. Oxford: Oxford University Press, 1925.

Oldham, John. *The Works of John Oldham*. London: Bettenham, 1722.

Parke, W. T. *Musical Memoirs*. New York, 1970.

Pepys, Samuel. *Diary*.

Playford, John. *An Introduction to the Skill of Music* [1674]. Ridgewood: Gregg Press, 1966.

Pope, Alexander. *The Works of Alexander Pope*. New York: Gordian Press, 1967.

Spinoza, Baruch. *The Ethics*.

Thomson, James. *The Poetical Works of James Thomson*. London: Bell and Daldy, c. 1860.

Wilson, John. *Roger North on Music*. London: Novello, 1959.

Wither, George. *Works of George Wither*. New York: Franklin, 1967.

Young, Edward. *Edward Young: The Complete Works*. Hildesheim: Olms, 1968.

3 Music in the Restoration Theater

Behn, Aphra. *Abdelazer*.

———. *The Amorous Prince*.

———. *The Emperor of the Moon*.

———. *The Forced Marriage*.

———. *The Lucky Chance*.

———. *Sir Patient Fancy*.

———. *The Young King*.

Congreve, William. *The Complete Works of William Congreve*. New York: Russell & Russell, 1964.

———. *The Double-Dealer*.

———. *The Judgment of Paris*.

———. *Love for Love*.

———. *The Mourning Bride*.

———. *The Old Batchelour*.

———. *Opera of Semele*.

———. *The Way of the World*.

Etherege, George. *The Man of Mode*.

Farquhar, George. *The Beaux Stratagem*.

———. *The Inconstant*.

———. *Love and a Bottle*.

Hawkins, John. *A General History of the Science and Practice of Music* [1776]. New York: Dover Reprint, 1963.

Lee, Nathaniel. *The Works of Nathaniel Lee.* Metuchen: Scarecrow Reprints, 1968.
———. *Constantine the Great.*
———. *The Duke of Guise* (co-authored with Dryden).
———. *Gloriana.*
———. *Mithridates.*
———. *Oedipus.*
———. *The Princess of Cleve.*
———. *Rival Queens.*
———. *Theodosius.*
Otway, Thomas. *Alcibiades.*
———. *History and Fall of Caius Marius.*
Sedley, Charles. *Bellamira.*
———. *The Orphan.*
———. *The Mulberry Garden.*
Steele, Richard. *The Plays of Richard Steele.* Oxford: Clarendon Press, 1971.
———. *The Conscious Lovers.*
———. *The Funeral.*
———. *The Tender Husband.*
Thomson, James. *Alfred.*
Vanbrugh, John. *The Complete Works of John Vanbrugh.* London: Nonesuch Press, 1927.
Vanbrugh, John. *Aesop.*
———. *A Journey to London.*
———. *The Pilgrim.*
———. *The Provoked Wife.*
———. *The Relapse.*
Villiers, George. *The Rehearsal.*
Wycherley, William. *The Gentleman Dancing-Master.*
———. *Love in a Wood.*

4 Music in Restoration Poetry

Butler, Samuel. *The Poetical Works of Samuel Butler.* New York: Appleton, 1854. II, 256.

Cowley, Abraham. *The Complete Works of Abraham Cowley.* Edited by Alexander Grosart. New York: AMS Press, 1967.

Crashaw, Richard. *The Complete Poetry of Richard Crashaw.* Edited by George Williams. New York: New York University Press, 1972.

Donne, John. *The Complete Poetry of John Donne.* New York: New York University Press, 1968.

Ekenside, Mark. *The Poetical Works of Mark Ekenside.* London: Bell and Daldy, 1845.

Gay, John. *The Works of John Gay.* London: Edward Jeffery, 1745.

Herrick, Robert. *The Poetical Works of Robert Herrick.* Edited by L. C. Martin. Oxford: Clarendon Press, 1963.

Lovelace, Richard. *The Poems of Richard Lovelace.* Edited by C. H. Wilkinson. Oxford: Clarendon Press, 1930.

Marvell, Andrew. *The Complete Works of Andrew Marvell.* New York: AMS Press, 1966.

Pope, Alexander. *The Works of Alexander Pope.* New York: Gordian Press, 1967.

Prior, Matthew. *The Literary Works of Matthew Prior.* Oxford: Clarendon, 1959.

Sedley, Sir Charles. *The Poetical and Dramatic Works of Sir Charles Sedley.* New York: AMS Press, 1969.

Shenstone, William. *The Poetical Works of William Shenstone.* Edinburgh: James Nichol, 1854.

Steele, Richard. *The Occasional Verse of Richard Steele.* Oxford: Clarendon, 1952.

Swift, Jonathan. *The Poetical Works of Jonathan Swift.* London: Bell and Daldy.

Thomson, James. *The Poetical Works of James Thomson.* London: Bell and Daldy, c. 1860.

Vaughan, Henry. *The Works of Henry Vaughan.* Edited by L. C. Martin. Oxford: At the Clarendon Press, 1957.

Waller, Edmund. *Edmund Waller, Poems*. Menston: Scolar Press, 1971.
Wycherley, William. *The Complete Works of William Wycherley*. New York: Russell & Russell, 1964.
Young, Edward. *Edward Young: The Complete Works*. Hildesheim: Olms, 1968.

5 Music in Restoration Prose

Browne, Sir Thomas. *Sir Thomas Browne's Works*. Edited by Simon Wilkin. London: Pickering, 1836.
———. *Religio Medici*.
———. *Enquiries into Vulgar and Common Errors*.
Congreve, William. *The Complete Works of William Congreve*. New York: Russell & Russell, 1964.
———. *Incognita*.
Defoe, Daniel. *The Works of Daniel Defoe*. New York: Henson, 1905.
———. *Augusta Triumphans: or, the Way to make London the Most Flourshing City in the Universe*.
———. *Memoirs of a Cavalier*.
Dekker, Thomas. *The Non-Dramatic Works of Thomas Dekker*. Edited by Alexander Grosart. New York, Russell & Russell, 1963.
———. *Lanthorne and Candle-Light*.
———. *The Divels Last Will and Testament*.
———. *The Seven Deadly Sinnes of London*.
———. *A Papisst in Armes*.
———. *The Dead Tearme*.
———. *Dekker his Dream*.
———. *Jests to Make you Merrie*.
Earle, John. *Microcosmography* [1628]. St. Clair Shores: Scholarly Press, 1971.
Farquhar, George. *The Complete Works of George Farquhar*. New York: Gordian Press, 1967.
———. *Adventures of Covent-Garden*.
Fielding, Henry. *The Adventures of Joseph Andrews*.
———. *The Life of Mr. Jonathan Wild*.

———. *The History of a Foundling [Tom Jones]*.
———. *Amelia*.
———. *The Adventures of Joseph Andrews*.
Fuller, Thomas. *The Holy State and the Profance State* [1642]. Edited by Maximilian Walten. New York: AMS Press, 1966.
Overbury, Thomas. *The Conceited Newes of Sir Thomas Overbury and His Friends*. Edited by James Savage. Gainesville: Scholars' Facsimiles, 1968.
Pope, Alexander. *The Art of Sinking in Poetry*.
———. *Memoirs of Scriblerus*.
———. *The Works of Alexander Pope* (New York: Gordian Press, 1967.
Prior, Matthew. *The Literary Works of Matthew Prior*. Oxford: Clarendon, 1959.
Richardson, Samuel. *Clarissa Harlowe*. New York: AMS Press Reprint, 1972.
———. *Sir Charles Grandison*.
———. *Pamela*.
Sedley, Charles. *The Poetical and Dramatic Works of Sir Charles Sedley*. New York: AMS Press, 1969.
———. *An Essay on Entertainments*
Swift, Jonathan. *The Prose Works of Jonathan Swift*. Oxford: Blackwell, 1957.
———. *A Discourse Concerning the Mechanical Operastion of the Spirit*.
———. *Gulliver's Travels*.
———. *Satires and Personal Writings of Jonathan Swift*. London: Oxford University Press, 1956.
Walton, Izaak. *The Compleat Angler*. London: Oxford University Press, 1935.

6 Restoration Philosophers on Music

Aubrey, John. *Brief Lives*. Edited by O. Dick. Ann Arbor, 1957.
Beer, E. *The Correspondence of John Locke*. Oxford, Clarendon, 1976.

Berkeley, George. *The Works of George Berkeley, Bishop of Cloyne.* Edited by A. Luce. London: Nelson, 1964.
Cooper, Anthony. *Reflections upon Ancient and Modern Learning.*
Harris, James. *Three Treatises.*
Hobbes, Thomas. *Leviathan.*
Hume, David. *The Letters of David Hume.* Edited by J. Greig. Oxford: Clarendon, 1932.
———. *The Philosophical Works.*
Hutcheson, Francis. *An Inquiry into the Original of our Ideas of Beauty and Virtue* (1729).
Locke, John. *The Works of John Locke.* [London 1823]. Aalen: Scientia Verlag, 1963.
Marvell, Andrew. *The Complete Works of Andrew Marvell.* New York: AMS Press, 1966.
Penn, William. *The Select Works of William Penn.* London: William Phillips, 1825.
Royce. *The Spirit of Modern Philosophy.* Boston, 1892.
Wotton, William. *Reflections upon Ancient and Modern Learning.*

7 Newton on Music

Newton, Isaac. *The Correspondence of Isaac Newton.* Cambridge: University Press, 1959.
———. *Unpublished Scientific Papers of Isaac Newton.* Edited by Rupert Hall. Cambridge: University Press, 1962.

8 Dryden on Music

Dryden, John. *The Works of John Dryden.* Edited by Edward Hooker. Berkeley: University of California Press, 1956.
———. *All for Love.*
———. *Amboyna.*
———. *Amphitryon.*
———. *An Evening's Love.*
———. *Cleomenes.*
———. *The Duke of Guise.*
———. *The Indian Emperour.*
———. *The Indian Queen.*

———. *King Arthur*.
———. *Love in a Nunnery*.
———. *Marriage A-La-Mode*.
———. *Oedious*.
———. *Secret Love*.
———. *Sir Martin Mar-all*.
———. *The Tempest*.
Grebanier, Bernard. *English Literature*. Great Neck: Barron, 1959.

9 English Views on Foreign Opera

Defoe, Daniel. *Robinson Crusoe*. Garden City: Doubleday.
Evelyn, John. *The Diary of John Evelyn*. Oxford, 1955.
Fielding, Henry. *The Adventures of Joseph Andrews*.
Gay, John. *The Works of John Gay*. London: Edward Jeffery, 1745.
Gildon, Charles. *The Life of Mr. Thomas Betterton, the Late Eminent Tragedian* [1710]. London: Frank Cass Reprint, 1970.
Gray, Thomas. *Correspondence of Thomas Gray*. Oxford, Clarendon Press, 1971.
Pope, Alexander. *The Works of Alexander Pope*. New York: Gordian Press, 1967.
Richardson, Samuel. *Clarissa Harlowe*. New York: AMS Press Reprint, 1972.
Rymer, Thomas. *A Short View of Tragedy*.
Sackville, Charles. *The Poems of Charles Sackville*. New York: Garland, 1979.
Shenstone, William. *Letters of William Shenstone*. Minneapolis: University of Minnesota Press, 1939
———. *The Poetical Works of William Shenstone*. Edinburgh: James Nichol, 1854.
Swift, Jonathan. *The Prose Works of Jonathan Swift*. Oxford: Blackwell, 1957.
Thomson, James. *James Thomson, Letters and Documents*. Lawrence: University of Kansas Press, 1958.

Vanbrugh, John. *The Complete Works of John Vanbrugh.* London: Nonesuch Press, 1927.
Wycherley, William. *The Complete Works of William Wycherley.* Edited by Montague Summers. New York: Russell & Russell, 1964.

10 Dryden on Opera

Grebanier, Bernard. *English Literature.* Great Neck: Barron, 1959.
Dryden, John. *The Works of John Dryden.* Edited by Edward Hooker. Berkeley: University of California Press, 1956.
———. *The Works of John Dryden.* Edited by Walter Scott. London: William Miller, 1808.

11 Restoration Journals on Opera

The Intelligencer
Nr. III, 1728

The Nonsense of Common-Sense
January 3, 1738
October 14, 1738

The Tatler
April 12, 1709
April 19, 1709
May 7, 1709
January 3, 1710
January 10, 1710
May 4, 1710
April 27, 1710

The Spectator
March 1, 1711
March 6, 1711
March 15, 1711
March 16, 1711
March 21, 1711
March 26, 1711

April 3, 1711
April 5, 1711
June 20, 1711
August 20, 1711
September 12, 1711
December 11, 1711
February 8, 1712
April 29, 1712
July 29, 1712

The World
November 14, 1754

12 Civic Music in the English Baroque

Ashton, John. *Social Life in the Reign of Queen Anne.* London, 1911.

Beaumont and Fletcher. *The Maid in the Mill.*

Bridges. "Town Waits and their Tunes." In *Proceedings of the Musical Association.* London, 1927–1928.

Browne, Sir Thomas. *Sir Thomas Browne's Works.* Edited by Simon Wilkin. London: Pickering, 1836.

Burney, Charles. *General History of Music.* New York, 1957.

Collinson, Francis. *The Bagpipe.* London, 1975.

Crewdson, H. A. F. *The Worshipful Company of Musicians.* London: Charles Knight.

Croft-Murray, Edward. "The Wind-Band in England, 1540–1840." In *Music and Civilisation.* London, 1980.

Dekker, Thomas. *Old Fortunatus.*

———. *The Non-Dramatic Works of Thomas Dekker.* Edited by Alexander Grosart. New York, Russell & Russell, 1963.

Evelyn, John. *The Diary of John Evelyn.* Oxford, 1955

Earle, John. *Microcosmography* [1628]. St. Clair Shores: Scholarly Press, 1971.

Ede, Mary. *Arts and Society in England under William and Mary.* London: Stainer and Bell.

Ford, John. *The Broken Heart.*

Hawkins, John. *A General History of the Science and Practice of Music* [1776]. New York: Dover Reprint, 1963.

London *General Advertiser* (October 21, 1744).
Marston. *The Dutch Courtezan.*
———. *The Malcontent.*
Middleton. *Mayor of Queenborough.*
Nichols, John. *The Progresses of King James The First.* London [1828].
Pepys, Samuel. *The Diary of Samuel Pepys.* London, 1924.
The Spectator, Nr. 18.
Walls, Peter. "London, 1603–49." In *The Early Baroque Era.* Englewood Cliffs: Prentice Hall, 1994.
Ward, Ned. *The London Spy.* Edited by Arthur Hayward. New York: Doran.

13 Music and English Manners

Butler, Samuel. *Characters.*
Cavendish, Margaret. *Sociable Letters* [1664]. Menston: The Scholar Press, 1969.
Evelyn, John. *The Diary of John Evelyn.* Oxford, 1955.
Gray, Thomas. *Correspondence of Thomas Gray.* Oxford, Clarendon Press, 1971.
Pope, Alexander. *The Works of Alexander Pope.* New York: Gordian Press, 1967.
Shenstone, William. *Letters of William Shenstone.* Minneapolis: University of Minnesota Press, 1939.
———. *Men and Manners.* Boston: Houghton Mifflin, 1927.

14 Pepys on Music

Pepys, Samuel. *The Diary of Samuel Pepys.* London, 1924.
———. *Private Correspondence of Samuel Pepys.* Edited by J. Tanner. London: Bell and Sons, 1926.

15 Restoration Journals on Music

The Spectator. Edited by Donald Bond. Oxford: Clarendon Press, 1965. *The Intelligencer*

III, 1728

The Spectator
March 1, 1711
March 21, 1711
April 3, 1711
May 1, 1711
May 21, 1711
May 25, 1711
June 7, 1711
June 16, 1711
December 26, 1711
January 18, 1712
March 17, 1712
April 7, 1712
June 24, 1712
June 27, 1712
August 5, 1712
September 1, 1712
September 24, 1712
September 28, 1712
November 1, 1712
July 21, 1714

The Tatler
April 12, 1709
February 14, 1710
April 1, 1710
April 11, 1710
August 15, 1710
September 9, 1710

About the Author

Dr. David Whitwell is a graduate ("with distinction") of the University of Michigan and the Catholic University of America, Washington DC (PhD, Musicology, Distinguished Alumni Award, 2000) and has studied conducting with Eugene Ormandy and at the Akademie für Musik, Vienna. Prior to coming to Northridge, Dr. Whitwell participated in concerts throughout the United States and Asia as Associate First Horn in the USAF Band and Orchestra in Washington DC, and in recitals throughout South America in cooperation with the United States State Department.

At the California State University, Northridge, which is in Los Angeles, Dr. Whitwell developed the CSUN Wind Ensemble into an ensemble of international reputation, with international tours to Europe in 1981 and 1989 and to Japan in 1984. The CSUN Wind Ensemble has made professional studio recordings for BBC (London), the Köln Westdeutscher Rundfunk (Germany), NOS National Radio (The Netherlands), Zürich Radio (Switzerland), the Television Broadcasting System (Japan) as well as for the United States State Department for broadcast on its "Voice of America" program. The CSUN Wind Ensemble's recording with the Mirecourt Trio in 1982 was named the "Record of the Year" by *The Village Voice*. Composers who have guest conducted Whitwell's ensembles include Aaron Copland, Ernest Krenek, Alan Hovhaness, Morton Gould, Karel Husa, Frank Erickson and Vaclav Nelhybel.

Dr. Whitwell has been a guest professor in 100 different universities and conservatories throughout the United States and in 23 foreign countries (most recently in China, in an elite school housed in the Forbidden City). Guest conducting experiences have included the Philadelphia Orchestra, Seattle Symphony Orchestra, the Czech Radio Orchestras of Brno and Bratislava, The National Youth Orchestra of Israel, as well as resident wind ensembles in Russia, Israel, Austria, Switzerland, Germany, England, Wales, The Netherlands, Portugal, Peru, Korea, Japan, Taiwan, Canada and the United States.

He is a past president of the College Band Directors National Association, a member of the Prasidium of the International Society for the Promotion of Band Music, and was a member of the founding board of directors of the World Association for Symphonic Bands and Ensembles (WASBE). In 1964 he was made an honorary life member of Kappa Kappa Psi, a national professional music fraternity. In September, 2001, he was a delegate to the UNESCO Conference on Global Music in Tokyo. He has been knighted by sovereign organizations in France, Portugal and Scotland and has been awarded the gold medal of Kerkrade, The Netherlands, and the silver medal of Wangen, Germany, the highest honor given wind conductors in the United States, the medal of the Academy of Wind and Percussion Arts (National Band Association) and the highest honor given wind conductors in Austria, the gold medal of the Austrian Band Association. He is a member of the Hall of Fame of the California Music Educators Association.

Dr. Whitwell's publications include more than 127 articles on wind literature including publications in *Music and Letters* (London), the *London Musical Times,* the *Mozart-Jahrbuch* (Salzburg), and 50 books, among which is his 13-volume *History and Literature of the Wind Band and Wind Ensemble* and an 8-volume series on *Aesthetics in Music.* In addition to numerous modern editions of early wind band music his original compositions include five symphonies.

David Whitwell was named as one of six men who have determined the course of American bands during the second half of the twentieth century, in the definitive history, *The Twentieth Century American Wind Band* (Meredith Music). A doctoral dissertation by German Gonzales (2007, Arizona State University) is dedicated to the life and conducting career of David Whitwell through the year 1977. David Whitwell is one of nine men described by Paula A. Crider in *The Conductor's Legacy* (Chicago: GIA, 2010) as "the legendary conductors" of the twentieth century.

> "I can't imagine the 2nd half of the 20th century—without David Whitwell and what he has given to all of the rest of us."
> Frederick Fennell (1993)

About the Editor

CRAIG DABELSTEIN began studying the piano at age seven and took up the saxophone at age twelve. Mr Dabelstein has Bachelor of Arts (Music) and Bachelor of Music degrees from the Queensland Conservatorium of Music and a Graduate Diploma of Learning and Teaching and a Graduate Certificate in Editing and Publishing from the University of Southern Queensland. He has held the principal saxophone chairs in the Australian Wind Orchestra and has been an augmenting member of the Queensland Philharmonic and Symphony Orchestras. He was a member of the Queensland Saxophone Quartet and has previously been a saxophone teacher at the Queensland Conservatorium of Music. He is a regular conductor of the Queensland Wind Orchestra and has been a research associate for the *Teaching Music Through Performance in Band* series of books. He is the editor of more than forty books by Dr. David Whitwell including *A Concise History of the Wind Band, Foundations of Music Education, Music Education of the Future, The Sousa Oral History Project, Wagner on Bands, Berlioz on Bands, The Art of Musical Conducting, Aesthetics of Music* (8 volumes) and *The History and Literature of the Wind Band and Wind Ensemble* (13 volumes). He currently teaches saxophone and clarinet, and conducts bands at St Joseph's College, Gregory Terrace.

Books by David Whitwell

- The Sousa Oral History Project
- The Art of Musical Conducting
- The Longy Club: 1900–1917
- La Téléphonie and the Universal Musical Language
- Extraordinary Women
- A Concise History of the Wind Band
- Essays on the Modern Wind Band
- Essays on Performance Practice
- A New History of Wind Music
- The College and University Band
- The Early Symphonies of Mozart
- Band Music of the French Revolution
- A Conductor's Diary

On Philosophy and Performance Practice

- Essays on Music of the German Baroque: Philosophy and Performance Practice
- Essays on Music of the French Baroque: Philosophy and Performance Practice
- Essays on Italian and Spanish Music of the Baroque: Philosophy and Performance Practice
- Philosophy and Performance Practice of Music during Jacobean England
- Philosophy and Performance Practice of Music during Restoration England

On Composers

- Wagner on Bands
- Berlioz on Bands
- Chopin: A Self-Portrait
- Liszt: A Self-Portrait
- Schumann: A Self-Portrait in His Own Words
- Mendelssohn: A Self-Portrait in His Own Words

On Education

- Philosophic Foundations of Education
- Foundations of Music Education
- Music Education of the Future

Aesthetics of Music

- Aesthetics of Music in Ancient Civilizations
- Aesthetics of Music in the Middle Ages
- Aesthetics of Music in the Early Renaissance
- Aesthetics of Music in Sixteenth-Century Italy, France and Spain
- Aesthetics of Music in Sixteenth-Century Germany, the Low Countries and England
- Aesthetics of Baroque Music in Italy, Spain, the German-Speaking Countries and the Low Countries
- Aesthetics of Baroque Music in France
- Aesthetics of Baroque Music in England

The History and Literature of the Wind Band and Wind Ensemble Series

- Volume 1 The Wind Band and Wind Ensemble Before 1500
- Volume 2 The Renaissance Wind Band and Wind Ensemble
- Volume 3 The Baroque Wind Band and Wind Ensemble
- Volume 4 The Wind Band and Wind Ensemble of the Classical Period (1750–1800)
- Volume 5 The Nineteenth-Century Wind Band and Wind Ensemble
- Volume 6 A Catalog of Multi-Part Repertoire for Wind Instruments or for Undesignated Instrumentation before 1600
- Volume 7 Baroque Wind Band and Wind Ensemble Repertoire
- Volume 8 Classical Period Wind Band and Wind Ensemble Repertoire
- Volume 9 Nineteenth-Century Wind Band and Wind Ensemble Repertoire
- Volume 10 A Supplementary Catalog of Wind Band and Wind Ensemble Repertoire
- Volume 11 A Catalog of Wind Repertoire before the Twentieth Century for One to Five Players
- Volume 12 A Second Supplementary Catalog of Early Wind Band and Wind Ensemble Repertoire
- Volume 13 Name Index, Volumes 1–12, The History and Literature of the Wind Band and Wind Ensemble

Ancient Voices

- Ancient Views on Music and Religion
- Ancient Views on the Natural World
- Ancient Views on What Is Music
- Contemporary Descriptions of Early Musicians
- Early Views of Music and Ethics
- Early Thoughts on Performance Practice
- Music Performance in Ancient Societies

Renaissance Voices

- Essays on Renaissance Philosophies of Music
- Renaissance Men on Music

www.whitwellbooks.com

www.ingramcontent.com/pod-product-compliance
Lightning Source LLC
Chambersburg PA
CBHW081349230426
43667CB00017B/2770